RUSSIA'S EDUCATIONAL HERITAGE

RUSSIA'S EDUCATIONAL HERITAGE

WILLIAM H. E. JOHNSON

Chairman of the Department of
Educational Foundations
University of Pittsburgh

With a New Introduction by

George S. Counts

1969

OCTAGON BOOKS

New York

Reprinted 1969
by special arrangement with William H. E. Johnson

OCTAGON BOOKS
A DIVISION OF FARRAR, STRAUS & GIROUX, INC.
19 Union Square West
New York, N. Y. 10003

LIBRARY OF CONGRESS CATALOG CARD NUMBER: 74-84175

Printed in U.S.A. by
NOBLE OFFSET PRINTERS, INC.
NEW YORK 3, N. Y.

To my Mother

Appreciation is expressed to the following publishers for permission to quote from the volumes named:

THE CLARENDON PRESS, Oxford, England, for *Russia From the Varangians to the Bolsheviks* (1918) by Raymond Beazley, Nevill Forbes, and G. A. Birkett.

E. P. DUTTON & CO., INC., New York, for *Russia and Reform* (1907) by Bernard Pares.

HARPER AND BROTHERS, New York, for *Roosevelt and Hopkins* (1948) by Robert E. Sherwood.

HOUGHTON MIFFLIN COMPANY, Boston, for *Russia and the Russians* (1901) by Edmund Noble; and for *Patterns of Culture* (1934) by Ruth Benedict.

ALFRED A. KNOPF, INC., New York, for *History of Russia* (1944) by Bernard Pares; and for *A History of Russia* (2 vols., 1924) by Alexander Kornilov (translated and extended by Alexander S. Kaun).

LITTLE, BROWN & COMPANY, Boston, for *U.S. Foreign Policy–Shield of the Republic* (1943) by Walter Lippmann.

LONGMANS, GREEN & COMPANY, New York, for *Rural Russia Under the Old Regime* (1932) by Geroid T. Robinson.

THE MACMILLAN COMPANY, New York, for *Home Life in Russia* (1913) by A. S. Rappoport; and for *New Minds, New Men* (1932) by Thomas Woody; and also to Allen and Unwin, Ltd., London, for *The Spirit of Russia* (2 vols., 1919) by T. G. Masaryk (translated by Eden and Cedar Paul).

POLISH INSTITUTE OF ARTS AND SCIENCES IN AMERICA, New York, for *The Origins of Modern Russia* (1948) by Jan Kucharzewski.

G. P. PUTNAM'S SONS, New York, for *Blood, Sweat and Tears* (1941) by Winston S. Churchill.

STANFORD UNIVERSITY PRESS, Stanford, California, for *Features and Figures of the Past: Government and Opinion in the Reign of Nicholas II* (1939) by V. I. Gurko.

THE UNIVERSITY OF BUFFALO, College of Arts and Sciences, Buffalo, New York, for *Education and Autocracy in Russia* (1919) by Daniel Bell Leary.

YALE UNIVERSITY PRESS, New Haven, Connecticut, for *The End of the Russian Empire* (1931) by M. T. Florinski; and for *Russian Schools and Universities in the World War* (1929) by P. N. Ignatiev; and for *A History of Russia* (1944) by George Vernadsky.

Dr. Nicholas Hans, University of London, for his *History of Russian Educational Policy, 1701-1917* (P. S. King and Sons, Ltd., London, 1931).

INTRODUCTION TO THE OCTAGON EDITION

The time is most appropriate for the publication of a second edition of this very important book. In fact, in terms of its content, it has no rival in the many volumes relating to Soviet education which have been published since we in America became interested in the spectacular rise of Russia during the twentieth century.

The special significance of this excellent study resides in the fact that it provides an indispensable background for understanding the development of organized education in the "Sixth Continent" since the Great October Revolution of 1917. It supports in detail the fundamental and inescapable truth that nothing can be understood in the realm of human affairs without knowing its history.

This principle applies with exceptional force to the achievement of genuine understanding of the nature of the Soviet state and the patterns of Soviet education. All students, when approaching the study of education in another country or age must realize from the beginning that education is never an autonomous process governed by its own laws and everywhere the same. On the contrary, it is always an expression of a given society with its power structure, its proclaimed goals, and its cultural heritage going back through the centuries. Many students of the Soviet Union have made the mistake of concentrating on the ideas and doctrines of Karl Marx. It is becoming increasingly evident that Bolshevism and the teachings of Lenin were deeply rooted in the autocratic tradition, the messianic vision, and the revolutionary movements of imperial Russia. This basic truth is supported in scholarly detail in *Russia's Educational Heritage.* It is also supported by the passing of the Communist monolith and the tendency of every so-called Communist country to pursue its own "road to socialism."

A final word should be said about the author. William H. E. Johnson is the outstanding American student of Soviet education. His background and experience, including three years of residence in and many visits to the USSR, embrace more than a generation of time. And he has been assisted throughout this period by his wife, Annette, who is also a scholar in her own right. This book should be on the reading list of every course in our colleges and universities dealing with Soviet education.

GEORGE S. COUNTS

Carbondale, Illinois
August, 1968

Foreword

This study of the major educational policies and programs characterizing the last three centuries of the Tsarist regime, although primarily concerned with the training of teachers, reflects the broader educational concepts of the era as well as much of the thinking and mode of life of the Russian people.

Many important connections between Empire and Soviet procedure are pointed out, indicating that instead of "smashing the old order," the Russian Revolution created a new state on the foundations of the old. The work reveals that the progressive educational theories and practices imported from abroad during the early years of the Soviet regime have been superseded by concepts and methods which were outlawed and despised in the 1920's.

The book also traces the interesting history of Tsarist Russia's famous trilogy—Orthodoxy, Autocracy, and Nationalism—and indicates how these same concepts dominate Soviet thinking today. Even though the Revolution produced a new "religion," a new sovereign, and a new patriotism, the demands of these institutions upon the ordinary citizen bear an astonishing resemblance to those once imposed by the Altar, the Throne, and the Fatherland.

The volume does not attempt to chart the future course

of Soviet education, nor even to explain the backgrounds of all the important details of its present organization. It has been written merely in the hope that, through an analysis of earlier Russian educational history, some light may be shed upon the motivations behind certain Soviet pedagogical procedures. Even though some of the documents of the past seem to have value in themselves, and a few appear remarkably prophetic of the future, the main purpose of the volume is to present an integrated view of the educational background of a great nation, expressly through its efforts to erect a satisfactory system of teacher education.

The approach, in the main, has been chronological. Chapters Two to Six, inclusive, cover the era from the fifteenth to the middle of the nineteenth century, and deal with the early Church schools, the establishment of state institutions of higher learning, the creation of state secondary and elementary schools, the unification of many of these agencies into a national system, and the disastrous period of reaction which characterized the second quarter of the last century. At this point a digression is made, in Chapter Seven, in order to provide an integrated historical review of the Main Pedagogical Institute which flourished in St. Petersburg during the periods described in all but the first of the previous chapters.

Returning to the chronological order, the next two chapters deal with the reforms during the latter half of the nineteenth century and the subsequent decades which led to the ultimate breakdown of the regime in 1917. Chapter Ten describes the status of teachers and teacher education during these last two decades, and Chapter Eleven outlines the philosophical and educational ideas of the Tsarist epoch which appear to have exerted the greatest influence upon Soviet pedagogy. A final chapter points out certain specific instances of the effects of this influence, and furnishes further evidence to support the views expressed in Chapter One.

The chief sources of data drawn upon in this volume are the official records of the various administrative organs which have controlled education in Russia since the first schools were established. Prominent among these agencies were the several early Church groups, the Holy Synod, the state and university councils, the ZEMSTVO boards, and, most important of all, the Ministry of Public Education after its creation at the opening of the nineteenth century. These records are supplemented by the writings of contemporary Russian philosophers, historians, educators, and journalists, the works of outstanding foreign authorities in the fields of politics, economy, and education, and in a few instances, the expressions of Soviet critics. It is hoped that through this wide assortment of primary and secondary records in several languages, a proper balance has been preserved between the exactitudes of scholarly exposition and the imponderables of personal interpretation.

During the years of travel and research upon which this book is based, the number of those who have assisted the author in one way or another is legion. While the author takes full responsibility for the views expressed, he would like to acknowledge the contributions of many friends and colleagues, both here and abroad who have aided in the completion of this study but who cannot, for reasons of space, be singled out by name.

There are two persons, however, who have given so much of their time and effort to the author that they must be granted special recognition. The first is Dr. George S. Counts, now Distinguished Emeritus Professor of Education at Southern Illinois University, who not only guided the entire course of the original edition but has honored this volume with a most gracious Introduction.

Secondly, there is the usual tribute to the wife of the

author, in this case no mere matter of form. From the background of her own long residence in the U.S.S.R. and her intimate knowledge of Soviet social institutions, Annette Fox Johnson has provided immeasurable assistance throughout the years of work on this volume. In addition, her constant—if sometimes impatient—encouragement has had a great deal to do with its ultimate completion.

William H. E. Johnson

Pittsburgh, Pennsylvania
March, 1969

Table of Contents

List of Tables in Appendix

List of Tables in Appendix

RUSSIA'S EDUCATIONAL HERITAGE

"Situated between the Orient and the Occident, leaning with one elbow on China, and on Germany with the other, we [Russians] should combine in ourselves two spiritual elements: imagination and wisdom. We should unite in our civilization the history of the whole world. But such has not been our lot. The experience of centuries does not exist for us. Anchorets of the world, we did not give anything to it, nor take anything from it. To the whole of human thought we did not add a single idea. We did not contribute in anything to the betterment of the human race, and we have warped everything that we have borrowed from progress. We did not invent anything, and from the invention of others we have adapted only deceitful appearances and superfluous luxuries. To call attention to ourselves we would have to expand from the Bering Strait to the Oder."

–Peter Y. Chaadaev in *Philosophical Letters* (1836)

"We Russians need have no doubts as to our political and state significance: only we, of all the Slavic tribes, have formed into a strong and powerful state. Both before and since the time of Peter the Great we have come through many a severe ordeal with flying colors. We have often stood on the brink of ruin, but have invariably ridden out the storm to reappear upon its crest with new and greater vigor and strength. . . . We envy our grandchildren and great-grandchildren who are destined to see Russia in 1940 standing at the head of the civilized world, giving laws to science and art, and receiving reverent tribute from all enlightened humanity."

–V. G. Belinskii in *A View on Russian Literature in 1846*, and *Almanac of 1840*

1

Introduction: The Enduring Past

ON THE MORNING OF MARCH 15, 1917 IT was announced to the world that Nicholas II, last Tsar of Russia, had abdicated and that a new form of government was to be established in that benighted country. The news organs carried the glad tidings that a Provisional Government had been formed to lead the Russian people into a new era of constitutional democratic self-rule.[1] This new Government was immediately welcomed by nearly all the nations then allied in the war against the Central Powers, the United States being the first to grant it formal recognition. At that time it seemed perfectly logical that the well established democracies of the world should joyously greet the advent of a new republic, especially one which promised the overthrow of absolutism, rigid censorship, and police terror, and at the same time sought to retain whatever good features existed under the old regime. Although the Provisional Government met with many trials during the next few months, the peoples of the democracies continued to hope that it would prove strong enough to endure.

These hopes were dashed on November 7, 1917, when the Provisional Government was overthrown by the most revolutionary elements of the populace under the leadership of about a quarter of a million members of the Bolshevik (majority) faction of the Russian Social Democratic Labor Party. A new government, dominated by the Bolsheviks, was founded with the avowed intention of completely smashing the old order and of installing entirely new ideas and machinery of democratic government. This new Government, unlike its immediate predecessor, was from the start regarded with fear and suspicion by the democratic nations. In a series of decrees in late 1917 and early 1918, sweeping and fundamental changes were ordered in Russian society. All private property in productive means was abolished, all land was taken from the former owners and given to the peasants, all factories were put under the administration of the workers, and the army was denuded of officers and placed in charge of ordinary soldiers elected by their comrades in arms.

These moves were shocking to most democratic peoples of the world, who began to think the new Soviet Government was "going too far" in its attack upon the past. Even though many Americans approved the Soviet decrees removing press censorship, making all levels of education free of charge, and dissolving the Established Church, most of them could not favor the abolition of private property or the institution of mass administration. But the chief objection of the people of the world to the early Soviet regime seems to have crystallized around the conception that it constituted a complete break with past Russian history. It is a rather quaint paradox that those free peoples who most despised the Tsarist regime should resent so strongly a Government which, both in words and deeds, seemed to be doing its best to wipe out the last vestiges of the hated past.

The only bright hope now held out to the democratic peoples was the view that such a completely revolutionary order could not last for long. In the belief that the November Revolution denoted a complete break with the past, many noted European and American commentators pointed out the impossibility of simultaneously abolishing the old and creating the new. This view was strengthened by Russian émigrés throughout the world who maintained that the Soviet regime "was a transitory creation, foreign to the life of Russia, not corresponding to the aspirations of the Russian revolution, imposed by a numerically insignificant minority, to a large extent the result of foreign intrigue." [2] Most observers seemed not only unaware of the irresistible force of custom and tradition which William Graham Sumner had described in his *Folkways* as early as 1906, but also oblivious to the fact that the people who were making this Revolution were themselves products of the very past against which they were struggling. Moreover, "a critical sense, based on comparative historical experience, indicated that a system so extreme in destroying the forms of the system itself, and at the same time so maximalist and dictatorial, that had arisen and was establishing itself on the ruins of Tsardom and on the ruins of antitsarist, liberal-democratic or socialist opposition, was the result of centuries and had a deep historical internal foundation. . . . The causal connection of Tsarist Russia with the developments that took place after her fall cannot be denied." [3]

However, not all adherents of democracy condemned the Soviet Government for its attempt to disavow completely its inheritance from the past. Many liberal thinkers in all the western nations hastened to applaud the new force dedicated so passionately to the obliteration of a regime which had been notorious for its imperviousness to liberal doctrines and practices. These people took the view that a new world had begun in Russia on November 7, 1917, a world which would never again know the hateful autocratism of the old order, with its violence, suppressions, malpractices and inhumanities. Some of these early adulators quoted such great Russian thinkers as Alexander Hertzen and Nikolai Chernyshevskii, who even in the middle of the nineteenth century prophesied that Russia might be the first home of modern socialist democracy for the very reason that its past was so evil as to offer no impediments to the establishment of a system completely new and unadulterated. Thus, both friend and foe of the new regime based their divergent aspirations upon the same basic concept, the former holding that the wholesale disregard of custom and tradition furnished the strongest base for its survival, the latter confident that such a breach would result in chaos and disintegration. Few there were who discerned the essential error in the fundamental approach to the problem, the error of assuming that a nation under any form of government can escape its social heritage.

In the words of one historian: "It was a tragic illusion to believe that the West was fettered by the past which was hindering its progress to the goal of the future, while Russia was free from any fetters, that she was able to effect a complete separation from the past, that in her collective soul she did not have the ballast of past centuries. Russia was shackled by her centuries-long enslavement . . . [which] had implanted in the peoples' minds the habits of despotism, love for arbitrariness, belief in the necessity of coercion, lack of respect for law and man's freedom, disregard for human individuality. That past created the conviction, difficult to eradicate, that man is a tool, material for the achievement of intended aims and the putting into effect of programs."[4] Nor is this error without its victims even today. An American professor recently pointed out that "most of the present-day writers on Russia find so much to hold their interest in the current scene that they are unable or disinclined to go deeper than the intriguing surface. But so striking a phenomenon as the Soviet Union must certainly have deep roots. As the visible structure of a tree is inseparably connected with the structure of the root, so the Russia of 1948 must have roots that reach back hundreds of years."[5]

One example of this connection between past and present is the principle of unanimity. Many democratically inclined people have been appalled at the lack of respect shown by the Soviet Union for minority political opinions. Long before the Revolution, Vladimir Ilich Lenin formulated his program of "democratic centralism" to govern the actions of the Bolshevik Party. This program, said Lenin, was "democratic" because it permitted free discussion of any problem up to the time a vote was taken, and "centralized" because after the vote the minority had to support the majority opinion just as if the vote had been unanimous.[6] But Lenin did not invent this policy: its roots lie very deep in Slavic history. "In early times the decisions of the people were unanimous. This does not mean that it was easy to arrive at a general agreement. Opinions were certainly as divided then as they are now. What is meant is only this—that, in case of a difference of opinion, the minority was forced to acquiesce in that of the majority. . . . In the Chronicle of Dithmar of Merseburg the 'unanimous vote' is distinctly stated to be a peculiarity of the primitive Slavic folkmotes. . . . In case some one refused to acquiesce in the common decision, he was beaten with rods. If any opposition to the vote of the majority arose after the assembly had been held, the dissentient lost all his property. . . . The unanimous vote is very often mentioned by contemporary chroniclers. . . ." [7] One has but to remember the insistence of the Soviet Union upon a unanimous vote in the councils of the United Nations in order to see remnants of this Slavic trait extant even today.

Lenin, moreover, was one of the few early Russian Communists who saw positive values in the great domestic and foreign heritage of his native land. In one of the most important speeches of his entire career, given in 1920 at a youth meeting, he urged the young citizens of the new Soviet state to study the past and make full use of its lessons. Lenin declared that "the tuition, training and education of the [present] youth must be based on the material that was bequeathed us by the old society. We can build Communism only on the sum of knowledge, organizations and institutions, only on the stock of human forces and means left to us by the old society. . . . You would be making a great mistake if you attempted to draw the conclusion that one can become a Communist without acquiring what human knowledge has accumulated." Speaking specifically about the Tsarist system of education, Lenin admitted that it had many faults and that it had to be abolished. "But does the fact that we must abolish it, destroy it, mean that we must not take from it all that mankind has accumulated for the benefit of men?" No, said Lenin, and replied further that "we must take what was good from the old school . . . , we must distinguish between what was bad in the old school and what was useful for us, and we must be able to choose from it what is necessary for Communism." [8]

Lenin selects Karl Marx himself as the prime example of a person who pursued this practice, in that Marx studied capitalism intently in order to evolve his theories of socialism. The same sources must be consulted, the same materials used, the same institutions studied, said Lenin, in the creation of the new "proletarian culture." He warned the young people that "unless we clearly understand that only by an exact knowledge of the culture created by the whole development of mankind, that only by re-working this culture, is it possible to build proletarian culture, unless this is understood, we shall not be able to solve our problem. Proletarian culture is not something that has sprung from nowhere, it is not an invention of those who call themselves experts in proletarian culture. That is all nonsense. Proletarian culture must be the result of the natural development of the stores of knowledge which mankind has accumulated under the yoke of capitalist society, landlord society and bureaucratic society." [9]

Thus, according to the founder of the Soviet state, anything that serves the cause of Communism must be treasured, even if it be borrowed from the past. Not only were there few revolutionaries in Russia who gave expression to this concept; there were few observers in the outside world who understood it, perhaps few who understand it even now. One of the greatest critics of the Soviet Union, Winston S. Churchill, saw this point at least as early as the autumn of 1939 when he declared that "the assertion of the power of Russia" was one of the greatest events of the first month of World War II. Churchill said that, during the past few years, Russia had "pursued a policy of cold self-interest." He continued: "I cannot forecast to you the action of Russia. It is a riddle wrapped in a mystery inside an enigma; but perhaps there is a key. That key is Russian national interest." The Soviet Union, said Churchill, will not deliberately do anything which is "contrary to the historic life-interests of Russia." [10] The British statesman might have added that anything requisite to those life-interests would be done.

The same thought has been put into more general terms

by an American observer, who says that while such life-interests "are not eternal, they are remarkably persistent. We can most nearly judge what a nation will probably want by seeing what over a fairly long period of time it has wanted; we can most nearly predict what it will do by knowing what it has usually done. . . . Even when [people] must adapt themselves to a new situation, their new behavior is likely to be a modification rather than a transformation of their old behavior." [11] How the people of Russia attempted to solve some of the educational problems which they encountered during the last three centuries of Tsardom will be described in the chapters to follow. Even the beginnings of their efforts may not be as far from the modern spirit as we are wont to think.

2

The First Steps Toward Enlightenment (15th – 17th Centuries)

"THE 'DIDASKALOS,' OR TEACHER, OF THIS school must be devout, judicious, humble, gentle, continent; not a drunkard, nor a fornicator, nor a usurer; not irascible, envious, ridiculous, nor foul-mouthed; not a sorcerer, nor a liar; not a party to heresy, but a promoter of piety, at all times conducting himself as a model of religious behavior. For the pupils will be imbued with the same virtues as their teacher."[1]

Thus begins Article I of the Rules affirmed in 1624 by the School of the Lutsk Brotherhood at Kiev, the first organization in Russia to define categorically the requirements for teachers. Many previous documents, however, had spoken of the need for general education among the peoples of Russia. As early as 988 A.D. (the year of the conversion of the Russian Church to Greek Orthodoxy) Vladimir, Metropolitan of Kiev, had expresed his desire that "intentional child offspring be permitted to commence on study books." [2] In the summer of 1028 the Prince of Yaroslav sent to Novgorod for 300 children's study books, and nine years later considerably increased his order.[3] Prince Vladimir Monomakh, in 1096, wrote a long letter to his children, offering them elaborate advice on how to become educated persons.[4] At the end of the fifteenth century Archbishop Gennadius of Novgorod and Pskov recommended that children study in schools rather than under the tutelage of a Master, because he had found children who were taught at home woefully lacking in the rudiments of education.[5] A few years later we find Gennadius' disappointment extended even to the clergymen. He complains that it had been impossible for him to find enough candidates for the priesthood able to read and write, and therefore he was obliged to ordain illiterate men who had merely achieved an approximate knowledge of church ritual through memorization.[6]

That the next half century brought little progress toward the establishment of any type of schools is indicated by the fact that the illiteracy of the clergy was a problem for discussion in 1551 at the meeting of the *Stoglav*, the hundred main representatives of the Church Council. In their own defense, the priests stated that their fathers and their masters had taught them the different church offices by word of mouth, but that there had been and was no one able to teach them to read. Disturbed by the prevalence of such a situation, the *Stoglav* decreed that schools be conducted in the homes of the better educated city priests to teach reading, writing and singing as well as the doctrines of the Church. While the purpose of these schools was primarily to provide elementary education for those children expecting to become priests, the children of all

Christians were to be made welcome. The *Stoglav* even went so far as to stress the necessity of "study books on all grade levels." [7] Despite the professed interest of this important Church group, it appears that the decisions were not widely carried out. "In large cities like Moscow and Novgorod, and perhaps in some of the larger monasteries, elementary parish schools were probably established, but this did not affect the general situation. Nor were the lower clergy very friendly to schools, books and learning." [8]

However, the *Stoglav* undoubtedly accomplished more than did its contemporary lay organization, the *Zemskii Sobor*, whose first convocation occurred also in 1551. This latter group of nobles, formed by Ivan IV to combine the activities of the *Duma* and the original *Sobor*, refused to pay any attention to education at all. Throughout its subsequent century and a half of existence, this organization considered practically every type of question of state policy, both foreign and domestic, except the enlightenment of the Russian people. "Illiterate as were their members, it is not surprising that the *Sobors* took no measure to increase the number of schools and educational establishments. They are probably the sole representative assemblies which never uttered a word about science or scholarship." [9]

The famous *Domostroi* books also attest to the great dependence throughout the sixteenth century upon home instruction. Parents too poor to employ a Master could find in these books rules to guide them in the basic elements of child education.[10] As the Russian historian, Paul Milyukov, has pointed out, "the demand for secondary and higher education developed much earlier than the need of elementary schooling. That one could learn to read and write without going to school was the general conviction." [11]

Throughout all these contemporary writings, one may

search in vain for any tangible reference to the qualifications of the teacher. It was usually "expected" that sufficient tutelage would be given in "God's Law," that the children would "study grammar," and that they would learn to become "honest, devout, and obedient." But, perhaps with good reason, no mention is made that the teacher should himself be aware of his duties and obligations. Two nineteenth-century historians,[12] looking back upon the School of Masters of Literacy which flourished in Moscow during the fifteenth, sixteenth, and seventeenth centuries, declare that "the teachers of this school, supported by means of receipts, were drawn from the clergy." (We have already seen that this fact did not necessarily assure their literacy.) The authors observe further that "the stern teacher, it seems, when it was necessary to read or write, did not like to go over twice what was said; he favored the birch rod or a cuff on the head, believing it thus easier and quicker to recall knowledge to the mind of the forgetful student." So far as "requirements" were concerned, we are told: "The birch rod and the leather lash were usually the primary needs of the teacher of that day."

This situation is not surprising, for the history of education in the western world reveals that in every nation the creation of a nucleus of a system of public instruction has antedated the establishment of any definite plan for the training of teachers. Despite the acknowledged dependence of the early schools upon the person of the pedagogue, it appears that the teacher was to be molded to fit the system, rather than the system to fit the teacher. Since "the Russian people had no school system at all prior to the sixteenth century," [13] we cannot expect to find any clearly formulated regulations concerning teacher qualifications prior to that period. Therefore, let us examine briefly the beginnings of these early schools.

"Schools, *as an Institution*, first arose at the end of the sixteenth century in southwestern Russia." [14] This region, which included Kiev, had long been under the cultural influence of western Europe. Many historians since have described the cultural life along the great river routes of the old Ukraine. One of the most scholarly of these writers, Professor Raymond Beazley of the University of Birmingham, England, declares that even by the middle of the twelfth century "a high level of material prosperity, active citizenship, and general culture, had been maintained by the men of Kiev. . . . The annals of this time bear emphatic testimony to the learning of the Russian princes of the great Kievian time, and to their zeal for culture—their knowledge of other tongues ('a thing foreigners admire in us', says Vladimir Monomakh), their wide reading, their book collections, their foundation of schools, their encouragement of Greek and Latin study, their reception of foreign scholars. Before the era of our Norman conquest something of a Russian Literature had been founded, and there are Russian manuscripts of the twelfth century which can almost be compared with really fine examples from the West." [15] But it is noteworthy that the greater part of all this learning was attained through private instruction. The same situation prevailed even during the reign of Boris Godunov (1598-1605), who was "the first Tsar to import foreign teachers on a great scale [and] the first to send young Russians abroad to be educated." [16]

However, by the time the annexation of southwestern Russia to the Muscovite domain took place in 1667 there were already flourishing in the former region several types of schools. The oldest of these were the church schools, where neophytes were instructed in the elementary religious studies; these schools, of course, were open only to those willing to take the religious vows and to devote the remainder of their lives to the service of the Orthodox faith.[17] The second type were the schools of various brotherhoods, where monks carried on individual study of religious doctrine and occasionally gave instruction in this same doctrine to the residents of the community. Another educational agency should be mentioned in this same connection, even though it hardly constitutes a school: that is the large number of private "Masters" who were employed by the wealthier citizens to teach children in the home.[18] This last-named group was probably the largest of the three but it was, by its very nature, unorganized, isolated, and subject to no unified direction or supervision. These three modes of instruction have their roots far back in the ancient history of Russia and other nations as well. Another type of school, encouraged by the revival of learning in western Europe, had a more recent origin: this was the Latin School, established in Russia in much the same form as it bore in Germany and in Poland. Despite their minor differences, the four prevalent forms of education—the church school, the brotherhood school, the private master, the Latin school—had a common general aim.[19] "These schools served the needs of the church, the society, and the state: that is, the needs of those classes which then predominated and filled from their own circles the offices of spiritual, legal and civil administration." [20]

But alongside these schools, there already existed schools in the native language, giving instruction in literacy to the wide masses of town and sometimes even village people. "Although these schools were institutions of the church brotherhoods, they were not always exclusively for churchmen. They did not prepare priests, or deacons, and if readers and singers went from their cloisters into the church, many also emerged simply as enlightened, literate people." Some foreign and native nobles, merely wishing their sons to become well-educated, sent them to these institutions.[21] With the rise of these schools, profound elements of educational progress began to assert themselves. First of all, there now existed agencies where instruction was carried on in the native language, thus increasing literacy in the communities served by the schools. Secondly, the various brotherhoods sponsored the instruction, and undoubtedly offered some semblance of unified supervision. Thirdly, the number of pupils reached by these schools far exceeded those served by the older agencies. And lastly, "these schools were created and supported by the people themselves, almost without interference on the part of the state." [22] Thus were laid two of the basic components of any system of public education: native language instruction, and wide public support. The fact that the teachers in these schools were responsible to their brotherhood organizations certainly had a great influence in the formulation of teacher qualifications. The Rules of the School of the Lutsk Brotherhood, quoted above, attest to the progress made in this direction by the second quarter of the seventeenth century.

For concrete evidence of the early concern of the Lutsk Brotherhood School for the capacities of the teacher, let us return to an examination of these Rules, which are important not only in themselves, but also because they "exemplify the character of Brotherhood schools in general, since all such schools were arranged more or less on the same basis." [23] The Rules consist of twenty articles describing in detail the aims, methods, curriculum and general regulations of the School. Nine of the articles refer directly to the responsibilities of the teacher. In addition to possessing the personal qualities enumerated in Article I,[24] "he must both teach and love all children alike; the miserable orphans and those who wander over the streets begging for food, as well as the sons of the rich. Teach them as much as each one is able to learn, according to his power, and not some more diligently than others. . . . The teacher is obligated to teach and set forth propositions for [the pupils], in writing, from the Holy Gospel, from the books of the apostles, from all the prophets, from the teachings of the holy fathers, from philosophers, poets, historians, and others, for 'whatever has been written down has been written for our instruction.' " [25]

The Lutsk teacher assumed full responsibility for the discipline, as well as the instruction, of the pupils, for the Rules state that "every morning the teacher must carefully observe in order that, if some boy be absent, he might immediately send for him and learn the reason why he had not come.[26] Did he get preoccupied somewhere in play? Was he lazing around the house? Did he oversleep and so did not come to school? The teacher must make inquiry concerning all these things, and bring the boy to school, for it is written: 'Save the sheep by fear and force.' " [27] Nor did the teacher's duties toward the pupil end with the school day. "After dinner on Saturday it is the teacher's duty to take not less but considerably more time than on other days in talking with the children, instructing them in the fear of God and the clean habits of youth: how they are to conduct themselves in church before God, at home with their family, and how they are to preserve virtue and purity, showing reverence and awe before God and the Saints, obedience to kin and the teacher, and, in general, humility and respect for all. . . . And these admonitions must be instilled in the children ever anew, for which purpose it will not hurt them to drink out of the school goblet [28] for their memory's sake. For it is written: 'Loving his son, a man chastises him more diligently; and not loving him, he spares the rod.' And again: 'Senselessness hangs upon the heart of a youth, but the rod and the punishment will drive it far from him'.[29] On Sunday and the Lord's holidays, when [the pupils] go to the liturgy, it is the teacher's duty to talk with them and instruct them concerning that holiday or holy day, and to teach them

God's will. And after dinner he must explain to them the Gospel and the apostolics of the holiday. For it is said: 'Blessed is he who studies God's law day and night.' "[30]

Much care was also taken in regard to maintaining co-operation between the teacher and the parents of the children, from the very day of the child's enrollment in the School. "A person bringing his son (or others) and giving him over to learning, should bring with him one or two of his neighbors, so that all talk may be held in the presence of these two or three witnesses; and so make an agreement with the teacher concerning the learning and its order of sequence according to the list set forth [in subsequent articles of the Rules]. And first of all he must have read the list, so that he might know in what manner his son will be taught, and so that the teacher may not hinder him in the order of learning but may assist the children by all means. . . .[31] And the teacher, having taken the child entrusted to him, must carefully teach him the useful subjects; must punish him for disobedience, not like a tyrant, but like an instructor, not in excess but according to the child's capacity, not with violence but meekly and gently. . . . So that the teacher will not stand guilty of negligence, envy or shyness—even toward one pupil—before Almighty God, before the kin of the pupil or before the pupil himself, in having taken the pupil's time and engaged him in subjects other than those agreed upon. For it is said: 'Sly and lazy slave, it seemed as if he put my money in trade but instead he took it for usury.' "[32]

The obligation of the teacher seems not to have ended even with the graduation of the pupil. "The teacher and the Brothers . . . must remind the parents concerning their sons (and the householders concerning other children) entrusted to them, that the children behave according to the injunctions learned at school, thus exhibiting their education and the politeness proper to their years and social class. And if anything has shown up in the children contrary to their education, it must be investigated whether the teacher, through neglect, or the relatives of the householder, through laxity, stood in the way of learning and good habits, so that the guilty one might be held responsible." [33]

The last article in the Rules emphasizes much the same qualities as does the first article, already quoted above,[34] and again directly connects the behavior of the teacher with that of the pupils. "If the teacher himself or any of his pupils were guilty of such behavior as the law not only does not prescribe but even forbids, if, for example, he were dissolute, a drunkard, a thief, scoffing at sacred things, careless, a lover of money, a slanderer, full of pride—such a man should certainly not be even a resident here, much less a teacher. 'Do not tempt,' said the Saviour, 'even one of these little ones who believe in My Name.' For if the teacher himself be an opponent of God's commandments, how can he keep others safe in virtue and instruct them to their profit? The Lord himself has said: 'Ye cannot, being evil, give tongue to goodliness.' And again: 'A tree, if it does not produce good fruit, is cut down, and thrown into the fire.' " [35]

It is noteworthy that among all these regulations stressing the necessity of piety, devotion, and diligence as the prime requisites of a teacher, there is not one mention of such attributes as wisdom, teaching ability, or knowledge of specific subject matter outside the realm of theology. However, these limited requirements are quite logical in view of the main objective of the School—to rear devout children—and its simple curriculum consisting of reading, writing, arithmetic, discourse and memorization.[36] Nevertheless, the pupils had to learn to speak, read and write in two foreign languages—Greek and Slavonic—as well as in Russian,[37] and certainly the teacher would be expected to have a command of these tongues. Yet the requirement is not included explicitly in the Rules. Evidently, since the teacher was invariably a member of the Brotherhood,[38] it was assumed that he possessed these skills.

More than half a century was to elapse before another important institution would attempt an improvement upon the teacher requirements established at Lutsk in 1624. Meanwhile, certain other institutions apparently carried on the educational process without setting up any definite written requirements for their faculties. The most important example of this tendency was the Lavr School established in 1631 by Peter Mogila to combat the increasing influence of the Jesuits. Its stated purpose was "to teach free knowledge in Greek, Slavonic and Latin, at the same time preserving the Christian truths of Eastern Orthodoxy." [39] Through long study of Western culture, including attendance at the Sorbonne, Mogila had come to the conclusion that the best way to conquer the prevalent heterodoxy was to fight it with its own weapons. Therefore, the eight-year curriculum of the Lavr School "was almost a copy of the Jesuit schools of Poland . . . and Latin was used both as the medium of teaching and as the language of conversation for the pupils. It was this institution which furnished the bands of scholars who corrected the sacred books of the Russian Church, and afforded a nucleus for the later work of Peter the Great. It was also the center from which came the translations of works of Western culture, and its graduates were among the first teachers of the following period." [40] Throughout the early years of its influence, the institution had a student body of more than two hundred and a faculty numbering at least four and perhaps even six or eight members. Mogila's ability to attract fine scholars known personally to him found recognition in the fact that, after an existence of only two years, the Lavr School received from King Wladyslaw VII of Poland "the privileges and title of 'Academy' " and was thenceforth known as the Kiev Academy.[41]

Simeon Polotskii, through whose influence the Moscow Hellenic-Greek Academy (later to be renamed the Slavonic-Greek-Latin Academy) was opened in 1687, was also a great scholar in his own right, although not as versed in Western thought as was Peter Mogila. Polotskii had served as tutor to the two elder sons of Tsar Alexis (half-brothers of Peter I) and was probably just as capable as Mogila of selecting his staff on the basis of personal knowledge. Nevertheless, the Patriarch Joachim, the real ruler of Russia during the early years of the reign of the child Peter I, left nothing to chance. Joachim's decree licensing the establishment of this Academy in 1682 (it did not open until five years later) is composed of a series of demands which in several respects go far beyond even the careful delineation of teachers' duties governing the School at Lutsk. Whereas the rules of the latter institution simply forbid the employment of magicians and sorcerers as teachers, the Moscow Academy regulations insist that if such heretics do manage to inject themselves into the staff, "without any mercy let them be burned." [42] The rules are explicit also regarding the positive attributes to be possessed by the faculty members at the Academy: "In our school we ordain that the guardian and teachers shall be pious, born of pious parents, and brought up in the Orthodox Christian Eastern faith of the Russian and Greek people." [43] Only students of this same faith were admitted to the school, and to these Orthodox lads great rewards were promised in return for the display of diligence in their studies: such were to obtain "meet recompense for their concern with the sciences, and upon completion of the liberal studies they will be graciously welcomed into the decorous ranks of wise men, according to their intelligence, and will enjoy our special Imperial generous mercy." All others, including the indolent and the irreverent, were barred forever from service to the state except in the army—children of nobles, however, were exempt from this proscription out of deference to their rank.[44]

Only a few of Joachim's eighteen specific regulations concern the relationship of teacher and student, most of them being occupied with the surveillance which the faculty was to exercise over the learned members of the Russian population and scholars visiting Russia from foreign lands. No person, for example, could keep in his own house a teacher of *any* foreign language "without the knowledge and permission of the School's guardian and teachers," nor could any child be educated in languages other than the Russian (even by his own parents!), lest "opposition to our Orthodox faith be introduced." [45] The School officials were to be on the watch for any citizen of the Empire suspected of entertaining even slightly unorthodox opinions, so as to expose him to shame and possible punishment. Particular obligations were laid upon the faculty members in the matter of the policing of foreigners, all of whom were open to suspicion: these persons were to be closely watched for heretical utterances and, if accused of such by the teachers, they "shall by our Imperial order be interdicted and subdued . . . , and tried without any remission by the proper civil courts." [46] The teachers were also charged with the registration of "all those who come from various faiths and heresies to our Orthodox Eastern faith," and were obligated to observe each case for evidence of dereliction. That this latter responsibility was in no sense a nominal or casual one is indicated by the penalties prescribed for those found guilty upon the testimony of a teacher: exile to Siberia for "failure wholly to keep our Orthodox faith and church traditions . . . [and] if any be found to hold to his former faith or heresy . . . let such be burned without any mercy whatsoever." [47]

One would think these duties, in addition to teaching, would be sufficient for the members of the Academy's faculty. However, according to the Regulations as set down by Simeon Polotskii, the chief energies of the teachers—and the most fiery wrath of the state—were reserved for the possessors of questionable books. "The guardian and the teachers [of the Academy] shall take great care that no spiritual or secular person of any rank whatsoever shall keep with him any books or writings of magic and enchantment and divination, or any books whatsoever that are blasphemous and hated of God and forbidden by the church, or act according to them or teach them. . . . Likewise, no person unlearned in the liberal teachings shall keep in his house Polish, Latin, German, Lutheran, Calvinistic or other heretical books, nor shall he read them. . . . All such heretical books shall be burned or brought to the guardian and teachers of the School. If any one be found to oppose [or to continue to disobey] this our Imperial command . . . , such a man, upon trustworthy testimony, shall be burned without any mercy." [48] In addition to these police powers, the School faculty also had the privileges of the judiciary. "If anyone of the foreigners or Russians, while banqueting or in any other place whatsoever, in the presence of proper witnesses, blaspheme our Orthodox Christian faith or church traditions or utter any reproving words concerning them, he shall be handed over for trial in this matter to the guardian and teachers of the School," who have the authority to condemn recalcitrants to the usual punishment, that is, to "be burned without any mercy." [49]

After such descriptions of the nonacademic responsibilities of the Academy teachers, it is somewhat anticlimactic to learn, in the last two regulations, that the faculty is expected to safeguard the State Library and maintain the school premises in proper order.[50] Nor does the rule requiring domicile and sustenance for the faculty within the Academy grounds [51] seem motivated entirely by considerations for their comfort; more likely it was to assure their constant surveillance of one another! Fortunately for all concerned, this state of affairs—if ever actually carried into practice—was short-lived; after several changes in the aims and organization of the Academy, a decree of Peter I in 1701 transferred the institution to the state and converted it into a completely Latin school.[52] Although the Academy was a step forward for Moscow, it "had no actual connection with Western science, and for a hundred years lagged behind the Kiev Academy, being far inferior to the latter as an actual educational institution. Even in the eighteenth century, Lomonosov [the greatest Russian scientist] went to Kiev after finishing at Moscow." [53]

In addition to the establishment of these three great schools (at Lutsk, Kiev, and Moscow), and others similar to them,[54] another event of tremendous educational importance occurred during the seventeenth century: the transfer of the Russian schools from a Greek-Slavonic basis to a Polish-Latin basis. This metamorphosis did not take place in all schools simultaneously, of course; a consensus of historical opinion dates the transformation as evolving during the period from 1630 to 1680.[55] By the latter date, Latin had become the language of nearly all the schools in Russia with the exception of the church schools for the higher clergy, of which the most notable example was the Moscow Academy (described at length above), which had been founded by a Greek brotherhood and therefore remained motivated by Eastern influences for a somewhat longer period. In direct opposition to the Moscow Academy, an interesting type of rural school arose. These agencies were known as Sextant, or "Old-Believer," Schools. Their opposition to the prevailing educational institutions was based not so much upon the matter of language as upon the growing centralization in Moscow of all power to define religious dogma. "From this schism arose the first 'people's schools'. . . . A new kind of 'teacher-master' appeared, followed soon after by the 'teacher-masteress'. . . , the latter being the first female teacher in Russia." [56] She went to the homes where parents entrusted her with the schooling of small groups of children. "Her school was completely religious in program and tasks; teach to pray, to read religious books, and to participate in divine service—these were the aims of instruction." The teacher observed the children in exercises such as these, and in return she was supported by the grateful parents. Remuneration of this type, however, "was not the same as paying for study, not the same as the fee—in the old sense of the term—demanded by the craft of the society of 'masters of literacy.' " [57] These "people's schools" represented a new type of education in Russia, a type which continued with very little change until the Bolshevik Revolution in October 1917.[58]

In view of these real and vital achievements both in clerical and lay education, it is quite unfair to assume that no progress at all was made in Russian enlightenment until the time of Peter the Great. One scholar claims that in Russia the seventeenth century ended "leaving in matters of public education nothing started and nothing accomplished, leaving no Russian school, no educational traditions, except the passive resistance of ignorance." [59] While it is true that several decades were to pass before Russia would actually possess *public* schools, and more than a century before these schools would be numerous enough to constitute a *system*, it should be obvious from the materials presented in this chapter that a real start had been made. As we shall see, the achievements of the seventeenth-century scholars provided the main groundwork for the educational enterprises of Peter I.

3

The Rise of the State Universities (1700–1760)

THE EIGHTEENTH-CENTURY EDUCATIONAL reforms were ushered in most auspiciously on January 14, 1701, by the decree of Peter I establishing the School of Mathematical and Navigation Sciences at Moscow. In this decree, Peter does much more than merely define the requirements of a teacher: he names the teachers whom he wants appointed.[1] Present-day Russian historians claim that this institution was "the first nonclassical school in the world," antedating by several years *Die Mathematische und Mechanische Realschule* which opened in Halle, Germany, in 1706.[2] Originally the School was intended to prepare naval officers, engineers, architects, and teachers of mathematics, and for several years it performed these functions.[3] The curriculum consisted of "arithmetic, algebra, geometry, trigonometry, geodesy, geography, the English language, navigation, engineering, and other sciences."[4] Its director and most of its teachers were foreigners, "for there existed no supply in Russia, and few of those sent abroad had acquired sufficient knowledge to teach."[5] Shortly after setting up this school in Moscow, Peter began to build his new Russian capital in St. Petersburg, and in 1715 he founded in the latter city the Naval Academy, which soon supplanted the School as an institution of higher learning. The latter then became a preparatory school for the new institution.[6]

In establishing the Naval Academy, Peter outlined a series of twenty-seven Instructions to govern its administration. Prominent among these rules was the stipulation that the authority of the teacher be unquestioned: the students "shall endeavor to learn what their teachers and professors teach, and they shall with all attention receive all the precepts which the said teachers and professors shall to them impart, and they shall have due respect for them under pain of punishment."[7] This statement is important, for its tone reveals a new attitude toward the teaching profession. Formerly, the teacher had been viewed somewhat as a respected menial, a trusted attendant to the young pupils, most of whom far outdistanced him in social standing. In the records of the early eighteenth century we note for the first time that the teacher in Russia is honored in a set of practical rules, rather than merely in a philosophical treatise. In addition, Peter established fourteen grades of officials and placed teachers at the tenth level from the top.[8] Though still not in an exalted position, teaching was now regarded as a profession.

This does not mean, however, that Tsar Peter was lenient in regard to academic obligations, for the Instructions state that "His Imperial Majesty commands the teachers and professors to be in the Academy at the same designated hours [as the students], and to endeavor to teach the Marine Guard everything which pertains to their rank, with all diligence and in the best reasonable manner, under pain of punishment." [9] Lest the staff become lax in these duties, "His Majesty Commands the Director of the Academy and the Commander of the Marine Guard to be in the halls and classrooms on all days . . . and to see that the teachers and professors teach, that the Marine Guards learn all the sciences, and that teachers and students perform their other respective duties." [10] In order to insure against possible collusion between students and faculty, "all teachers and professors are forbidden to accept any gift, either in direct or devious manner, from the Marine Guard, under the penalty of returning it four-fold for utilization at the discretion of His Imperial Majesty; and whoever in any way falls into such error, will receive corporal punishment." [11] Just a few years before, the main concern of disciplinarians had been about the indoctrination of heresies; [12] Peter's anxiety about acts of bribery seems much more practical in view of the level of teachers' salaries even in those days. Moreover, the ultimate penalty imposed during the preceding century invariably robbed the pedagogical profession of a much-needed member, while that decreed by Peter permitted the retention of the wayward teacher and at the same time augmented the Tsar's treasury.

Such reforms merely illustrate an attitude for which Peter I has already received much credit from historians. In a large sense it is true that he opened "a window on the West," thus encouraging the influx to Russia of more progressive ideas from her European neighbors. But it was not alone the personality of the Tsar that led to the reforms. New foreign trade agreements were straining the rather primitive Russian industry, which in turn placed greater demands upon the educational agencies. More people had to be trained for the further exploitation of natural resources, for the reorganization of military affairs, and for the modification of Russian civil laws along the lines of those of the more advanced nations. Although the government brought in many foreign specialists, it was nevertheless incumbent upon Russia at least "to think of preparing her own workers" for these gigantic tasks. Thus "there arose a new service for the nobility: the teaching profession." [13] Promising young Russian men were sent abroad to study at the highest levels, with the expectation that they would return to become leaders in education. Textbooks were imported, translated into Russian, and reissued in large quantities for use in the schools.[14] For the first time in Russia, the work of preparing teachers began to be conducted on a secular plane.

But the Church did not remain oblivious to the new activity in the field of education. "Simultaneously with the solicitude of the government for the training of its necessary specialists, the higher clergy (the majority of whom up to that time had been educated in the Kiev academies) began to be concerned about the systematic training of better educated church officials. Until the middle of the eighteenth century there was in Russia no special educational institution for preparing priests. The neophyte practically prepared himself to enter on the road to candidacy by working in a church as reader, clerk, or deacon. He learned simply by hearing and remembering. Even at the beginning of the nineteenth century one met illiterate priests." [15] Just as the government found itself in need of trained personnel, so did the Church come to realize the advantage of well educated disputants in the ranks of the clergy. A number of archbishops opened elementary schools for novitiates, either in their own courtyards or under the direct supervision of the monasteries. "The teachers were usually drawn from Kiev, and the program was based on the model program of the southwestern church schools, formerly the

Brotherhood schools."[16] By 1724 there were forty-six such church schools, from which developed the theological seminaries of the later eighteenth century.[17]

But Peter, even at the turn of the century, already seems to have had in mind not only a renovation of the Church educational programs but also a reorganization of the Church itself. When the Patriarch Adrian died in 1700, "Peter declared that the choice of a successor was so important that it must be deferred for full consideration. No appointment was ever made. . . ."[18] However, in 1721 Peter signed the famous document entitled "Ecclesiastical Statutes"[19] which abolished the Patriarchate and erected the Holy Synod in its stead.[20] Peter's chief collaborator on this document, and its probable author, was Feofan Prokopovich, a progressive, erudite archbishop who had several heresies to his credit. A graduate of the Kiev Academy, Prokopovich had been appointed by Peter as Rector of that institution after several years of study in Europe. Thus he brought to his new role of author the traditions of the Kievian church scholars, some of the "liberalism" of the West, and a devotion to Peter's concept that the State should dominate the Church, rather than the other way around.[21]

The Ecclesiastical Statutes are important because they prescribe the new form which the Church administration is to take, and set forth the new methods of education which it must employ. Although they undoubtedly express the views on education held by both the Tsar and Prokopovich, the Statutes also reflect much of the new "spirit of the time" which has been described briefly above. Characteristically, they include a disparagement of previous educational efforts: "Meet it is to know that from the 500th to the 1400th year, that is for 900 years, throughout all Europe almost all learning was in great decay and neglect. . . . After [that] there . . . began to appear the most inquisitive and therefore the most skillful teachers, and little by little many academies did gain very great strength. . . . But many schools remain in their previous mire so that, while they offer rhetoric and philosophy and other sciences, they possess not the real essences." [22]

Therefore, continue the Statutes, should His Imperial Majesty judge it fitting to found an Academy,[23] "the Ecclesiastical College [Holy Synod] would deliberate what teachers to appoint and what manner of teaching to indicate to them, so that the Sovereign's expenditure might not be in vain, and that instead of the expected benefit there might not be vanity worthy of ridicule." [24] After this explicit delegation to the Holy Synod of full authority in matters regarding appointment of teachers and selection of methods, the Statutes then brazenly enunciate twenty-six "helpful rules, lest it be difficult [for the churchmen] to proceed skillfully" toward these ends. These rules are important enough to deserve rather full analysis, but a few excerpts will be sufficient to delineate their main characteristics.

The first four rules apply to the number and qualifications of the teachers to be appointed, stating that "there is no need, at first, of many teachers, one or two being sufficient for the first year; these would teach grammar, that is, the correct knowledge of Latin or Greek or both. The second and third years, proceeding to greater teachings, let a larger number of teachers be added while still retaining the original staff for instructing new pupils." [25] The process of selecting teachers is proposed in rather specific terms: "In every case of him who wishes to be a school teacher, test him out in his work. For example, desiring to know whether he is skilled in Latin, bid him translate a Russian composition into Latin, and likewise translate into Russian the words of some author celebrated in the Latin tongue. Then bid someone skilled therein examine and attest to his translations, and at once it will appear whether he be perfect or mediocre, or even lower than that, or wholly naught. There are also trials proper to other disciplines which may be specially transcribed." [26]

Practical as this test appears, there is no definite statement regarding just which of the four degrees of skill mentioned must be demonstrated by the teacher. In fact, the succeeding admonition makes it clear that the candidate's possession of an agile mind may sometimes temporarily compensate not only for ignorance but for laziness as well: "And though he show himself unskilled in the required discipline, but it be known that he is keen-witted and manifestly failed to qualify because of sloth or a bad teacher, bid him study half a year or a year from authors skilled in the work, if the teacher so desire. This do only because of the scarcity of people; better would it be not to resort to such." [27]

Having offered these concrete but still rather inconclusive suggestions, the Statutes go on to describe the basic methods to be utilized in the actual instruction of the pupils. Since theology, naturally, was to be the most important course in the Academy, a brief description of the procedures proposed for that course will afford a conception of the entire methodology. "In Theology [say the Statutes], it is proper to order that the chief dogmas of our faith and the divine law be taught. The theology teacher should read the sacred scriptures and teach the rules governing the knowledge of the straight and true Power, and the meaning of the Scriptures; and should fortify all the dogmas with the testimony of the scriptures. And to aid in this matter he should read assiduously the books of the Holy Fathers, and of those fathers who have written diligently concerning the dogmas because of disputes that have arisen in the Church, including attacks on opposing heresies." [28] Contrary to the restrictions upon teachers imposed, for example, by the original Moscow Slavonic-Greek-Latin Academy less than forty years earlier,[29] these Statutes specifically declare that "the theology teacher may also seek aid from the most modern teachers of other faiths, although he must not teach from them nor rely upon their sayings. . . . The theology teacher must teach . . . according to his own knowledge; and, choosing the proper times, should now and then show the books also to his pupils, so that they too may be sure and may not doubt whether their teacher speak the truth or a lie."[30]

Despite such ideas relating to the higher and more ethereal realms of education, most of the schools actually opened during the era of Peter's reforms were of a purely vocational, or even "narrow-specialty," character. For example, the Moscow Navigation School mentioned earlier prepared students exclusively for the Azov Sea fleet, and it set the pattern on which many similar schools, such as the St. Petersburg Naval Academy, were later modeled. The "cypher schools" were established in 1714 to provide the government with semi-skilled technical workers, "acquainted with arithmetic, geometry and geodesy," so that the tremendous program of military and public construction could go on. Teachers for these schools were drawn from among graduates of the Navigation School and, later, the Naval Academy. In several towns, "garrison schools" prepared the children of soldiers to become noncommissioned officers. The enumeration of these types of schools might lead one to conceive their total scope to have been much broader than it actually was. As a matter of fact, "the government looked upon its tasks in the affairs of public education from the utilitarian point of view: it opened only those schools which prepared the specialists it required."[31] Even in 1724, a year before Peter's death, there were only 110 secular elementary schools in all of Russia, a nation of 13 million people, and 40 of these were "cypher schools" attended by a total of about two thousand pupils.[32] It is true that in 1719 literacy was made mandatory for the children of the nobility and the clergy, and compulsory State examinations were conducted for all well-born youths. A gentleman was forbidden to marry unless he had either graduated from elementary school or could otherwise prove himself able to read and write. Although this law could not be fully enforced, an illiterate son of a noble or priest was penalized by the loss of certain privileges and might even find himself conscripted into the army for life.[33] But "the matter of instruction in literacy and general education was regarded as the private affair of the citizenry. . . . Thus was organized government care of the schools, but not of the dissemination of education." [34]

The government program, however, did instigate the translation and publication of a greater number of books, an increase in the number and circulation of newspapers, and the opening of several museums.[35] While the immediate beneficial effects of these innovations accrued directly only to those persons already literate, there was undoubtedly an influence therefrom on the various types of schools in the western part of Russia, at least. Certainly the Academy of Sciences, soon after its opening in St. Petersburg in 1725, began to exert a profound influence upon the few secondary schools in the Empire. Although the Academy was actually opened after Peter's death, he had begun, some ten years before, a "correspondence with [Christian] Wolf, the German philosopher, and with [Gottfried Wilhelm] Leibnitz, and had organized a plan for the creation of seventeen professorships, and a gymnasium which was to serve as a feeder for the Academy. That is, it was to be at once a learned society, a university, and a secondary school." [36] It is probable that Peter himself wished the new Academy to be an institution solely of higher learning, for his 1724 decree establishing it makes no mention of a gymnasium, stating only that the Academy will consist of two levels, or "forms"; the University to train Russian scientists, and the Academy to pursue higher research and supply "professors" for the University.[37] The need for the gymnasium seems to have become apparent only in the very year of the actual opening of the Academy, and the solution of this problem and its numerous ramifications during the next decade constitutes one of the most fantastic stories in educational history. Although the full details of the complex situation are still not clear, the works of several reliable authors[38] attest to the following sequence of events.

It was discovered rather late that no Russian scientist of that day possessed the qualifications necessary for appointment to professorial rank, so in 1726 seventeen German scientists were imported to fill the number of posts specified in Tsar Peter's decree. The conditions of their appointment required them to give lectures and, since few Russian students studied German, the professors were to lecture in Latin. Then the gymnasium was established in order to insure that the Russian students would know sufficient Latin.

Now a new problem arose: no Russian students already accomplished in Latin applied for admission to the lectures, and the beginning students in the gymnasium were not yet proficient in that language. Since it would be highly irregular for a university to exist without students, eight Latin-speaking youths were imported from Europe to serve in this capacity. All would have been in order had not the Russian Government, sorely in need of trained young scientists, immediately employed all eight lads on practical projects, leaving the University still bereft of students. At the same time, the Government insisted that the seventeen professors observe strictly the terms of their contracts regarding the giving of lectures.

Nothing was left for the miserable scholars but to lecture to one another. This situation soon became obviously ridiculous, so lectures were abandoned altogether and the professors devoted full time to research. The staff became noticeably excited in 1732 when twelve students were brought to the University from the Moscow Theological Seminary (the former Slavonic-Greek-Latin Academy). But their delight was short-lived, for the Government soon sent all of the twelve on a scientific expedition which was leaving immediately for Kamchatka. By the time twelve more graduates of the same school could be rounded up, in 1736, they found they could learn nothing at the University because the professors could no longer be persuaded to give lectures at all!

Although the fortunes of the University improved in later years, it was long in becoming the kind of institution which Peter I had envisioned: "In 1760 when the first great Russian scholar, [Mikhail V.] Lomonosov, became Rector of the University, he divided it into three faculties: the philosophical, the juridical, and the medical. He established dormitories, he compelled the professors to deliver lectures; but the students never exceeded the number of twenty, and in fact in 1782 there were only two students. . . . Nevertheless, even if the classroom work amounted to nothing, the St. Petersburg University, by reason of the very existence of a scholarly faculty, had a considerable influence in the eighteenth century." [39]

Thus Peter I had enormous direct influence upon the secular and religious educational institutions of his time. We note also that he was acutely aware of the value of good teachers in these schools, for his decrees, unlike many previous edicts on schools, invariably insisted that qualified teachers be sought. But what did other influential men think about the teacher and his specific role in molding the minds of the new generation? The answer exists in a treatise by Vassili Nikitich Tatishchev, who was as close a collaborator with Peter on pedagogical affairs as Feofan Prokopovich in clerical matters, and who is described as being even more liberal than the latter in his social philosophy.[40] In 1733 Tatishchev published his "Dialogue on the Benefits of Science and the Schools"[41] which, in the form of more than a hundred questions and answers, defends the principles of free scientific inquiry and teaching. In a discussion regarding military schools, one of the queries is "What qualifications are required in teachers?" In reply Tatishchev outlines views which undoubtedly summarize the attitudes of the progressive thinkers of the mid-eighteenth century who were beginning to free themselves of the chains of the Orthodox dogma.

Teachers, says Tatishchev, "must be judged partly upon their knowledge and partly upon their social standing. In accordance with the principles of the Divine Law, they must be sufficiently learned in the rules of true theology as well as in morality; not hypocritical nor superstitious, but of good judgment; and if monks not less than 50 years old and of good mode of life be not found, there is no objection to using for the purpose secular persons having wives. Military officers shall be the main teachers even though foreigners are used because of lack of sufficient learned persons in our country. . . . Teachers of all other sciences [except Theology] may be foreigners provided that each is not only sufficiently learned himself in his science but also has adequate ability to instruct; for not every learned person is suited for teaching others, persons of truculent or arrogant character especially being unfit for the instruction of youths. Both for teaching in the state schools and in private schools, instructors must be prepared from among Russians so that foreign teachers may not always have to be contracted at great loss [of money]. Apprentices may be appointed from the gymnasiums to assist the foreign teachers, two such persons being chosen for each science;

in this way it is hoped that we shall attain in time enough suitable teachers of our own."[42]

In the foregoing tract it is possible to see certain new ideas of the century in contrast to the old: a knowledge of the scriptures important but not decisive; piety subordinate to intelligence; foreigners utilized extensively even in military schools, and unwelcome only for financial, not ideological reasons; and finally the concept that erudition is not the only criterion of the ability to teach. It was such ideas as these which formed the foundation of the educational progress made during the remainder of the eighteenth century.

As mentioned above, the near half-century of Peter's reign (1682-1725), with its progressive economic doctrines, church reorganization, and civil reforms, also encouraged the higher classes in Russia to look toward western Europe for ideas and for institutions. For a long time certain members of the Russian nobility had perceived the need for a well-organized program of education for their younger children. At this time the law of primogeniture still prevailed in Russia. The eldest son of a noble inherited the title and all the property, while the younger children faced the prospect of having to support themselves. Hence the need of a practical education for the latter.[43] These nobles learned of the Cadet Corps in France and the Knightly Academy in Germany, both established at the end of the previous century with the aim of giving fundamental instruction of high quality to the children of the upper classes.

So, in 1731, there was opened the Noble Cadet Corpus, housed in a magnificent building on the banks of the Neva River at St. Petersburg, which was to serve "200 children of noble birth from 13 to 18 years of age."[44] They were to be prepared for military and civil offices, and toward this end they were given a surprisingly secular course of study, similar to that of the finishing schools of Europe. Latin was relegated to a minor place in the curriculum, while the modern languages—French, German, Italian and Polish—were stressed. In like manner, the usual philosophical and philological studies gave place to the exact sciences such as mathematics and physics—subjects which laid a foundation for the students' future careers in military strategy, artillery and fortifications. Nor were the arts neglected: "dancing, singing, music, rhyme-making, and finally, the art of horseback riding and the mastery of swordsmanship—matters of absolute necessity to any young nobleman of that time"—were required courses at the Cadet Corpus. Since a virile but gentlemanly spirit prevailed, "torture, coercion and beating" of students by the teachers were strictly forbidden.[45]

In addition, "the desire was growing, on the part of the nobility, for a higher education. New interest in foreign countries and languages resulted in the sending of children abroad and the importation of foreign tutors, as well as the establishment and growth of private boarding schools, established by foreigners, which sprang up in large numbers during the reign of Elizabeth (1741-61)," daughter of Peter I. "By 1764 there were some 27 such institutions giving higher education to some 6000 pupils." [46] A start had already been made on this program under Peter, of course, and his widow, the Empress Catherine I, had carried to fruition the Academy of Sciences during the brief two years of her reign. The Empress Anne (1730-40) contributed the Cadet Corpus, although the real organizer of this institution was Count Burkhard Christoph Münnich, a German who had been among the last foreigners brought into Russia by Peter.[47] However, not one of these establishments really fulfilled the most essential need in Russia at that time: a well-organized university equipped with a broad curriculum, staffed by competent native teachers, and devoting all of its time to the higher education of selected students. "It was felt that, with more and better facilities provided by the state, with more and better teachers who were also Russians, the growth of the private schools would cease." [48]

The opening of the Moscow University in January 1755 —"the first real Russian University" [49]—was, therefore, the crowning event in the eighteenth-century efforts toward higher education in Russia. The university possessed three faculties: philosophy, law, and medicine. The professors were obligated not only to lecture to the students, but also to give public addresses; however the public profited little from this provision until 1768, when French was made optional with Latin in the contracts. From the very beginning, French and German had been used in the classrooms, for most of the teachers were, of course, foreigners, although vacancies on the faculty were soon filled with Russians who had studied abroad.[50] "Strict supervision was exercised by the State over the actual instruction." [51] The original student body consisted of a hundred young men from the Moscow Theological Seminary [52] and, since one of the founders of the new institution, Mikhail V. Lomonosov, regarded a university without a gymnasium as "a fertile field without seed," a preparatory school was established to provide a continuous supply of students.[53]

It will be recalled that the University of the Academy of Sciences at St. Petersburg had also drawn its original native students from the Seminary, and likewise had set up a gymnasium as a source of future students.[54] Yet the St. Petersburg plan failed to work out in this regard, while at Moscow University "the number of students during the eighteenth century was always between eighty and one hundred." [55] What was the secret of the success of the latter institution? Was it that in the two decades separating the founding of the respective universities the Russian people had become more aware of the values of higher education? That explanation obviously does not provide the answer, for the St. Petersburg institution was floundering throughout the very years that its Moscow counterpart flourished.[56] Unfortunately, the reason lies in the continuing social backwardness of the people, rather than in their progress toward intellectual emancipation. For there was not just one gymnasium attached to Moscow University, but two: "one for the nobility, and the other for the lower ranks except landlords." [57] Such discrimination seems to have satisfied "the social prejudices of the nobility . . . for in 1758 a similar double gymnasium was established at Kazan. . . . Indeed, the failure of the nobility to attend [the St. Petersburg gymnasium] has been explained by just this fact, that it was not exclusively an upper class institution." [58] When Lomonosov became Rector of the University of the Academy of Sciences at St. Petersburg in 1760, he reorganized its faculty structure on the Moscow model, but refused to create a double gymnasium. The result, as we have seen, was that for the next quarter-century his student body numbered between two and twenty.[59] The following year, 1761, the death of the Empress Elizabeth necessitated a reshuffling of state affairs and personnel, and the cause of education was for a time neglected.[60]

4

The Creation of State Schools (1760–1800)

FROM HER ACCESSION IN 1762 UNTIL HER death near the end of the century, the Empress Catherine II followed through many of the educational reforms initiated by her illustrious predecessor, Peter I. During her reign was established a whole network of special schools modeled on the Cadet Corpus, and "there arose women's institutes which were the last word in pedagogical thought of that time." [1] Before Catherine, girls had been educated only at home or in convents. The first, and for a long time the most important, of these schools for women was The Educational Society of Noble Girls, established at the old Smolny Monastery in St. Petersburg in 1764. Like the better boys' gymnasiums of that period, it had two divisions: one for the well-born ladies, the other for daughters of the middle class. The curriculum in both divisions required four years and had certain studies in common such as Russian, foreign languages, arithmetic, geography, and history; but the noble girls studied courtly manners, while those of lesser birth took household management and domestic science. French was the language of instruction from the founding of the school until 1783 when, in line with Catherine's establishment of the Russian Academy of Letters to purify the Russian language, the courses became based on the native tongue.[2] Although the teachers were expected to maintain a high standard of instruction in subject matter, their main concern was to be with the proper upbringing of their charges, whose ages ranged between six and eighteen years. Toward this latter end it was ordered that "the Headmistress and the teachers are obliged to take great care, in order that the girls by no means speak among themselves in church, but stand in awe and with proper decorum. For at the slightest transgression during the prayers or the divine service, the teacher shall, after the return to the chambers, take severe measures in the presence of the whole class, or in an assembly of all the pupils, so that shame alone may serve once and for all to deter others from similar conduct." [3]

Such meticulous behavior was demanded not only in the presence of the Deity, but also in the mundane affairs of life. "The Headmistress and teachers must show the young girls the right way to sit at the table and eat neatly, and also the decorous deportment and pleasant courtesies [required] in speaking among themselves, so that they are able to condescend to their very servants with affectionate treatment." [4] Nor did nightfall bring relaxation to the harried faculty, for the four pupils' bedrooms (one for each grade or class) were placed between those of the headmistress and teachers "in order that the bedchambers of the pupils be under constant supervision." [5] These responsibilities were made even more difficult to fulfill by the stipulation that they must be carried out in a very clever manner: "The Headmistress and teachers, while not separating themselves from the girls, shall in no way interfere in anything; on the contrary, they shall appear at all the innocent games and diversions of the pupils as if they do not notice them." [6]

Catherine's concern for the education of women was in itself a progressive characteristic in those days, and it was only logical that she should have used female teachers to instruct them. But the Empress did not stop there; so pleased was she with the work done at the Educational Society (later known as the Smolny Institute) that she conceived the idea of employing women to supervise the younger boys in the Cadet Corpus at St. Petersburg. In 1766 she revised the Rules of this institution to include one headmistress and ten female teachers to look after the first group (aged 5-9 years) of noble youths.[7] Naturally, extreme caution had to be exercised in selecting women for this work: "Their duty is so important that at all times assignments to it should be made only after diligent scrutiny of their morals. It is incumbent upon them to observe unceasingly the young nobles and not to part from them either by day or by night. To treat their pupils, and to instruct and teach them, with all tenderness, patience and love—these are especially enjoined upon them. They shall keep table together with their pupils, be inseparable from them at all their games and amusements, and never part from them except for the most legitimate cause. Great care must be taken that the pupils never have any communication with the servants." [8]

Only men teachers were permitted to deal with the boys in the next two age groups (9-12 and 12-15 years) and it was ordered that "professors for the nurture and instruction of [these] cadets should be appointed with great circumspection. They shall show them, over and above the sciences designated for the cadets, the experience gained in all other branches of knowledge which are necessary for . . . these two age groups. They should proceed in all other respects in accordance with that which is prescribed for teachers in the preceding age groups." Just as the headmistress commanded the teachers in the youngest group, "there must be an inspector who shall supervise the order, administration and conduct of the professors and the cadets . . . in the second and third age groups." [9]

Catherine, again like Peter, looked abroad for ideas. Having established a type of secondary schools for the nobility, she became interested in organizing a system of schools for all classes. As early as 1770 she began to lay plans for an eight-month school year which would be compulsory for all males.[10] Three years later the French philosopher Denis Diderot visited Russia at the earnest behest of the Empress, after a fervid correspondence about ideals, aims of a state, and functions of society in general. By the time the Encyclopedist arrived, however, Catherine's passion for political radicalism had considerably cooled because of the Pugachev rebellion and resultant internal strife. Nevertheless, Diderot was given a cordial reception, and assigned to compose a plan of organization for the lower secondary schools, universities, and women's educational establishments. The distinguished guest complied, and in a few months prepared his *Plan d'une universite pour la Russie*, which "demanded general compulsory and free education in the elementary schools, [offered] a sensible program for gymnasiums which was full of useful knowledge, and [outlined] a project for university education carefully worked out even as to faculties and chairs." [11]

Diderot also suggested that anatomy be included among the subjects taught both girls and boys; paradoxically, this seems to have been the proposal which most offended the tender sensibilities of the erotic Catherine! At any rate, she permitted Diderot to return to France, and proceeded to carry out her own plans as before. Her decree of 1775 increased the number of *guberniyas* (provinces) to fifty, set up in each a Board of Public Assistance,[12] and ordered these boards to establish and maintain schools in all the towns and larger villages. But Catherine expected too much from the meager financial assistance she gave the boards, so the project soon failed. The same decree attempted to put all private schools under state control, and required that all foreigners desiring to teach should pass examinations at the Academy of Sciences. Again, insufficient funds were provided for inspection, only 15,000 rubles being awarded each of the fifty *guberniyas*. So these measures never actually materialized.[13]

Once more Catherine cast her nets abroad in the hope of finding someone who combined practical administrative talent and agreement with her educational theories. She invited the German-French writer, Baron Friederich Melchior von Grimm, to Russia to supervise a plan. Perhaps Grimm had heard of Diderot's experience; at any rate, he declined the invitation. It is interesting to note that, while Catherine was persistently searching for foreigners to fulfill her ambitions regarding a system of popular education, she was disregarding one of her own subjects who was undoubtedly the greatest Russian educator of the eighteenth century. Nikolai Ivanovich Novikov was "a truly remarkable public figure," whose work laid the foundations for the "philosophy of education . . . and the beginnings of popular education [which] took form and began to develop consistently in the 1860's," nearly a century later.[14] The activities of Novikov, ex-guardsman and son of a noble family of the Moscow region, were known early to the Empress, for in 1767 she had appointed him to a minor political post. Some years later Novikov entered the field of journalism, and in one of his articles on education violently attacked the pedagogical ideas and practices of Catherine.[15]

Thus he forever closed the door on opportunities in the state administrative system.

Nevertheless, Novikov found many other channels through which to expound his views. He published several newspapers, and in 1777 he used the profits of these enterprises to set up two progressive schools in St. Petersburg, where "the children were not only instructed but were imbued with humanitarianism and community spirit," and where all forms of corporal punishment were prohibited.[16] Two years later he moved to Moscow and leased there the University Press in order to propagate further his concept that a system of education must grow out of community interest and support, rather than be set in motion by bureaucrats, however enlightened. Novikov already had many powerful friends in Moscow, one of these being a Professor Schwarz of the Moscow University, a German who had come to Russia from Transylvania in 1776 and who was later to become Inspector of the pedagogical seminary attached to that institution.[17]

"One of [Novikov's] main ideas concerned the importation of qualified teachers from abroad and the preparation of better Russian teachers." [18] In 1782 he founded The Friendly Learning Society, "one of whose aims was to raise funds to educate Russians at home and abroad." Nikolai Karamzin, destined to become the leading Russian historian of the nineteenth century, was one of the beneficiaries of these funds; but it is ironical that he was never able to secure a teaching position in a Russian university.[19] The Society was extremely active. It brought together many middle-class people who felt that education was too much a province of the nobility, the clergy, and the state, as indeed it was. "It opened the first public library in Russia and also the first bookstore . . . [and] organized on a cooperative basis a pedagogical seminary in which the 'new' teachers were trained." As a publisher, Novikov established several journals and newspapers, put out nearly 450 books of which well over half "were of a lay character in contrast to the predominantly religious content" of most of the literature of the time, and established the first Russian magazine for children.[20] His greatest scholarly undertaking was the compilation and publication of the *Ancient Russian Library*,[21] a collection of Russian writings selected with a view toward providing the literate public with material on the history, geography, and literature of their country, and thus inspiring a love and respect for Russia to counteract the current "enthusiasm for everything French." [22]

Such widespread radical activities were preordained to encounter the enmity of the throne, particularly since Novikov was also closely connected with the Society of Free Masons, a group Catherine saw as the embodiment of those French revolutionary ideas which she had begun to fear and hate. So, in 1791, Novikov found himself sentenced to fifteen years in prison. Although he was freed immediately after Catherine's death in 1796, he emerged broken in health and spirit.[23] The fate of Russia's foremost educator up to 1800 thus foreshadowed the destiny of many others like him in the years to come.

Meanwhile, the Russian Empress was continuing her efforts to locate a foreign scholar to head the new educational system. Emperor Joseph II of Austria recommended to Catherine "an accomplished Serbian educator, Jankovitch de Mirievo, who had reorganized the public school system of Hungary," [24] and who was familiar both with the Russian language and the Austrian school system which Catherine wished to use as a model for her own.[25] In 1782 Catherine created the Commission for the Establishment of Schools, which was to concern itself also with the procuring of teachers and textbooks, and de Mirievo became a member of it.[26] The following year a normal school for teachers was set up in St. Petersburg under his direct supervision, and one hundred theological students were enrolled therein.[27]

The resultant plan for a school system was the product of four years of study, during which de Mirievo and the Commission appear to have enjoyed full moral and financial support from Catherine. Twenty-seven German and Austrian textbooks were translated into Russian and published in sufficiently large editions.[28] The plan itself was approved and published in 1786 under the title "Statutes for Public Schools in the Russian Empire." [29] Its preamble is weighted down with noble sentiments and wholesome generalities, but nevertheless it indicates the emergence of a social concept of education, the concept that the true aim of education is to prepare people not only to live, but to live with others:

"The bringing up of the youth has been, among all enlightened peoples, of such great importance that it has been considered the one means of strengthening the general welfare of the citizenry; and it is indisputable that the subject of education includes a clear and intelligent understanding of the Creator and His divine law, the basic rules of firm belief in the state, and true love for the fatherland and one's fellow-citizens. Education enlightens the mind of a person by the revelation of other knowledge, and beautifies his soul; it inclines his will toward doing good, guides him toward the virtuous and worthy in life, and, finally, provides that understanding which a person requires to live with others. From this it follows that the seeds of such needs and useful knowledge must be sown in infancy, so that they will grow throughout the years of developing maidenhood and young manhood, ripening, and bearing fruit for society. But such fruit, if it is to develop to its full capabilities, must be placed only in those institutions where the basic subjects will be taught the youth in the native language. Such institutions must exist in all guberniyas and localities of the Russian Empire, under the name of public schools which will be designated as Main and Minor." [30]

The 113 articles of the Statutes are much more practical, and reveal a high degree of imitation of the Austrian system. The plan in its early stages envisioned three types of schools: a 'minor school' of two years' instruction, a 'middle school' of three years, and a 'main school' of two years. Further consideration and experiment, however, indicated no need for the 'middle school,' and so this level was absorbed by the 'main school,' increasing the term of the latter to five years. Thus the Statutes actually call for the establishment of a two-level system. 'Main schools' were to be established in the cities and the more important towns, while the 'minor schools' were to serve the smaller towns and villages. Each 'main school' would prepare teachers for the 'minor schools.' [31] Control of the system was placed nominally under the Commission, but was usually delegated to the local Boards of Public Assistance which Catherine had set up in 1775 to administer one of her previous educational projects.[32]

Elaborate regulations were included in the Statutes regarding the number of teachers required in each type of school, their teaching duties and hours of work, and their general responsibilities to their students and to their communities. Because the Statutes represent the supreme achievement of Russian educational thought up to the opening of the nineteenth century, it is worthwhile to describe at some length the rules on teachers before turning to an examination of the concrete results of the plan.

Each minor school was to employ two teachers, one for each of the two grades, unless the enrollment was so small as to require the services of only one. Subjects to be taught during the two-year course included reading, writing, arithmetic, catechism and sacred history, and Russian grammar. If neither of the regular teachers was capable of giving instruction in drawing, a special teacher could be employed for this purpose. The number of teaching hours for each member of the staff depended, naturally, upon whether one, two, or three teachers were available.[33]

Each main school was to have six teachers, their respective duties and hours of work ranging from the teaching of one subject (such as drawing or foreign language) for a total of 12-18 hours a week, to teachers instructing in as many as seven different subjects for 29 hours a week.[34] In addition, "one of the teachers of the higher classes of the main school will take upon himself, by designation of the director, the duties of librarian, having the books under his care."[35]

Chapter Three of the Statutes is composed of thirty articles devoted entirely to the specific duties of teachers. Every teacher in the new school system was required to have a roll-book containing the names of all his pupils according to their grade in school, and strict record had to be kept of all pupil absences and the reasons therefor.[36] Monthly reports to the director by the teacher were to contain "information concerning the conduct, application and success of his pupils, indicating when they came into his care, what they knew upon entering, what was imparted to them in the class of the school and privately in his own apartments, and with what success."[37] Since the schools were tuition-free to all classes as well as to both sexes, the teachers were cautioned "not to disdain the children of poor parents, but always to bear in mind that they [the teachers] are preparing members for society."[38]

All teachers were expected to complete the requisite material for each grade in one year, except for the fourth grade in the main schools which covered two years. Furthermore, the amount of material was specifically prescribed as being the entire content of the textbooks selected by the Commission. Nor was individual initiative encouraged in the classroom, for the Statutes admonish the teachers to "teach exactly according to the rules" which were printed either in the textbooks themselves or in the teachers' manuals, as well as to confine themselves to the official materials and methods. "In imparting instruction the teachers shall not intermingle anything extraneous and irrelevant to the subject taught, nor shall they undertake anything whereby the continuation of instruction or the attention of the pupils might be arrested. . . . All the teachers shall in everything conform to the prescribed method of instruction and shall not employ other books than those designated in this statute." [39]

Teachers were expected to report to work on time, of course, and to remain for the number of hours required each day. In cases where "sickness or any legitimate reason" prevented the teacher's presence in class, he was obligated to report this information far enough in advance for the director to assign a substitute to his class, "so that the pupils be not idle." Those teachers living in school quarters had to get permission from the director to spend the night elsewhere, and also to have overnight guests in their apartments.[40] Exceptions to the latter rule were the pupils themselves, for the teachers were encouraged to spend as much time as possible with their charges: praying with them several times a day; indoctrinating them with such ideas "as may dispose their hearts to virtue and their souls to right thinking; . . . showing them how to sit decorously, to walk, to bow, to make requests courteously and speak affectionately even to . . . servants." In order to preserve the students' self-respect and to insure the best use of their time in study, it was forbidden for teachers to use them for housework or send them on errands. "Above all, it is required that the teachers shall, by their own conduct and actions, give to the pupils examples of piety, good morals, friendship, courtesy and application, avoiding before them both in word and in deed, all that which may cause temptation or give occasion for superstition." [41]

In addition to these obligations incurred by all teachers, the teachers in the main schools had several special responsibilities. One of these was to assist in the selection of teachers for all schools, both public and private, of the Empire. "Inasmuch as those persons seeking teachers' posts either in the public or in household schools must first be examined by teachers of the main schools, not only in those same disciplines which they wish to teach, but also in the method of teaching them, the teachers of the main school are in duty bound to assist them" in learning both the necessary subject matter and the accepted manner of teaching it, as well as how to prepare reports.[42]

Distasteful as this duty might have been to the already overworked teachers in the main schools, there was another (reserved, it is true, for the teachers only of the two higher classes) which was probably even more odious. Yet it now seems remarkably modern both in purpose and in procedure: "In order that the history of the Russian State may in time have trustworthy monuments from which to borrow evidence of events touching the propagation of knowledge, it is incumbent upon the teachers of the [two] upper classes . . . with the assistance of the director, to keep by common effort a record of the public schools established in their region." A mass of material is demanded: exact dates, names of particular persons involved on all levels, personal data on all teachers, number of pupils each year in each school, results of examinations, status of libraries, "how many teachers for the minor schools were prepared in the main school, when and to what posts they were appointed, . . . at what times and by what noted persons the schools were visited, and anything worthy of note that occurred in such circumstances." Each January, a report of progress on this task was to be sent to the Head of the Commission, with a copy retained in the school's own library.[43] Nikolai Novikov, seated at his desk in his

Moscow publishing house, must have rejoiced at this official program demanding that all teachers take part in the exhaustive study of their own communities! But, alas, few of the teachers had the time to do more than attend to their instructional duties, and to the attendant responsibilities of character training and conduct supervision demanded by the remainder of the rules.

There was one general obligation for all teachers, however, the discharge of which should have taken nothing from the time nor the energies of even the busiest member of the staff. The statement of this obligation, here quoted in full, gives evidence of an extremely modern approach to the problem of relationships among teachers themselves. "In general, it shall be required that the teachers aid each other by deed and counsel, and display before the pupils the respect due one another. Both in the main schools and in the minor schools, let the teachers of the higher classes by no means disdain the teachers of the lower classes, and let them not belittle the subjects taught by them before the pupils or outside persons; for all teachers and all subjects taught are equally necessary parts of one chain; in response whereto the teachers of the lower classes shall also by their courtesy give precedence to those teachers who excel them in knowledge." [44]

These statements constitute the ideals, aims and goals of the system of education created by Catherine II and Jankovitch de Mirievo upon the foundations laid, in an institutional sense, by Peter I and, in a broadly social sense, by such men as Novikov, Schwarz, and other members of the Friendly Learning Society. One question which naturally arises is: How well did this system work in practice? Statistics reveal that the school situation showed a remarkable improvement immediately after the new plans went into effect: a great numerical increase in schools, teachers and pupils took place in the very first year (1786).

Schools increased from 12 to 165 (13.7 times); enrollment leaped from 1,491 to 11,088 (7.4 times); and teachers rose from 38 to 394 (10.4 times). Such rapid progress certainly indicates that the plans of the Commission were indeed well worked out in advance; as a matter of fact, de Mirievo had devoted all his time to this project since his arrival in Russia four years before. It is also significant that the number of both new schools and new teachers in that year rose to a greater degree than did the number of pupils, thus providing the youth with more adequate equipment and instruction. Whereas in 1785 there had been more than 120 pupils per school and 39 pupils per teacher, the 1786 average was a school for every 67 pupils and a teacher for every 28. The following year even this ratio was slightly improved in both respects: schools became 1 to 62 and teachers 1 to 26. But there real progress stopped for the remainder of the century; although the ratio of both schools and teachers to pupils did increase sporadically in the next decade and half (reaching, in 1794, for example, 1 to 55 and 1 to 22, respectively), this increase was due more to declining enrollment than to the provision of greater facilities.[45]

What, then, halted the onrush of the public education movement which started in 1786 with such splendid prospects? The reasons for the deceleration are, of course, numerous and complex; therefore, only the more significant causes can be touched upon here. These causes of failure have been summarized by one observer as follows: lack of funds, lack of supervision, lack of support from the nobility and the local communities, and lack of teachers.[46] Certainly one more reason may be added, and that was lack of students. It was very hard to find students for the two higher classes (grades III and IV) of the main schools, due largely to the competition of the private schools—usually run by foreigners—and the practice of employing foreign tutors in wealthy homes.[47] The Empress Catherine herself unwittingly added to the prestige of this imported instruction when, in preparing the ground for the advent of her system of free indigenous schools, she ordered the Commission on the Establishment of Schools to make a thorough investigation of all foreign teachers in the Empire in 1784. The Commission's report revealed those schools operated by foreigners to be far superior to those run by Russians, "only one of the former and all of the latter being [thereupon] closed." [48] Nevertheless, all private schools were placed under the supervision of the Commission, and no new ones were to be opened except upon charter granted by the Commission, "who were first to be satisfied concerning curriculum, methods, and teachers. This is the beginning of the later strict supervision of all educational activities proceeding from other than state authority. While this action did much to set a standard for education, low as it was, it also prevented the experimentation in the nature of the different types of education suited to the character of the different classes of Russian society, and permitted the universal rule of one type, imposed from above, and suited best to the ideas of the upper classes." [49]

In regard to higher education, the system was much the same. "Every incentive was given to raise the number of students at the universities. Each student, regardless of his social station by birth, was presented with a sword upon entrance to the university . . . , assured a good position upon entrance into the service of the State, and allowed to count the years of his study as years of service. Free instruction and free quarters were given to many but, in spite of all these efforts, the number of students seeking instruction at the universities was not large. The whole scheme was still in advance of the needs and demands of the people." [50] In one sense, this last statement is undoubtedly correct. Russian admiration for and dependence upon

Western culture had actually increased through the very methods employed by Peter I and Catherine II in the hope of strengthening the indigenous culture. Slavish worship of the West spread still further the already rather prevalent fashion of sending wealthy young men abroad to travel or study. "Glasgow, Leipzig, Göttingen, Edinburgh, Oxford, Paris, Strassburg—all contained Russian students. . . ." [51] And this at a time when exactly two students were enrolled at the University of the Academy of Sciences at St. Petersburg! [52]

But there is still another explanation of the paradox which obviously existed in the fact that so many youths studied abroad and with tutors while the Russian public school system and universities were disintegrating through lack of students. That reason is the poor quality of teaching provided in Russia. Whereas the Austrian system of public education, which de Mirievo sought to imitate, regarded normal schools as the foundation of the network, only one such institution was established by the Russian Government. Instead, teachers were brought in from theological seminaries, and in many cases pupils themselves actually served as instructors in the absence of any teacher at all.[53] Such a condition should be expected if one realizes that the "Statutes for Public Schools in the Russian Empire"* of 1786 called for a six-teacher school in each of the fifty main towns and a two-teacher school in each small town.[54] With a maximum average ratio of 2.6 teachers per school throughout the Empire before 1800,[55] some schools naturally found themselves with no teachers at all, even though in a few large centers the new schools did very well.[56]

In addition to the small number of teachers and the low quality of their preparation, it is also interesting to consider an account of the personal characteristics and mode of life of the Russian schoolteacher at the end of the eighteenth century, as recorded by a critic of the age:

"Pitiable was the situation of such a teacher. Overburdened with an enormous household, he received in all 100 rubles a year assigned wages. Poverty forced him to carry out his duties as guardian of the pupils. He arose very early and walked to the market for provisions. Then, in the winter, he chopped firewood and heated the stoves, and in summer he turned up the soil in his little kitchen-garden. The pupils did free him from sweeping out: the first arrival took the broom from the corner and swept the classroom. Winter and summer, the teacher wore the same baize frock-coat and, instead of stockings, he twisted paper around his legs. But we cannot say that he was completely devoid of spiritual interests, although there might have been excuse for such in his difficult conditions. He was friendly with the village priest, and often they talked together, in Latin, over a cup of tea. Frequently the teacher sat up late at night reading books and writing much, but no one knows just what he wrote. . . . At his death, an inheritance of five coppers was left to his wife and five children." [57]

In summarizing the contributions of the eighteenth century to the course of Russian education, several points of view must be taken into account. One author is inclined to believe that "all in all, the whole eighteenth century, in spite of efforts on the part of both Peter and Catherine for the lower and middle classes, had really bettered only the nobility to any appreciable degree. The clergy and the upper classes of cultured men and women had prospered and progressed, but largely at the expense of the other portions of the whole society. The nobility and their class ideas had prevented the full fruition of a comprehensive system for the education of the classes below them,—and one class, the serfs, had received no attention at all. Indeed, for several generations yet to come, until late in the nineteenth century, no effective scheme was to be found for them. It is estimated that out of the whole population of Russia at the end of the eighteenth century, only one in

800 was receiving any education." [58] Taking this estimate at face value and accepting the popular estimate of Russia's population as 36 million in 1800,[59] one arrives at the figure of 45,000 persons enjoying some form of education: in state schools, private schools, religious institutions, higher educational establishments, under tutors in their homes, and, perhaps, even those studying abroad. Of this total, it has been shown that about 20,000—or less than half—were enrolled in schools of the new system, even fifteen years after its creation!

However, a number of other historians offer much praise for the progress made under the enlightened monarchs, Peter and Catherine, although most of these accounts do not attempt to isolate the degree of educational advancement from that of the indisputable improvement in economic affairs, political administration, and philosophical judgment.[60] On the topic of education itself, there is some value in the commentaries of an early Soviet educational critic to whom reference has already been made several times in this and preceding chapters.[61] This writer freely admits that not all of the eighteenth century pedagogical efforts found lasting place in Russian culture. After the powerful personality of Peter I departed the scene, the demands for specialists of the type produced by the "cypher" and "garrison" schools declined, for Peter had stressed the utilitarian and technical aspects of education largely in order to augment the military power and the productive forces of the State. Therefore, these schools soon closed, as did others of similar type.

But "the academy gymnasium and university lived to become a real gymnasium and a real university as independent establishments." These schools, the latter especially, supplied eighteenth-century Russia with a number of scholars interested in "the study of Russia and the spreading there of truly scientific knowledge." This was a valuable achievement, even though many of these scientists felt it necessary to continue their studies abroad.[62] The schools founded by the archbishops also showed great improvement and lasting virtues: "originally wretched, they by degrees became transfigured into real theological seminaries which later offered a whole course of instruction, not only in the more priestly and episcopal subjects but also in the secular sciences and social life." Even the most progressive writers of the following century (Speranskii, Chernyshevskii, Dobroliubov) praised the quality of the instruction in these seminaries.[63]

Although Catherine II carried on much of the work begun by Peter, she did not share his views regarding the aims of education. To her, education was a social force which could mold the future, produce cultured citizens, form character, and control behavior—in short, its purpose was to shape both body and mind. While some of her schemes came to naught, there is no doubt that her achievements in the field of education left a profound impression on the substance of Russian learning, and may even have charted some of its subsequent channels. Her encouragement of the Cadet Corpus, founded several decades prior to her coronation, contributed much to the longevity of that type of establishment: it was "a real class institution, dedicated to the task of cultivating the ideals and outlook of a definite class. Its basic features were retained for 150 years in the Cadet Corpus itself and in other privileged 'closed' schools such as the lycée, the law schools, and the women's institutions." [64]

The Moscow University, which opened a few years before Catherine came to the throne, reached a high point of liberalism during her reign, largely, it is true, because she was too occupied with other matters to chasten the faculty there until rather late in the century.[65] However, Catherine took a very positive attitude toward such reforms as education for women, the necessity for training native teachers, the creation of learned societies, the control of private schools, and the insistence on learning the Russian language—and during her reign a great deal was accomplished toward all of these ends.[66]

Important as were all these educational advances, both of Peter and Catherine—and certainly they constitute a record of notable progress for Russia in a single century—there was one institution created during the period which outranks them all in the history of Russian social development: that is the system of free elementary and secondary schools (the 'minor' and 'main' schools) established by Catherine and de Mirievo. Although the actual influence of these schools on curriculum and method was less than that of the gymnasium; although their programs underwent constant revision and their administration constant change; although for a long time such schools served only the towns, ignoring the villages where dwelt more than 90 per cent of the Russian people[67]—still a great forward step had been taken when these schools were projected by an autocrat for the benefit of both sexes and all classes. "For the first time [in Russia], education became a state responsibility."[68] From the point of view of the average laborer or peasant of that time, the gain was small. In an institutional sense, however, the achievement was important enough to usher in a new era in Russian pedagogical thought and practice.

5

The Forging of a School System (1800-1825)

IT HAS BEEN POINTED OUT THAT CATHERINE II's receptive attitude toward social reforms, always limited to the espousal of action from above, began to cool soon after the peasant revolts of the 1770's. The last fifteen years of her reign, though by no means devoid of progress, witnessed a number of restrictions imposed to prevent the further infiltration of radical sentiment from abroad. Catherine had closed all the private printing presses in Russia, with the result that the new and vital publishing industry declined rapidly. Under her son and successor, Paul I, there occurred an entirely reactionary period of five years' duration (1796-1801). Each year fewer books were published, and the importation of foreign volumes was forbidden in 1798.[1] The same year another decree called home all young

Russians studying abroad "because of the rise there of the pernicious precepts of a licentious and depraved philosophy which inflames immature minds." [2] Furthermore, "it became almost impossible for foreigners to enter the country. Paul energetically persecuted every outward manifestation of liberalism. . . . Officials suspected of the least sympathy with progressive ideas lost their posts." [3]

Fortunately for the cause of social progress, Paul was soon succeeded by his son, Alexander I, whose first act was the abrogation of these restrictive decrees on printing presses, importation of books, Russians studying abroad, and foreigners wishing to enter Russia. The new Tsar also reorganized the political-administrative system of the country, setting up co-ordinated ministries to do the work formerly done by councils, commissions, and other isolated agencies.[4] In line with this reform, the Ministry of Public Education was established in 1802 to supplant the Commission on the Establishment of Schools, created by Catherine II.

Count Peter Vasilevich Zavadovskii, formerly chairman of the Commission, was selected by the Tsar to head the Ministry.[5] One of Zavadovskii's chief assistants, and the person who did most of the important work, was Mikhail Nikitich Muraviev (1757-1807), who had tutored Tsar Alexander in the latter's youth and who soon became Curator of the Moscow Educational Circuit. The new Ministry was given jurisdiction over all public libraries, museums, public and private printing presses, and most of the educational establishments; in addition, it was charged with the censorship of all printed matter. Schools which did not come under the supervision of the Ministry included the military and naval schools, the Cadet Corpus, the Holy Synod schools, and certain women's institutions which Alexander placed under the personal protection of his mother, Empress Maria.[6] One unfortunate result of this division of authority was that a number of educational budgets, reports, and investigations remained outside the scope of the Ministry of Public Education.[7]

Nevertheless, the reorganization brought many advantages to the school system. "In fact," says one historian, "there was no such thing as a school system before Alexander I; there were schools but no system."[8] Inasmuch as Catherine II and de Mirievo had created an actual network of schools which numbered more than three hundred at the turn of the century and served nearly twenty thousand pupils,[9] this statement appears unjust. However, from the point of view of co-ordination between all levels, the accusation must be accepted, for the Statutes of 1786 made no attempt to bring the gymnasiums and higher schools into the same system with the 'main' and 'minor' schools. In this sense, Alexander's plan was a great advance, for it called not only for the inclusion of the existing gymnasiums and universities but also for the establishment of several more. Moreover, these universities were to be the very core of the entire system, sharing authority even with the Ministry itself. It is not surprising, therefore, that even a Soviet critic would later see fit to call the project "the most complete and satisfactory plan for the organization of public education that the Russian government was to offer until 1917."[10]

Immediately upon its inception, the new Ministry of Public Education started to work on its plan for the reorganization of the school system. Intending from the very beginning to revise Catherine's procedure of organizing school districts on the basis of the fifty political-administrative units (*guberniyas*), and also to give the universities a leading role, the Ministry studied first the problems of organization and administration. In January 1803 the results of this study were outlined in a tract entitled "Preliminary Rules for Public Education" and codified into law in a special legislative act.[11] According to these Rules, the country was to be divided into six "educational circuits" (*uchebnye okrugi*), with a university in each of the following cities as the center of its own circuit: St. Petersburg, Moscow, Vilna, Dorpat, Kazan, and Kharkov. At the time the Rules were published, Russia possessed only three universities–at Moscow, Vilna, and Dorpat–and "of these Moscow alone was really Russian, for Vilna and Dorpat represented Polish and German civilization." [12] In conformity with the Rules, universities were soon established at Kazan and Kharkov, but that at St. Petersburg was delayed until 1819 because the Main Pedagogical Institute, set up there in 1804, was already preparing teachers for the lower schools.[13] Since it was recognized that previous educational projects had failed partly because of the lack of good teachers, the Rules stipulated that to each university there be attached a training school, the students of which would be supported by the State upon agreeing to teach for six years after graduation.[14]

This preliminary plan was considerably reinforced in November of the following year, 1804, when a decree outlined specifically the "Regulations of the Moscow, Kharkov and Kazan Universities and the Educational Establishments Under Their Jurisdictions." [15] Chapter XII of these Regulations is devoted entirely to the subject of the pedagogical or teachers institutes existing or to be set up at each of the three universities, and opens by explaining that such institutes "train teachers for the gymnasiums and schools within the university's [educational] circuit, under the leadership of a Director chosen by the Council [16] from among the staff of Ordinary Professors." [17] In turn, "the Director of the Pedagogical Institute, at half-year intervals, submits for the consideration of the General Meeting [18] a study plan [course of study] designed to fit the purposes of the institution. Not only must he [the Director] see to it that this plan is carried out exactly, but he himself must observe the behavior of the students, direct them in their studies, point out the best writers on those sciences of most concern to the students, and insist upon the teaching of those sciences in a clear and systematic manner." [19]

Most of the attention of these pedagogical rules, however, is directed toward the students rather than toward the faculty. Several new privileges, and some new obligations, were added to the lot of the students. In the first category is the provision that "candidates who remain three years at the Institute and at the new examinations demonstrate clearly that they have acquired the necessary knowledge to teach the sciences to others, as well as the ability to teach, receive the second University degree, or are sent as Junior or Senior Teachers into the schools of the surrounding circuit, where their merits are observed." [20] Furthermore, "Masters of the University and Senior Teachers of the gymnasium who have served at least three years are given preference over outsiders for promotion to university instructorships (Adjuncts) whenever such vacancies exist, provided that the General Meeting, after proper examination, finds them deserving." [21] But by far the most attractive innovation was the practice of sending abroad the two outstanding students, with all expenses paid, for a period of two years "during which they endeavor to improve their knowledge." Every two years a pair of such students was to be chosen by the University, recommended by the Curator, and approved by the Minister of Public Education.[22]

On the other hand, as was mentioned earlier, graduates of the pedagogical institutes were expected to remain in the teaching profession. The Rules state that "candidates who receive their degrees and wish to leave the University in order to begin work as teachers in another institution under the Ministry of Public Education, must sign a written pledge that they will remain at these duties for at least six years . . . [while] those who qualify for the Master's degree and remain at the University are obligated to teach the Student-Candidates, and, if the Council so decides, to teach in the University auditorium at specific days and hours."[23] In such manner did the newly established Ministry of Public Education embark upon its long-term program to attract superior students to the teaching profession, and to hold them in their duties despite the undoubtedly numerous temptations to enter other fields of work.

Although the Preliminary Rules also forecast the several types of secondary and elementary schools to be created or reorganized under the new system, these types are considered in much greater detail in the official "Regulations for Educational Establishments Under the Jurisdiction of the Universities," which was published on the same day as the rules for pedagogical institutes just described.[24] At the same time, the publication of the University Code of 1804 gave concrete authority to the projects in higher education proposed in the Rules.

The Regulations are 155 in number, and cover every important phase of educational organization, administration, supervision, and curriculum on both elementary and secondary levels, as well as the duties of teachers and pupils. As mentioned previously, Russia was divided into six "educational circuits," and a "curator" (*popechitel'*) was named for each circuit to share responsibility with the rector of the central university in the management of all the schools of the circuit. However, the six curators all lived in St. Petersburg in order to take part in the regulation of educational affairs on a national plane; they were expected to keep in touch with their respective provinces through periodic visits and tours of inspection.[25] Each curator was also a member *ex officio* of the Educational Council of his circuit which had charge of the provincial university. In turn, each university was responsible for the administration of all gymnasiums and other secondary schools in its circuit, although the direct supervision of these schools was in the hands of a Schools Committee consisting of the rector of the university and six professors elected annually from among the members of the university faculty.[26] Further down the administrative ladder, we find that the directors of the gymnasiums in the main provincial towns were also in charge of all the elementary schools in their respective circuits, while the principals of the elementary schools had supervisory powers over all the other schools in the surrounding parish.[27]

The Regulations are quite specific concerning the number and types of schools to be established, the aim being to provide each circuit center with one university, each main town or city with one or more four-year gymnasiums, each district with some type of two-year secondary or elementary school, and each parish (or two parishes) with a one-year elementary school.[28] Taking a lesson from the meager financial support given previous educational schemes, the Ministry appropriated 2.8 million rubles for the first year of this project. From this sum, each of the six universities received 130,000 rubles, for a total equal to the entire educational budget of Catherine II in her most generous years. The remaining two million rubles was apportioned in fixed amounts to the secondary and elementary schools.[29] From the standpoint of organization it can hardly be denied that the plan was carefully and intelligently worked out. The administration was as logically coordinated as the structure, and considerable funds were provided to bring about the desired integration. "This project foresaw an actually unified system of schools connected successively from bottom to very top, wherein all levels represented not only a natural continuation but also a veritable pedagogical bond." [30]

Nor did the Regulations overlook the fact that the

teacher is at least as important a functionary as is the administrator or supervisor. On the contrary, an entire section of the document is devoted to a description of the value of the teacher and his attendant duties and responsibilities. To begin with, the Regulations require each teacher —regardless of level, grade, or subject—to "observe punctiliously the school hours assigned by the director in the arrangement of school subjects" and never to absent himself at such hours "without notifying the . . . authorities in good time . . . and giving valid reasons for such absence." [31] Furthermore, the teacher "must strive with all his might that his pupils understand clearly and accurately the subjects he teaches, and he must rely more on his own diligence and orderly methods than on the excessive labor of his pupils. For young children he endeavors to make his teaching light, pleasant and entertaining, rather than burdensome to them." [32]

In line with these injunctions comes the admonition to "make more effort concerning the education and sharpening of the reasoning powers of all students, and especially the older ones, than of the cramming and exercising of their memory." For "the most important aspect of the instruction of youth is to train them in assiduity, inspiring in them the eagerness and devotion to learning which, upon their leaving school, will cause them to continue toward even further improvement of themselves. Show them the way to learning, make them feel its value and its use, and thus make them suitable for any vocation. And, especially, give their minds and hearts the proper direction, establish in them the firm foundations of honesty and morality, and correct and overcome in them any bad tendencies." [33]

The teachers are warned that, to the pupils, they stand in the place of parents, and therefore must act this role with all the attributes of good parents. They must be stern but not harsh, kind but not indulgent, "so that they may invite neither hatred nor contempt." Reprimands or even punishment must follow transgressions, but these "must never be meted out in passion or in anger, nor before a proper inquiry into the guilt of the pupil." Despite the fact that the teacher is a representative of the parents, he must not autocratically impose his own will upon the pupils, for "the parents, sharing their power with the teacher, think not of relinquishing it themselves." Therefore, the teacher must cooperate with the parents "in joint effort and counsel for the best upbringing of the child." [34] Another means suggested toward this end is that the teacher take as his first objective the task of "learning well the traits and characters of the children, . . . trying from the very beginning to acquire authority over them, . . . instilling in them respect, love and obedience toward himself." He is cautioned always to speak the truth and to lead the children to do likewise, as well as to set a good example in the direction of courtesy and neatness. In case these exhortations prove inadequate, the teacher is referred to a more voluminous set in the teachers' manuals.[35]

That the fulfillment of these obligations was not left to chance is indicated by the requirement that teachers in all three types of schools—gymnasiums (or city schools), district schools, and parish schools—"assemble on the first Sunday of each month with the director, for pedagogical counsel. Each teacher tells the assembly of the notes made by him in the course of the past month, [including] the diligence and success of his pupils, his opinion on how to make instruction more interesting, and also concerning the best methods of improving his teaching." It was felt that "this mutual sharing of opinions, these discussions of the methods of teaching—the hardest of all the arts—give the director an opportunity to learn perfectly the intelligence of the teachers, their diligence in duties, and their pedagogical aptitudes." [36]

The gymnasium teachers, as might be expected, are charged with certain responsibilities which teachers on the other two levels do not incur. Chief among these is the revival or continuation of the "community study" projects described in the 1786 "Statutes for Public Schools in the Russian Empire." [37] However, the new plan, while still encouraging explorations into local culture, places greater emphasis upon topographical and economic surveys. It also provides that "this labor is numbered among those accessory obligations of teachers for which they may expect special reward, provided it is worthy of esteem." Inspection of such work is placed in the hands of the director of the school, who in turn reports to the supervising university in the circuit.[38] A second extra duty also stems from the past, antedating even the Statutes of 1786. Under the Regulations, all persons "seeking teaching positions in public or private schools must first be examined by gymnasium teachers, not only in the subjects which they desire to teach, but also in the methods of teaching them. Therefore, in case an applicant possesses inadequate knowledge of either, the gymnasium teacher must assist him not only in the elements of public instruction, but also and particularly make clear to him the obligations belonging to the teaching profession." [39]

Few privileges accompanied these many responsibilities. It is true, of course, that the social status of the teacher, which had begun to rise just a century before, was considerably greater than ever. Teaching was now recognized as a profession which accorded special, even though flexible, civil rank to a young man or woman. Moreover, the Regulations of 1804 include little of the "guardian" type of duties laid down in the documents of previous decades. The enormously increased expenditures on public education provided much better salaries at all levels of the profession.[40]

Perhaps the most encouraging note of all, however, was struck by the provisions of the new Regulations regarding the possibility of promotion in rank within the profession, that is, from one level or type of school to a higher. Teachers in parish schools could "go into the district schools as teachers if they have the necessary knowledge therefor and do not hold an ecclesiastical post." In like manner, teachers in district schools were encouraged "to improve their knowledge in those subjects which are taught in gymnasiums" so that they may enter the latter "in case of open vacancies." [41] Finally, since "according to the rules of universities, teachers in gymnasiums may enter vacant positions of instructors in the universities, therefore must they strive for the expansion of their knowledge in those sciences whose basic elements are taught in the gymnasiums, in order that they might become worthy of such promotion." [42]

Such were the main elements in the new plan in regard to organization, administration, finance, and teaching procedures. But the curricula were also modernized, particularly in the gymnasium, where courses in logic, aesthetics, psychology, ethics, law and jurisprudence, and political economy were added to the old curriculum in an effort to provide a good general education for those not going on to a university.[43] Although the system represented the best effort which Tsarist Russia was ever to make toward the realization of a true "ladder" arrangement, wherein each level was co-ordinated with the level immediately above, there was also the desire to make each level in itself provide a certain amount of socially valuable training. Peter I had viewed education in a purely utilitarian sense and had wanted vocational training extended to every one of his subjects. Catherine II saw education as much broader in purpose, with its chief aim being the inculcation of the principles of good citizenship; but she considered only a small minority of people to be capable of profiting from such training. The several plans and decrees issued in the first few years of the reign of Alexander I indicate that "education was for the first time recognized as a social need." [44] Not a social need of the individual, but a need of society itself! This new concept was expressed in 1804 by one Russian philosopher and journalist, Ivan Petrovich Pnin (1773-1806), as follows: "Education, as accepted in the present sense, consists in that each member of society, no matter what profession he finds himself in, knows and fulfills thoroughly his responsibilities; that is to say, when the superiors on their part sacredly carry out the obligations of the power entrusted to them and when the lower class people inviolately live up to the responsibilities of their obedience. If these two classes do not transgress their bounds but preserve the proper equilibrium in their relations, then education has attained the desired aims." [45]

On paper, then, the 1804 system of public education had much to insure its success. For the practical aide, most historians agree that the choice of Zavadovskii as first Minister was a good one, and that all six original curators were able men.[46] Yet progress was slow, many difficulties being encountered on each level. It has already been mentioned that no university was founded to head the St. Petersburg circuit (the most important of the six) until 1819, thus seriously delaying the work in that region. Although the other universities received numerous applications for faculty posts after the University Code of 1804 guaranteed self-government of these institutions, many of the new and old appointees resigned when they discovered the autonomy to be largely theoretical. There was also much dissatisfaction over the continued use of Latin as the language of instruction by many of the foreign teachers, since so few entering students were adequately prepared in this tongue.[47] Finally, the nobility still resented the presence of the lower classes in the universities. This rancor was so strong as to make necessary the erection of special dormitories for the rich at some of these institutions and the founding, during the first fifteen years of the century, of four new higher learning establishments: the Forestry Institute (1803) and the Institute of Ways of Communications (1810) in St. Petersburg, the Commercial Academy (1810) and the Lazarev Institute of Oriental Languages (1815) in Moscow.[48] Meanwhile, in 1809, there were only 450 students in all five of the state universities of the Empire.[49]

The same type of class antagonisms existed at the secondary level, where the gymnasiums of the Ministry of Public Education had to compete with the preparatory schools for nobles and other private schools. Most famous in this group was the Lycée of Tsarskoe Selo, which was set up in 1811 by the government as a state-supported school to offset the tendency of many noble families to have their sons prepared for the university by private, and usually foreign, tutors at home.[50] Nor was this competition confined only to obtaining students; the private institutions paid better salaries and therefore secured the best teachers. The additional courses in the curriculum, while placed there for a worthy purpose, resulted in either too long a course or a curriculum crammed too full for proper assimilation. The district schools suffered the effects of being at the bottom of the administrative ladder: they did not get sufficient funds, they were plagued with teachers who could not find employment elsewhere, and there was a constant shifting of students who went on to better schools.[51] But the parish schools, dependent entirely upon the generosity of the local community and the village landlords, suffered most of all. One historian says that "they remained a pious wish, but a dead letter on the statute book"; another declares that "they almost disappeared a few years after" the decree which ordered their creation; a third states categorically that they "were never actually brought into being [but] the lower grades of the 'minor schools' simply continued to exist as before."[52]

Despite these difficulties some real progress did result from the plan. The upper grades of the 'main schools,' established in the previous century, were gradually absorbed into the new gymnasiums, while the lower grades of the 'main schools' combined with the upper grades of the 'minor schools' to form the new district schools.[53] The following table reveals the degree to which the new system had achieved its quantitative aims by 1808.[54]

EDUCATIONAL CIRCUIT	NUMBER OF MAIN TOWNS	NUMBER OF GYMNASIUMS	STUDENTS	NUMBER OF PROVINCIAL TOWNS	NUMBER OF DISTRICT SCHOOLS	STUDENTS
St. Petersburg	5	3	294	43	5	1066
Moscow	10	10	447	116	44	2356
Vilna	8	6	1305	89	54	7422
Kharkov	11	8	477	109	18	1747
Kazan	13	5	315	129	5	248
TOTAL	47	32	2838	486	126	12,839

It is difficult to estimate fairly the success of the new system purely on the basis of the above table. In the first place, no figures are given for the circuit of Dorpat. Secondly, no comparison is possible with the achievements of the previous century (see Table No. 1 in Appendix), for the reason that the 1786 system included *all* public schools, even those in parishes, while the above table is limited to only two types. Therefore, the only sensible approach is to compare the results with the purposes outlined in the 1804 Regulations themselves, which declared the goal of the new system to be the establishment of a gymnasium in every main town and a school in every district town. How much of these aims had been achieved after five years? The answer is by no means encouraging. Fifteen out of forty-seven main towns were still without state gymnasiums, the Moscow circuit alone having reached its goal. Furthermore, enrollment in the existing gymnasiums varied from an average of less than 45 in Moscow to more than 217 in Vilna. In regard to the district schools, the situation was obviously much worse, barely one-fourth of the requisite number of schools having been established. At this level, too, conditions varied with the locality: well over half of the provincial towns in the Vilna circuit possessed schools, while in Kazan circuit only one town in twenty-six was so fortunate. Even in the Moscow and St. Petersburg circuits the plan had hardly begun to function, although the number of private schools in these territories compensated to some extent for the failure to establish the required number of public institutions. Thus there is certainly some justification for the statement of one historian that, by 1810, the whole program had failed.[55]

Even the unity of organization, "the most important feature of the new system,"[56] was short-lived. Although the real reaction was to come a few years later, after Russia's war against Napoleon and Alexander's creation of the "Holy Alliance," the ground for it was laid in 1810 when the reactionary Count Sergei Semenovich Uvarov became Curator of the St. Petersburg circuit and began to mold the new system to suit his own limited ideals. "He advocated the study of such subjects in the gymnasium as were appropriate to the age and conditions of the students, leaving the advanced legal and philosophical studies for the university. This meant concentration on religion, the mother tongue, history, geography, mathematics, literature, grammar, and the classical languages."[57] Furthermore, Uvarov firmly believed that the aim of the gymnasium was to prepare students for the universities, rather than to provide a general education for those unable to continue their studies. Latin, therefore, was once more to be a required study so that students entering universities could understand the professors.[58]

The burning of Moscow in 1812 by Napoleon was a great shock to the Russian people, and they reacted immediately in two ways. First, they revived their ancient distrust of foreigners, since it was outsiders who had pillaged their country and their great city. Second, they turned with greater fervency to religion, since God had saved them and once more flung out the horde of invaders. In a short time, these two reactions fused into one large concept: devout adherence to Russian Orthodoxy and hatred of all that opposed it. In such a psychological situation it was inevitable that the secular education nourished for the past century would be challenged. Actually, it was not only challenged but defeated. The spearhead of the new religiosity was Prince Alexander Nikolaevich Golitsyn, head of the Russian Bible Society and Chief Procurator of the Holy Synod. In his youth Golitsyn had been a friend of Tsar Alexander and somewhat of a "freethinker," but in his later years he became a complete mystic. He had established branches of the Bible Society throughout Russia in order to campaign for the extension of sufficient elementary education so that everyone could read the Scriptures. Golitsyn was appointed Minister of Public Education in 1816 and, on the basis of the previous work of such men as himself, Admiral Shishkov and Count Uvarov, began to force all education back into the administrative, as well as ideological, channels of the Church.[59]

In 1815 Tsar Alexander, inspired by the success of his armies against Napoleon and his own new role as Savior of Europe, formed in Paris the famous "Holy Alliance" which united the reactionary monarchs of several nations in a drive against all expressions of liberal thought.[60] Specifically, Alexander saw in the Holy Alliance a union between Church and State which would strengthen the moribund feudal system in Europe and, incidentally perhaps, the position of the Tsar himself both in this world and the next. Returning home, Alexander immediately began to direct his own country along the new lines of endeavor. "How can we serve the Holy Alliance," he asked, "if its commencement is left standing alone and does not pervade the hearts of the people?"[61] The handiest inoculating device was obviously the new system of public education, and Alexander's ministers lost no time in utilizing it for this purpose.

In 1817 the Tsar published his "Manifesto Concerning the Establishment of the Ministry of Spiritual Affairs and Public Education." This document explained that "since Christian piety should always be the foundation of all true education, it is deemed proper to unite the work of the Ministry of Public Education with the affairs of all creeds."[62] Moreover, the new Ministry was directed "to find itself in the exact relationship to the Holy Synod as does the Ministry of Justice to the Senate"—in other words, responsible to the Church rather than to the State. Thus was State control of education, so long fought for and so briefly enjoyed, forsaken. In its place came religious domination of education by one of the most bigoted and backward sects in all Europe: the Orthodox Church of the Russian Empire.

Domination is not too strong a term in this instance, for the Holy Synod did not stop with the mere delineation of ministerial duties. In 1819 the gymnasiums and district and parish schools were ordered to place the study of the catechism and other religious writings foremost in their curriculums.[63] The same year Minister Golitsyn sent an emissary to investigate Kazan University. He chose for this work a man named Leonti Magnitskii, a member of the Educational Council and a former colleague in the Bible Society. Some insight to Magnitskii's views on education is provided by one of his earlier statements: "The whole mischief which has been observed in our universities has been caused by the education, the books, and the men we have imported from the German universities. There the infection of unbelief and revolutionary principles, which started in England and gained additional strength in pre-revolutionary France, has been erected into a complete . . . system. . . . The learning and literature of North Germany are so infected with this poison that they can be used only with the greatest caution." [64]

Upon completion of his investigation, Magnitskii strongly urged that Kazan University be closed, but both the Tsar and Count Uvarov opposed such an extreme measure. A compromise was reached whereby Magnitskii was appointed Curator of the Kazan Circuit, and was permitted to reorganize the university. This reorganization was carried out with a heavy hand indeed: eleven professors were summarily dismissed, a special Director of Morality was installed, and the curriculum was remodeled along the lines of a theological seminary.[65] The new curator also excluded from the university library even "books of the most reasonable content, forbade the teachings of the theories of Buffon and the systems of Copernicus and Newton as contrary to the Scriptures, and ordered the Professor of History to take as his model the work of Boussuet. Dissection was forbidden as disrespectful to the dead. Economics was to be a 'politico-moral' study, showing how material good can be transformed into spiritual. Nikolsky, the professor of geometry, represented the triangle as the emblem of the Trinity." [66] The classics, the sciences, and history had to be made to agree with the teachings of the Bible, and "disobedient students were confined in cells and forced to wear cards with the inscription 'Sinner' upon them." [67]

The orders for the above changes were contained in a long document, written in 1820 by Magnitskii himself and entitled "Instructions to the Director of Kazan University." This missive begins with the flat statement that "the aim of the government in the education of students is the bringing up of true sons of the Orthodox Church, loyal subjects of the State, good and useful citizens of the Fatherland." [68] As one means toward this end, the Director of the University was specifically instructed to make sure of a student's "devotion to the sacred evangelical studies before admitting him to lectures in philosophy, history, or literature."

Similar repressions were put upon other universities and, in turn, upon the gymnasiums under their jurisdictions. Both at Kharkov and the newly established university at St. Petersburg a number of professors were discharged, "one being accused for teaching the philosophy of Schelling, and another of 'Robespierrism' for having criticized serfdom and the excessive issue of paper money." [69] The Jesuits were expelled from Russia, even though their six schools had been approved in 1804 and their university at Polotsk had been declared in 1812 equal to the Russian universities.[70] Russians were forbidden to leave the country for the purpose of studying, and professors who had studied abroad were declared ineligible for posts in Russian universities.[71] The six excellent curators originally appointed in the early years of the creation of the system (1804-1810) were replaced by confirmed reactionaries of Magnitskii's type.[72]

The immediate result of this virulent campaign was the decline of the prestige and authority of the universities, so that they "became even less capable of directing the course of education and culture in Russia." [73] Enrollment at Kazan University dropped to ninety-one in 1822, barely what it had been fifteen years earlier. At Kharkov University the number of professors fell from twenty-eight to eight. During the first two decades of its existence (1819-1837) the University of St. Petersburg graduated only 365 students. However, at Moscow, Dorpat and Vilna, the new policy seems to have had no deleterious effect upon either staff or students.[74]

In any case, the reign of Alexander I shows a net increase in educational progress at all levels. In 1809 Russia had possessed five universities with a total of only 450 students, while by 1825 there were six such institutions enrolling 1691 students in all.[75] The increase in gymnasiums was indeed phenomenal: 42 were opened during Alexander's reign alone, and in 1825 their number stood at 48 with an enrollment of 5,500.[76] The figures regarding district schools are not so easy to analyze: one historian says that 405 were opened on direct orders from Alexander, while another writer reports that in 1825 only 337 such schools existed and that these were attended by about 30,000 pupils.[77] This discrepancy appears quite reasonable, however, when it is realized that a number of such schools were opened for a short period and then closed or combined with other local schools. In summary, the year 1825 presented the following picture: There were in Russia 686 towns with a total population of 3.5 millions; the rural population came to about 52 millions. At the service of these people were "1095 schools of all kinds, while at the same time there were 4266 churches and monasteries." [78] Obviously, public education had made hardly a dent in the Orthodox hide of Russia, a fact which was shortly to be demonstrated in practice as the Church once more took over the system of education.

In regard specifically to the preparation of teachers, the reign of Alexander I attempted little and accomplished still less. The creation of Pedagogical Institutes as annexes to the universities has already been described, as have the efforts to secure better methodological training for teachers. For the first time in Russian educational history, a real effort was made to instill into the prospective teachers a *social* conception of education based on the one hand upon an understanding of child psychology, and on the other upon an acceptance of the teacher's responsibility to the community. The six-year obligation to teach, the sending of students abroad, and the new promotion program also contributed to an improved system of teacher education, although the political reaction invalidated many plans in these directions. One move of the Ministry of Public Education which had far-reaching effects in the teaching profession was concerned immediately only with higher education in general: this was the matter of standardizing academic degrees. The problem first arose in 1816 with the setting up of specific requirements for the degrees in jurisprudence, but it was decided then to make no general rulings until further study of the situation had been made. Thus the first basic regulations covering several faculties were confirmed only in January 1819 when a Ministerial decree outlined in some detail the requirements for the various degrees and the privileges of educational institutions to award them.[79]

According to this decree, academic degrees were to be awarded in four fields: Divine Law, Philosophy, Law, and Medicine.[80] Degrees in Divine Law could be conferred only by institutions approved both by the State educational administration and the Holy Synod: these included theological academies, seminaries, and the like, of which four are specifically named. In Medicine, only the Imperial Medical-Surgical Academy was listed as qualified, but all existing Law faculties were granted the right to award degrees after sufficient study in any of the several aspects of the subject. As usual, the Philosophical faculties are considered in two divisions, Physico-Mathematical and Ethical-Philological, and as many as nine aspects were acceptable for major study toward a degree.[81]

Four types of degrees were established: (1) Degree Student, (2) Candidate, (3) Master, and (4) Doctor. To pass from the first degree to the second, the student had to complete the entire university course with excellent marks, get his diploma, and stand another examination. Candidates wishing to become Masters had to display full knowledge of their entire field of study, in an examination or otherwise. The Doctor's degree was reserved for those who acquired "a fundamental and deep knowledge of science." [82] But these transitions could not be accomplished merely at the volition of the student: one year had to elapse between the granting of a diploma and the award of the degree of Candidate, two years had to intervene between the granting of Candidate and the conferring of Master, and three years between the degrees of Master and Doctor.[83] Specific civil rank accompanied each degree: a Degree Student held rank of XIV; a Candidate, XII; a Master, IX; and a Doctor, VIII.[84] The great importance of these measures to the teaching profession will be described in subsequent chapters.

One more effort of this period in the field of teacher education should be considered here, not so much because of its lasting values as because it indicates the traditional autocratic manner of dealing with educational problems. The case regarding degrees, outlined just above, reveals how the Ministry of Public Education was striving to make higher education more attractive and more valuable, at the very same time that it was permitting such programs as that of Magnitskii to drive good teachers and students out of the universities. A similar paradox is noted in an action instituted two years earlier: although it was well known to the Tsarist government that the majority of teachers were opposed to the administrative amalgamation of Spiritual Affairs and Public Education, the first act of the newly formed Ministry was a decree designed to attract more and better trained persons to the teaching profession. In a long speech made the day after the combined Ministry was established, Prince A. N. Golitsyn (who had been retained as head of the new agency) reviewed the previous efforts of the government to deal with the problems of teacher education, and he pointed out the salient faults in these programs.[85]

Golitsyn recalled that it was Catherine II and her Austrian adviser, Jankovitch de Mirievo, who in 1782 had made the first attempt to co-ordinate teacher education with the needs of the public schools. Four years later the "Regulations for Public Schools" ordered each 'main school' to prepare teachers for the surrounding 'minor schools.' The next important step, said Golitsyn, occurred in 1804 when the new "Regulations for Educational Establishments under the Jurisdiction of Universities" required that gymnasiums prepare teachers for the district and parish schools. Thus the main schools rendered the same service to the minor schools as did the gymnasiums to the lower institutions in the later system. Furthermore, the universities were charged with preparing teachers for the gymnasiums, which in turn supplied students for the university, while the gymnasiums received pupils from the schools to which their graduates had gone to teach. Golitsyn admitted that such an arrangement appeared entirely logical. But, said he, the results had never been satisfactory, due largely to three causes which he described in some detail.

The first reason was that the children of nobles and officials, after graduating from the gymnasiums, nearly always went on for further study in the higher institutions, while the children of lower social ranks went directly into employment, usually in the same type of work as that pursued by their fathers. Thus very few graduates of the gymnasium desired to teach in the lower schools. Secondly, even the few who did become teachers soon took advantage of their new positions to find other employment in occupations offering better chances of economic and social advancement. Thereupon, the schools faced a lack of teachers and could not provide the quality of instruction expected of them. Thirdly, Golitsyn pointed out that, under these circumstances, the Curators of the circuits were forced either to consolidate two schools into one in order to have an adequate teaching staff, or to permit the principals to assign double loads of duty to the remaining teachers. In either case, the school system suffered a reduction in standards which became progressively worse as these conditions continued.

To remove these evils, Golitsyn suggested three measures: (1) the establishment of a Second Division in the Main Pedagogical Institute at St. Petersburg whose sole task would be the training of teachers for the district and parish schools; (2) the creation within this Division, and at other pedagogical institutes, of a system of State scholarships to attract able and reliable young people to the teaching profession; and (3) to strengthen the requirement that the recipients of these scholarships teach in the public school system for six years after graduation. Golitsyn's plan was immediately approved, and a special budget was assigned to provide funds for the additional expenses involved in carrying it out.[86] However, the plan did not work out in practice: in 1819 the Main Pedagogical Institute itself was reorganized into the University of St. Petersburg, and three years later the Second Division was abolished. Thus the reign of Alexander I, whose early years had promised so much in the field of public education, ended with a school system established but no stable agency to supply the system with teachers. Unfortunately, the regime that followed was also concerned with many other matters than teacher education.

6

The Long Period of Reaction (1825–1855)

THE REACTION THAT BEGAN IN THE realms of high politics as early as 1815, when Alexander I assumed the leadership of the Holy Alliance, was soon felt in educational affairs, but for a time it was confined to the upper administrative levels and the universities. Important as were the changes that occurred in the educational system between 1817 and 1825, these changes did not disturb the foundations of the system itself. Moreover, the reactionary leaders were clever enough to realize that their new administrative and curricular policies were being carried out within a framework designed for an entirely different type of education. The coalition of Holy Synod and Ministry of Public Education was in itself a superficial move, and so was soon abandoned. By the time Admiral Alexander

Semenovich Shishkov became Minister of Public Education in 1824, the Ministry had regained its administrative integrity only in order that the State could have a free hand in carrying out really profound revisions on every level and in every sphere of the educational system. The new minister had long been an intimate friend of Tsar Alexander, and had been his companion in Bible-reading ever since Alexander's return from Paris after the founding of the Holy Alliance.[1] Also, Shishkov had advised the Tsar on censorship of the press, and his new duties appear to have included the continuation of this activity.[2] With this as his background, Shishkov embarked on a program which in one decade was to supply Russian pedagogy with new aims, new methods, and new structure.

In a speech delivered in St. Petersburg during the first few months of his administration, Shishkov described some of his views on the question of public education. Knowledge, he said, is a good thing "only when, like salt, it is utilized and handed on in correct measure. . . . To instruct all the people, or even a disproportionate number of them, in literacy would do more harm than good. To teach rhetoric to the son of a farmer would make him a bad and useless citizen, if not a really dangerous one. But instruction in the rules and principles of Christian conduct and good morals is needed by everybody." [3]

Later in the same year, Shishkov offered his "Proposal for Working Out a New Plan of Education," in which he stated that, after observing "the course of affairs," he had come to the conclusion that "the Ministry itself has no steadfast plan by which it might always be guided." [4] Conditions in the schools themselves were also far from satisfactory to the Admiral: no standard textbooks had been prepared and "teachers generally follow their own wills and understanding in the admonition of the youth." Insufficient attention was being paid to piety and religious devotion. Moreover, instruction was sometimes actually conducted in languages other than Russian, for example, in schools situated in Polish, Lithuanian, and German districts. All these "evils" were to be remedied immediately, declared Shishkov. Hereafter, "the education of all people throughout our whole Empire, notwithstanding diversity of creed or language, shall be in Russian." Furthermore, the schools must take as their major aim the bringing up of "true sons of the Church and loyal subjects, persons devoted to God and Tsar."[5]

Although Alexander I died in 1825, the year following Shishkov's appointment, his successor, Nicholas I, saw no reason to alter his brother's choice of a Minister of Public Education. In fact, it was Nicholas who insisted upon the official establishment of Shishkov's views in regard to both education and censorship. In 1826, the new Tsar approved Shishkov's extremely repressive Statutes on Press Censorship, which consisted of 230 specific prohibitions as against the 47 in the 1804 decree on that subject,[6] and also appointed him as head of a Commission to revise the educational system. While the severity of some of the measures confirmed by Nicholas might have been heightened by the famous "Decembrist" uprising at the end of 1825, it is quite likely that the Tsar would have carried out such a program in any case. Most historians agree that Nicholas had very definite ideas regarding the role of education in an autocratic regime, and that he regarded even the remnants of the 1804 system as far too liberal.[7] In 1827 he addressed to Admiral Shishkov a letter stating that he strongly disliked the "ladder system" which allowed peasant youth to go from one level of education to another, and that he disapproved also of permitting students of all classes to mingle in the same school. Furthermore, he felt that too much stress had been placed on the dispensation of knowledge at the expense of the building of character in the children.[8]

Honoring fully such views as these, Shishkov's commission published in 1828 an entirely new set of "Rules of Gymnasiums and Schools Under the Jurisdiction of the Universities." [9] Numbering 325 articles, they are nearly twice as numerous as the Regulations of 1804 which they were designed to supplant. "The first principle of the new system was that schools should not be arranged in a sequence, one leading up to another, the primary to the secondary, the secondary to the college or university; but rather to make of the schools independent units adapted to the social position of the social class from which the pupils came. The village school was to have in mind exclusively peasant children; the country [district] school, children of the merchant class; gymnasiums and universities, children of the nobility." [10] All private schools were to be inspected so that the government could rigidly control all agencies of education. The classical gymnasiums were frowned upon because of their concentration upon civic matters and because their courses referred to "republics"; by the middle of the century, only eight of these institutions remained in existence. "The Pedagogical Institute [at St. Petersburg] was closed, 'being unnecessary,' and unnecessary it really was in Nicholas' reign." [11]

Separate categories were established to distinguish secondary school teachers from those in higher institutions, and "even private tutors were required to have a certificate of their character and political trustworthiness from one of the universities." [12] No particular social status was required of teachers in the parish schools, but posts in the district schools and gymnasiums could be held only by "persons of free estate." However, even in parish schools, only those teachers who were freemen could attain the fourteenth civil rank, though that was the lowest level in the entire hierarchy.[13] Instead of the channels of promotion established by the Regulations of 1804, unusual zeal or success in teaching was now rewarded by small cash presents, bestowed with the consent of the landlords of the community.[14] Corporal punishment, banned even in the days of Peter I, was revived, but teachers were cautioned to resort to it only when more gentle means failed.[15] Several of the Rules warn the teachers that they "must under no circumstances lose sight of the chief, that is the moral, aim of education . . . [and] must strive so that the children entrusted to them understand . . . the importance of their present and future duties to God, to themselves, their neighbors, and those in authority over them." [16]

The above quotations indicate that the concept of complete subservience to dogmatic forms had once more found its way into the teacher-pupil relationship. But the new system did not rely on blind obedience alone to accomplish its aims. To insure the carrying out of all the regulations, a special office—the Monitor—was created, and the longest Rule in the entire series of statutes is devoted to a delineation of the duties of these officials who had charge of the dormitories attached to some of the gymnasiums. This Rule requires all Monitors to: [17]

1 keep vigilant, continual watch over their charges;
2 be with them continuously in the hours free of classes, sitting with them at meals and taking turns spending the nights with them;
3 take turns also with them going to classes;
4 have day-by-day knowledge of all that was heard in class, seeing to it that their charges prepare the lessons given them and review what they learn; and in their free time occupy the pupils with reading, or set them to translating or making abstracts of what they have read;
5 observe their charges even in their talk with one another, noticing and correcting their mistakes in language, decorum, or taste;

6 give a verbal account each morning to the inspector regarding conditions in the dormitory; however, the inspector must be informed immediately of any unusual happenings so that, if necessary, the report can be carried even to the director;

7 keep a day-book, marking down in it not only the progress of the pupils in their studies, but also their behavior, noting their traits of character and any evidence of their diligence, and for what subjects they have the most inclination, as well as into what transgressions they fall most often, what kind of assistance they are in special need of, etc.; these day-books are presented at the end of the month to the inspector, and from him they go to the director and to the Honorary Trustee; [18]

8 see that the pupils do not read books disapproved of by the inspector, and in general do not permit themselves to do anything improper for noble and well-reared youths.

Thus was real police-control of students restored in the schools, and under a special officer responsible not to the faculty but to another disciplinary official, the Inspector.

The latter official stood in somewhat the same relation to the teachers as did the Monitor to the pupils. There was an inspector in each school regardless of its type or level. In the parish school, the inspector was charged with "making inquiries concerning the qualities of [the teachers'] characters and conduct, making an effort to ascertain beforehand whether they be capable of discharging their duties without bringing harm to the pupils." [19] Thus the inspector was in a key position in regard to the selection of the teachers for interview. His approval was also required for the granting of rewards and bonuses to teachers.[20] In the gymnasiums, as has already been pointed out, the inspector was in direct charge of all the monitors; this really gave him a staff of his own which was also one step removed from the director. In addition, the teachers now gave their monthly reports not to the director, but to the inspector, who in turn discussed them with whomever he wished.[21] However, the inspector seems to have had nothing directly to do with the appointments of teachers, these being "designated by that university in the jurisdiction of which the gymnasium is located." [22]

It was at the level of the district school that the inspector assumed greatest authority. "Teachers are required to render obedience to him in everything which is not contrary to the law or to the articles of these Rules and the orders of the highest school authorities. He makes the appropriate reprimand to the teacher who is not diligent in his post or who is stubborn in character . . . ; in case of failure to improve, he informs the director. The inspector gives directions to the teachers concerning teaching . . . ; he watches over the progress made in training and also sees that the planned course of each class ends at the designated time." [23] Here, too, the inspector receives reports from the teachers and then he himself decides upon promoting the pupils to a higher grade and issuing certificates of completion of the course.[24] The inspector is charged with restraining the teachers from "occupying themselves excessively with certain pupils," and also with "the preservation of punctilious justice in punishments." [25] Finally, it is now the inspector, rather than the director, who presides at the monthly meetings of the teaching staff.[26]

Thus was the power of the Supervisor first established in Russian education and, still more important, the practice of rigid surveillance over both students and teachers initiated in the secular schools. Although varying in its intensity in future decades, it was destined never again to disappear entirely. In view of so many repressions, the inauguration of two minor practices advantageous to teachers seems trivial; but they are at least worthy of mention. One was a proviso in the Rules declaring that "the house in which the [parish school] teacher lives is released from the requirement of serving as a military billet, and the house which he himself owns is absolved of all other obligations," such as taxes, which now became the responsibility of the school itself.[27] The second concession was also economic in character, but applied only to the widows of directors, inspectors, and teachers of gymnasiums and district schools. Such widows, "whose husbands die in service before completing the required twenty-year term for half-pension, receive assistance in a lump sum equal to one year's salary of the husband; the widows of those who have served twenty years and more are allotted the pensions due their husbands." [28]

It has been reported in at least one history of the period that these Rules of 1828 "suppressed all private boarding schools and educational enterprises." [29] That this impression is erroneous is proven by the fact that an entire chapter of the Rules is devoted to regulations "Concerning Private Educational Institutions and Teachers not Employed Within the Jurisdiction of the Ministry of Public Education." [30] Moreover, one of the articles states explicitly that "the usefulness of well-conducted private educational institutions is so important and so manifest that local authorities are obligated to aid in their maintenance and improvement." [31] It is true that the private schools were required to observe the same general rules as did the state schools in matters such as moral education, keeping of records, selection of teachers, examinations of students, and courses of study.[32] In addition, each private school, according to its location, was subordinate either to the director of a gymnasium or to the inspector of a district school.[33] On the other hand, private institutions could operate either on a day-school basis for boys and girls, or a boarding-school basis for one sex or the other. To the minimum course of study they could add "whatever sciences, foreign languages or arts which are in keeping with the local need and the special purpose of the institution," and could request permission to use whatever special textbooks were needed beyond those approved by the state.[34]

The rules on private-school teachers were a bit more lenient than those in state schools; although some credential from a university or gymnasium official was required of most candidates, exceptions were made in the cases of clergymen teaching religious subjects, teachers with not less than three years' experience in state schools, and teachers of art.[35] The determination of the state to extend its authority over *all* teachers is, however, indicated by the fact that even family tutors in private homes had to abide by the general regulations for all teachers, and all school authorities were told to "take proper measures so that no one without the right to teach may take such a post . . . even in private families."[36]

Such control of elementary and secondary education was rather easily established because the prevailing mood of the Russian people not only countenanced but actually encouraged the return to nationalism and orthodoxy. On the throne was a Tsar who "made it his paramount task to educate his people for an autocratic regime."[37] Between these two—ruler and people—was an officialdom which saw education chiefly as a means of making the masses satisfied with their status in life. Admiral Shishkov, Minister of Public Education from 1824 to 1828, has already been quoted on this point.[38] Count Uvarov, who came to this ministerial post in 1833, held no more enlightened a concept of education's purpose. Uvarov had been Curator of the St. Petersburg Circuit from 1810 to 1821, when he ran afoul of the notorious Magnitskii's drive to wipe out the universities. Although a reactionary himself, Uvarov was more capable and enlightened than most of his colleagues, and he had staged a valiant struggle both to establish a university at St. Petersburg and to retain the services of certain professors who had incurred Magnitskii's distrust.[39] But the years had deepened Uvarov's nationalistic and religious prejudices to such an extent that, in a report he drew up for Tsar Nicholas in 1832, he declared: "The younger generation can be turned into useful and zealous instruments of the Government if thoughtful guidance be brought to bear on the development of their spirit and attitude of mind. . . . They can be led into a mood of devoted and humble love for the existing order." The basic principles of this order Uvarov defined as "Orthodoxy, Autocracy, and Nationalism"—terms which have since become famous in the annals of Russian educational history.[40] Upon his accession to the Ministry the next year, Uvarov stated that his objective was to construct "dams to hold up the flow of new ideas into Russia, and thus prolong the period of her youth."[41] He is also reported to have declared that he would die happy if he could "retard the development of the country by fifty years."[42]

It is ironical that the man who had done most to defend the autonomy of the universities in one decade should in the next be the chief instrument of their degradation, yet such was the role of Uvarov. It is true that during his administration the University of Kiev was founded in 1833, but this institution merely replaced the one at Vilna which had been closed in 1831 on account of the Polish Rebellion. The educational system was further bureaucratized in 1835 by the removal of the universities from the administrative channel and the vesting of all power directly in the hands of the six curators, who now became responsible only to the Ministry of Public Education. In addition, the new law put severe restrictions on the independence of the universities: although they retained the right to appoint their own professors, all such appointments had to be approved by the Ministry.[43]

One chapter of the "General Regulations of Imperial Russian Universities," issued in 1835,[44] was devoted to the so-called "special institutions" existing therein, namely, (1) the Pedagogical Institute, (2) the Medical Institute, and (3) the Learned Society.[45] The aim of the Pedagogical Institute is defined as being "the training of teachers for the gymnasiums and the district schools." [46] Each such institute is required to offer "not less than twenty student scholarships which are awarded to outstanding scholarship pupils from the gymnasium on a competitive basis. [However], if there is an insufficient number of such competitors, the surplus funds can be granted to nonscholarship students. . . .[47] In addition to attending the university lectures, the students of the Pedagogical Institute receive individual guidance in the selection of their major branch of study, exercise in the composition of judgments, and practice in the giving of experimental lectures and lessons. Supervision of these tasks is conducted by three or four professors of the major subjects which the student is preparing to teach. Should a student fail to display sufficient achievement in two half-year courses, he is bereft of his scholarship. . . . Upon completion of their training, students of the Pedagogical Institute are obliged to serve not less than six years in the school system." [48] The only ominous article in this section of the Regulations concerns student discipline: "The moral and financial affairs of the Institute devolve on the Inspector of Students, he being assisted in the former matters by his Assistant and in the latter by the Steward." [49] Thus was control of student behavior left in the hands not of the teaching faculty but of the supervisory staff. On the other hand, certain former rules were relaxed in order to permit any student of the university to take pedagogical courses and obtain teaching practice at the Institute if he "expressed a desire to teach in the school system." [50]

Another encouraging note in teacher education was struck later in the same year (1835) when a decree was approved "On the Training of Scholarship Pupils for Teaching Posts in the Siberian Guberniyas." [51] Previous chapters of this volume have indicated that the Tsarist government had been concerned almost exclusively with the educational establishments of European Russia, and, even more narrowly, with those of the larger cities and towns. The present decree notes the fact that in May 1834 the Committee of Ministers had suggested that the Tsar ask "the Minister of Public Education to turn his special attention to the lack of teachers in the Tomsk *guberniya*, and to take into consideration the fact that Kazan University refuses to admit Siberians unless they obligate themselves to teach for at least fifteen years in Siberia." The Committee of Ministers also pointed out that several Siberian educators had mentioned the advantage of having natives "who are used to the climate" prepared for the teaching profession either in the gymnasiums of Siberia or at Kazan University.[52] This decree attempts to remedy the situation by assigning a certain number of pedagogical scholarships to the Siberian gymnasiums, although the Ministry recognized the inadequacy of this move, since only two such schools existed: one at Tobolsk and the other at Irkutsk. The former was ordered to provide for ten trainees, the latter for eight. Tomsk and Yenisei were to offer four scholarships each "when their gymnasiums are erected"; meanwhile, their quotas were to be added to the responsibilities of the two existing gymnasiums. Upon graduation from these institutions, the best students were to be admitted to the university. Those students who went into teaching direct from the gymnasiums were required to serve in that capacity for eight years, while those graduating also from the university had to teach ten years.[53] Feeble as was this legislation, it at least indicated an effort by the government to improve the quality of public education and teacher education in remote as well as metropolitan areas of the Empire.

Although the independence of universities was restricted by the "General Regulations" of 1835, it was in 1848 that the really severe blow fell upon these institutions, in connection with the government's drive against all forms of liberalism. "Thoroughly alarmed by the events in France and by the revolutionary movements in other countries, the government embarked at once on an orgy of repression, calculated to crush the rising intellectual movement and stifle all signs of life in Russian society." [54] Even the already harsh rules of censorship administered by the Ministry of Public Education were deemed inadequate; additional proscriptions were ordered, and a special committee was appointed to keep the newspapers and publishing houses in line.[55] University professors were required to send in to the Ministry not only the lists of books used for collateral reading in their courses, but even advance copies of the lectures they planned to give! Nor was this just a matter of formal compliance: the deans were instructed to see that the lectures as given in class were identical with the filed copies, and to report even the slightest discrepancies, no matter how harmless.[56] The university curriculums were purged of such courses as social statistics, logic, and metaphysics. European Public Law was discontinued because "rebellions in foreign lands have disfigured this science and shattered its very foundations." Comparative Constitutional Law was withdrawn because of "the weakness of its principles and its unsatisfactory results." [57] Courses in philosophy and psychology could be taught only by Greek Orthodox professors of theology, and had to be in strict accordance with the Church creed as well as expressive of the truth of revealed religion.[58]

University students suffered by direct legislation as well as through the effects of the above academic restrictions. It has even been suggested by some historians that the University Statutes of 1848 were designed primarily to make conditions intolerable in such institutions.[59] The quota of students was cut in all faculties except theology and medicine, tuition fees were greatly raised, and the number of textbooks limited in all courses. Students were required to wear special military uniforms, to cut their hair in a certain fashion, and to conduct themselves in public according to a set of specific rules. Finally, an Inspector of Morals was appointed in all state universities, just as had happened at Kazan nearly three decades earlier.[60]

The secondary and elementary schools were also changed to conform to the more exclusive pattern. The course in the gymnasiums was extended to seven years instead of four, and two more years were added to give the district schools a five-year curriculum.[61] The following year (1849) a further reorganization of the gymnasium took place, this time on an internal plane only. The course was divided into a "general" section common to all students, and a "special" section beginning with the fourth year which permitted the students to specialize in the classics, law, or mathematics. Once more the government decided that study of the classics was too dangerous for any except those able to reach the higher classes of the gymnasium, so Latin was required only for admission to the universities and Greek only for students of philology.[62]

The law putting this change into effect was almost the last official act of Count Uvarov. Realizing that his program had seriously damaged the cause of higher learning, he resigned as Minister of Public Education in the latter part of 1849. But this move did not help the situation, for his successor, Prince P. A. Shirinskii-Shikhmatov, was even more reactionary than he.[63] The classical gymnasiums, once the pride of the secondary school system, remained in disgrace, and by the end of the reign of Nicholas I in 1855 only eight were still in existence.[64]

The status of elementary education remains to be considered. Historians of the period are extremely vague on this question, for few records were kept and even these are not always reliable. It is probable, however, that this level of education suffered most of all, especially in the rural districts. Here the Ministry of Public Education attempted little and accomplished less, even with the parish schools which were nominally under its jurisdiction. After 1830 the Ministry of Public Domains made some efforts to establish schools in the villages to train peasants in clerical skills, and it is reported that "by 1853 there were some 3,000 of these schools with an average of 50 pupils" in each.[65] The total number of pupils derived from these figures would be 150,000, which seems large in comparison with the information provided for the year 1853 in Tables Nos. 12 and 13 in the Appendix to this volume. But some support is given this figure by a Soviet educational historian, who says that such schools admitted between one-tenth and one-twentieth of the school-age population.[66] There were also a number of informal locally organized "literacy schools" scattered over the countryside which instructed peasants of all ages in the rudiments of reading, writing and counting, and these were destined to become the bases of the *zemstvo* schools of the 1860's.[67]

Perhaps the best summary of the situation has been offered not by an educational historian but by an authority on the status of the peasant in Tsarist Russia. This author states that in the half-century preceding the Emancipation (1861) "some progress was made in establishing official primary schools among the peasants. In addition to these official schools, there existed an indeterminable number of unregistered primary schools, maintained sometimes by the peasants themselves and sometimes by the landlords. A beginning had thus been made, but the great mass of the serfs on the private estates and of the peasants on the State domains had hardly been touched by the cultural changes which since Peter's time had so deeply affected the nobles and the bourgeoisie. Some few of the serfs, most often from the 'courtyard people', were, however, selected and trained for higher things. If the landlord maintained a school on the estate, it was likely to be devoted to the preparation of clerks and bailiffs, and perhaps to the preliminary education of other serfs who were destined to serve on the estate as barber-surgeons, surveyors, solicitors, or in some such technical capacity. Sometimes it pleased the proprietor to nurture the arts among the peasantry—to have some of them instructed in architecture, painting, poetry, music—to organize them into orchestras, ballets, opera troupes or dramatic companies. To send a serf to a gymnasium or a University was forbidden in 1827, and again in 1843 (unless he was to be set free), but occasionally a proprietor even sent a favorite abroad to study—perhaps to become more cultivated, more European, than himself."[68]

Yet some progress had been made even during this thirty-year period of darkest reaction, chiefly, it is true, in the realms of secondary and higher rather than elementary education.[69] Although the district schools had not grown at all in number or enrollment, the gymnasiums had increased from 48 to 78 and the number of students in them had quadrupled; in addition there were many more private schools with a greatly increased enrollment over that in 1825. Yet the number of students in higher educational establishments showed an increase of less than 64 per cent between 1830 and 1858, despite the fact that the number of such establishments had more than doubled.[70] The University of St. Vladimir at Kiev was founded in 1833 but, as has already been mentioned, it added nothing to the total because that at Vilna had been closed two years before. However, Nicholas I had set up several higher technical schools on the model of the Institute of Technology at St. Petersburg (1828) and the Moscow Institute (1844). In addition, there was the Demidov Law School in Yaroslavl which had been established in 1805 with private funds but which attracted few students until the 1820's, and the Historico-Philological Institute of Prince Bezborodko in Niezhin (1820), supported from similar sources.[71]

Progress was also made during this period in the matter of strengthening the requirements for, and consequently the value of, academic degrees. The previous chapter described the initial legislation taken in this direction in 1819. In 1837 a new regulation brought about still stricter standardization in the requirements but, aside from this, also granted more liberal privileges to the students.[72] The 1837 decree limited the number of faculties qualified to confer degrees to three in each of the five existing universities: the faculties of Philosophy, Jurisprudence, and Medicine in the Universities of St. Petersburg, Moscow, Kharkov, Kazan, and St. Vladimir.[73] On the other hand, the arbitrary periods between degrees were abolished, permitting the students to pass from one degree to the next as fast as they could qualify. For example, students completing the university course with distinction could immediately stand the examination for Candidate instead of having to wait a year as formerly.[74] Penalties for failure were no longer so severe: two chances were permitted the student to pass a given degree examination, but in such cases the attempts had to be separated by a year.[75] After receiving the degree of Candidate, the student now had the option of attending the university as a Regular Student or working out an individualized program preparatory to standing the exams for a higher degree.[76]

Standards for work toward all degrees were ordered raised, with more attention paid to the quality of instruction.[77] Hereafter, two types of examinations were to be given for each degree (of Master or Doctor), the first being in the major fields and the second in several related fields.

For example, a Master's degree in Philosophy required a major examination in Philosophy, General History, and General Literature, with a minor examination in Greek and Roman history and literature.[78] Another vitally important innovation was the requirement that for the degrees of Master or Doctor a dissertation had to be written and publicly defended.[79] Furthermore, all such degrees, though still granted by the university, had to be approved by the Curator of the circuit and confirmed by the Minister of Public Education.[80] One more item indicates the relative value placed by the Ministry upon Russian degrees: provision was made permitting persons with Doctor's degrees from foreign universities to be granted the immediate status of Master and, after three years of additional study in a Russian university, to take the local examination for the degree of Doctor.[81]

Certain changes were also made in faculty titles and ranks, during the decade 1832-1842, which enhanced the opportunities for younger teachers on university staffs. Two illustrations of such legislation will suffice for the purposes of this study: the first example deals with the creation of the title of Professor Emeritus and the subsequent restrictions on its privileges; the second is concerned with the establishment and expansion of the rank of Docent.

A law of November 9, 1832, had permitted university teachers bearing the rank of either Ordinary or Extraordinary Professor to retire on pension after twenty-five years of service and to assume the title of Professor Emeritus. Because of the great shortage of experienced university professors, the law stated that these "retired" teachers could still continue in their old jobs at full pay. However, it was soon discovered that there might be widespread abuse of the spirit of this law, in that men could be retained after their real usefulness had passed. Therefore, in August 1833 another decree restricted this privilege of continuing work after retirement to those special cases approved by the Minister of Public Education, the Curator of the circuit, and the Council of the University concerned. The new decree pointed out that a quarter century of teaching is enough to drain most of a man's energies and that he should thereafter devote himself to less active pursuits. Furthermore, said the decree, the actual retirement of the older professors permits the advancement of younger teachers to posts of responsibility.[82]

The category of "Docent" was established at the University of St. Vladimir at Kiev in June 1842 as a university rank for those teachers possessing the Master's or Doctor's degree but failing to meet other requirements for the rank of Professor.[83] In October of the same year this rank was adopted at the University of Dorpat, and in June 1843 the remaining four universities (at St. Petersburg, Moscow, Kharkov, and Kazan) were also authorized to award the rank. Moreover, the 1843 decree permitted each University Council to set up its own requirements for the rank and to appoint as many Docents as it needed or could afford to employ. The decree reviewed the great difficulties which the Ministry had encountered in obtaining university teachers because of the restrictive policies regarding appointments, and stated that such formal restrictions had driven many able teachers into foreign universities or private instruction, and had also prevented both foreign and native scholars from joining the staffs of Russian universities.[84]

Another event of prime importance, especially in the history of Russian teacher education, occurred in November 1850: this was the establishment of special chairs in Pedagogy in all the universities except Dorpat. Such a chair had been created at the Main Pedagogical Institute ten years before,[85] and the Minister of Public Education stated in the present decree that both the Tsar and he recognized the value of this move "for the theoretical and practical preparation of students for the teaching profession." [86] Therefore, said the Minister (Prince P. A. Shirinskii-Shikhmatov, who had recently succeeded Count Uvarov), it had been decided to effect the following procedures: "(1) to set up a chair of Pedagogy within the Historical-Philological faculties of each of the five universities; (2) to place in each of these chairs an Ordinary Professor, with the same salary as that given the corresponding position in the Main Pedagogical Institute; [87] and (3) to require attendance at the lectures on Pedagogy, aside from students of the Historical-Philological faculties, not only of all scholarship students preparing to teach in gymnasiums and district schools but also of all non-scholarship students expecting to become private tutors." [88]

Despite this somewhat enlightened attention directed by the new Minister to the subject of Pedagogy, the agencies of teacher education were spared neither the criticism leveled against educational institutions in general nor the stringent moral censorship imposed on all establishments of higher learning. Ever since Magnitskii's notorious "Instructions to the Director of Kazan University" in 1820, the hold of the State and the Church upon educational aims and principles had been growing tighter. Following both the spirit and the letter of Magnitskii's words, Minister Shirinskii-Shikhmatov on January 23, 1851, addressed a series of "Instructions" to the Directors and Inspectors of the Richelieu Lycée, the Demidov Lycée, the Prince Bezborodko Lycée (the last two being private institutions), and the Main Pedagogical Institute. Regarding the status of the last-named institution, the Minister directed his invective toward the lack of supervision and co-ordination on the part of the leadership, the inadequacy of the program as a whole, the deplorable quality of the instruction provided, and the low standards set by the examinations. [89] For these alleged shortcomings, the Minister had in mind a definite program of remedies. Henceforth, all professors were to be required to file advance outlines of their courses with the Director, who in turn would co-ordinate these courses and see that they were taught in a logical manner.[90]

In erecting the entire program the Director and the Council were to bear in mind four main objectives: (1) each subject should be planned with a view toward its contributions to the whole field of pedagogical training; (2) each subject should stress strongly both the academic and the moral aims of instruction; (3) each subject should be purged of all materials not in agreement with the ideals of the Church; and (4) each subject should include everything possible to encourage devotion to the Church, loyalty to the Tsar, and love of the Fatherland.[91] The Inspector must be constantly on guard against the possibility of any professor teaching "untruths," and he must report all such cases to the Director. Mere suspicion of such transgression warrants both the Director and the Inspector to investigate and censor the lectures of the professor. Should an accused or suspected professor refuse to submit to such supervision, or decline to mend his ways, an account of the case must be sent to the Ministry of Public Education.[92] Finally, say the Instructions, while it is primarily the job of the Inspector to see that the examinations are of the necessary difficulty and scope, the Director is in the end responsible for the examinations as well as all other activities of the Institute. Therefore, either of these officials has the right and duty to check all examinations to determine whether they are suitable to the given course, and to revise them if necessary.[93]

From the above decree, one can observe the culmination of a policy of stifling professors which had been gaining ground for more than three decades. Granting that there were undoubtedly grave flaws in the program of the Main Pedagogical Institute, and granting also that several of the

Minister's requirements (such as his first two "main objectives") were not only sound but even rather advanced for the time; nevertheless, the "Instructions" constitute an order of censorship which few self-respecting professors would willingly endure. While several of the prescriptions and proscriptions bear the tone of the early eighteenth century, there is one new, and ominous, trend—the growing power and scope of the office of the Inspector. In previous decrees he has appeared as omnipotent in the area of discipline and moral instruction; in this document he emerges as the eyes and ears of the Director in all academic affairs.

Undoubtedly these restrictions upon the higher schools exercised a deleterious effect upon their standing even among Russians willing to dedicate themselves to Orthodoxy, Autocracy, and Nationalism. As one writer puts it: "The class and political aims of education at this period were fully developed, and the formula of Uvarov . . . [was] so literally accepted and followed that the schools under [the government's] domination became a mere department of internal affairs." [94] The same author acknowledges, however, that "during the 1840's there was one bright spot. The University of Moscow became the center of liberal thinking in history, law, philosophy, science, and literature." [95] On the same subject the great Russian novelist, Ivan Turgenev, had written in 1844: "Never in any country has any institution been comparatively more useful and more fertile of results. Today it is rare that a man who writes his own language correctly, an honest and enlightened official, or an upright and firm magistrate, has not at some time been a student in the University of Moscow." [96] Nearly all the liberal thinkers of the period were products of this institution—Hertzen, Belinskii, Bakunin [97]—as well as most of those educational philosophers who in the next few decades were to create a new era of progress in Russian pedagogy.

7

Brief History of the Main Pedagogical Institute at St. Petersburg (1725–1858)

FREQUENT MENTION HAS BEEN MADE IN PREvious chapters of the existence in St. Petersburg of a special agency to train teachers for the schools of Russia. Wherever such references have occurred they have been connected, more or less directly, with a change in the general system of higher, secondary, or elementary education. However, this special agency undoubtedly had an important history in its own right during the many decades already covered in this volume. Therefore, it is well to interrupt at this point the chronological story of the development of the Russian educational system as a whole, and to concentrate our attention momentarily on the creation, the growth, the struggles to survive, and the consequent influence of this institution which passed through many vicissitudes during the period 1725-1858. Thenceforth, its history can be interwoven with the main theme.

The first *civil* agency established explicitly for the training of teachers in Russia was the Gymnasium created along with, and attached to, the Academy of Sciences in 1725.[1] In 1782, Catherine II and Jankovitch de Mirievo converted the remnants of this agency into the first Teachers Seminary, which was designed to be the progenitor of a network of similar regional institutions. But this plan never worked out; on the contrary, four years later the Teachers Seminary was bereft of much of its original responsibility by the decree ordering the regional 'main schools' to prepare teachers for the 'minor schools'.[2] As a result, the Seminary was reduced almost to its original status of a Gymnasium, and not a Teachers Gymnasium at that, for at times "there was not one student [there] preparing to become a teacher."[3] In connection with the establishment of the Ministry of Public Education and the consequent plans for the reformation of the entire school system, the agency was revived under the name of the Teachers Gymnasium in 1803. Count P. V. Zavadovskii, who had become the first Minister of Public Education after serving since 1782 as Chairman of Catherine's Commission on the Establishment of Schools, made a speech announcing the revival and describing the plans to make the institution more important than ever. Zavadovskii declared that Novosiltsov, President of the Academy of Sciences and Curator of the St. Petersburg Educational Circuit, had drawn up designs for the reconstruction of the building which would increase its capacity to one hundred students, all preparing to be teachers. Nearly 20,000 rubles was to be appropriated for this reconstruction, and an additional 24,000 rubles would be provided for the tuition and maintenance of the students.

As Minister, Zavadovskii directed Curator Novosiltsov to make special efforts to have the building ready for occupancy by the following September (1803), and asked that several of the most capable teachers in the Empire be released from their present duties in order to join the new faculty.

Since the project had the Tsar's support as well as his own complete approval, Zavadovskii promised to use his influence with the Theological Seminary and the University of St. Petersburg in persuading these institutions to transfer some of their best students to the Teachers Gymnasium. The Department of Public Instruction, highest division of the Ministry of Public Education, confirmed these proposals and embodied them in an official resolution.[4] That the Minister was not exaggerating the high sources of support accorded the plan was evidenced in January of the following year when the budget of the resuscitated Teachers Gymnasium was approved by the Ministry of Public Education. Out of the 20,000 rubles mentioned earlier by Zavadovskii, more than 15,000 was assigned to faculty salaries. The Director of the Teachers Gymnasium was to receive 2,500 rubles a year, as against 2,600 for the directors of the four most important universities of the Empire, 2,500 for the directors of the Pedagogical Institutes at the universities of Moscow, Kharkov, and Kazan, and 2,000 for the Curators of the six educational circuits. Moreover, the rank of Professor at the Teachers Gymnasium drew the same salary (2,000 rubles) as that assigned to the professors at the universities, and the Language Teachers got even more (1,000 rubles as against 600 rubles).[5]

But this elevation was not all that was in store for the Teachers Gymnasium. In April 1804, Zavadovskii announced that this institution was to be reorganized into a

Pedagogical Institute and attached to the projected University of St. Petersburg as a separate division. According to the Minister, this move would afford the agency even more authority and autonomy. Pursuant to this decision, a full set of "Regulations for the Pedagogical Institute at St. Petersburg" was drawn up, modelled on the statutes for the universities themselves.[6] The Regulations consist of ten chapters subdivided into 136 articles, as follows: I-Internal Structure (art. 1-9); II-Conference and General Meeting (art. 20-34); III-The Director (art. 35-50); IV-Duties of Faculty Members (art. 51-76); V-The Academic Secretary (art. 77-81); VI-The Library (art. 82-89); VII-The Students (art. 90-107); VIII-The Housekeeper (art. 108-119); IX-The Inspector (art. 120-133); and X-The Physician (art. 134-136). The Regulations state that the purpose of the Institute is to prepare teachers for the leading gymnasiums, which desire "to obtain skillful teachers of all subjects." Therefore the Institute must accept two grave responsibilities: "(1) to admit only those students possessing superior talents and adequate training in scientific literature and foreign languages; and (2) to teach each one of these students the subjects of the gymnasiums with the greatest possible breadth." [7] A teaching staff of eleven professors and teachers is provided for, and the following courses constitute the curriculum of the Pedagogical Institute: [8]

Pure and applied Mathematics, Logic, Metaphysics, Moral Philosophy, Geography, Natural History, General History, Experimental Physics, Chemistry, Russian History, Political Economy, Aesthetics, Commercial Science, Rural Domestic Arts, Latin language and literature, French language and literature, German language and literature, Drawing and Design. [The last four subjects are designated as "most important."]

The course of study is to be three years in length, with rigid examinations after each year.[9] The Director is to be in complete charge, with the Inspector second in command. The latter official must be approved by the Curator of the Circuit, must reside at the Institute, and take charge of all students. All other professors and teachers must be confirmed in their appointments by the Minister of Public Education.[10] The "Conference" or "General Meeting" is composed of the leading professors of the Institute; it meets both regularly and on call of the Director, and acts as his advisory council.[11] The chief method of instruction is dictation, which not only best teaches the subject but also trains the memory: "for the most part, the youth retain in the mind only that which they write down at dictation." [12] The budget of the new agency was raised considerably above that of the preceding year: 44,928 rubles overall, of which 18,700 rubles was assigned to faculty salaries on much the same individual basis as in the original fund, a Librarian and a third professor being added to the staff.[13]

Four years later, in 1808, another effort was made to increase the prestige of the Pedagogical Institute by rewarding the outstanding students with foreign travel fellowships. The plan was carefully organized and elaborately worked out, and called for the assignment of an annual fund of 18,000 rubles to finance the study and travel abroad of twelve students for a period of three years each, at an average sum of 1,500 rubles per year per student. Not only were the students very carefully selected (their names appear as part of the decree itself) but special courses of study had to precede their journeys, and an individual itinerary was set up for each student. Evidently all the great universities of Europe had been evaluated by the Ministry of Public Education, for specific colleges are recommended for each subject: Göttingen for political science and philosophy, Heidelberg for civil law, Berlin and Paris for chemistry. The decree frequently refers to particular professors at these institutions, and in some cases even designates scholars who devote themselves exclusively to private teaching. Students who received these awards were required to submit reports every four months to the Conference of the Pedagogical Institute, and were expected to abide by any changes in study plans or itinerary suggested in reply. One admonition to students of philosophy has particular significance for this volume, even though Pedagogy was not one of the twelve fields selected for foreign study. Nevertheless, a paragraph of the decree urges "the young philosopher who has an excellent encyclopedic knowledge and the desire to use the findings of science for the benefit of mankind . . . to turn his attention to the rules of the nurture, learning, and education of youth," and at the end of his travel and study, "to occupy himself with Pedagogy." [14]

In 1810 Count Zavadovskii was succeeded as Minister of Public Education by Count A. Z. Razumovskii, who immediately set about insuring for students of the Pedagogical Institute all the privileges to which other university students were entitled. The "Rules of the Academy of Sciences" which were adopted in 1803 had provided for the selection of as many as twenty university and gymnasium students to serve as scholarship students in the classes of the Academy. Such students were to be awarded the fourteenth civil rank upon admission, and could elevate this to the twelfth rank after standing certain examinations.[15] In June 1811, Count Razumovskii announced that students of the Pedagogical Institute were thereafter to be included in the plan; in fact, he stated that three such students were already studying successfully at the Academy in the fields of astronomy, chemistry, and political economy and statistics. Now, however, the opportunities were to be broadened even further: students could raise their civil rank from twelfth to ninth, and their monetary allowances from 400 rubles a year to 550 or even 750, by serving as substitute Senior Teachers in the Teachers Gymnasium while carrying on their studies at the Academy. Upon completion of these studies, such students were to be given preference in the filling of any vacancies arising at the Teachers Gymnasium.[16] This move on the part of the Ministry indicated both the government's interest in encouraging superior individuals to enter the teaching profession, and the ability of Pedagogical Institute students to compete successfully with other university students. Despite these attractions, however, several schools even years later were bemoaning the lack of qualified teachers.[17]

Still further efforts were soon made to broaden the scope and authority of the Pedagogical Institute at St. Petersburg. In 1816, its name was changed to the Main Pedagogical Institute,[18] and instead of preparing teachers only for the gymnasiums and schools of the St. Petersburg educational circuit, its task became that of "training teachers, masters, adjuncts, and professors for all the schools of the Empire functioning under the Ministry of Public Education, as well as headmasters for private schools or boarding schools, and private tutors." [19] Furthermore, the Main Pedagogical Institute was designated as the center of teacher education for all of Russia, and all other pedagogical institutes were to co-ordinate their work with its program.[20] Two separate curricula were set up in the Institute, the first consisting of only two years for those students wishing to enter ordinary government jobs, and the second of six years for candidates for the teaching profession.[21] The latter course was divided into three main units: (1) the preliminary course of two years; (2) the higher, or concluding, course of three years; and (3) a sixth year devoted particularly to the study of Pedagogy.[22] Twenty-one departments were created, as follows: [23]

(1) Divine Law
(2) Philosophy
(3) General Law
(4) Statutory Law
(5) Political Economy
(6) Mathematics
(7) Physics
(8) Chemistry and Technology
(9) Zoology
(10) Botany
(11) Mineralogy
(12) History
(13) Geography
(14) Statistics
(15) Greek Literature
(16) Latin Literature
(17) Arabic Literature
(18) Persian Literature
(19) Russian Literature
(20) German Literature
(21) French Literature

The academic year in both the Preliminary and Higher courses consisted of eleven months, and the curriculum for each course is given below. No formal curriculum is listed for the sixth year, which was to be devoted entirely to the study of Pedagogy on an individual basis, with much actual practice in the schools.[24]

Curriculum in Preliminary Course (2 years) [25]

Logic and Mathematics; Pure and Higher Mathematics; Mathematical and General Geography; Physics; Survey of General History; Ancient Geography; Mythology and Origins of Peoples, especially the Slavic Peoples; General Rhetoric; Arts: * Civil Architecture, Drawing and Design, Music, Fencing; Languages and Literatures: Greek, Latin, Russian, German, French.

* These Arts taught also throughout the Higher Course. Listed as subjects "strictly required for all pupils" are Divine Law, Russian Literature, and Latin Literature.[26]

Curriculum in Higher Course (3 years)[27]

Section I (Philosophical and Juridical Sciences)

1. Speculative and Practical Philosophy
2. Law
   - A. General
     - a. encyclopedic
     - b. natural
     - c. political
     - d. civil and public
     - e. commercial
   - B. Statutory
     - a. criminal
     - b. Roman
     - c. Russian
       - 1. civil
       - 2. criminal
       - 3. Russian legal procedure
3. Political Economy

Section II (Philosophical and Mathematical Sciences)

1. Mathematics, pure and especially higher and theoretical
2. Astronomy
3. Physics
4. Chemistry and Technology
5. Natural History
   - or a. zoology
   - b. botany
   - c. mineralogy

Section III (Historical and Literary Sciences)

1. History, general; and especially the Russian Government
2. Geography, general; and especially that of Russia
3. Statistics
4. Languages and Literatures:
   - Greek
   - Latin
   - Arabic
   - Persian
   - Russian
   - German
   - French

Note: The course in Arts (see Preliminary Curriculum) continues here, and "above all is the course in Divine Law which continues throughout the Higher Course."[28]

The decree provides that, for the Higher Course, there shall be on the faculty twenty qualified teachers possessing higher-education degrees, including Ordinary Professors at a salary of 2,000 rubles, Extraordinary Professors at 1,600 rubles, and Adjuncts (substituting for Professors) at 1,000 rubles. In this group there must be one teacher of Divine Law with the rank of Professor and a salary of 1,500 rubles. In addition, there are also to be six Masters or Lecturers at a salary of 700 rubles, and six more Adjuncts (besides those substituting for Professors) at 800 rubles who will be used for various teaching duties.[29] Each Section (see Curriculum for Higher Course above) must have one Senior Ordinary Professor, elected for a term of three years by a conclave of Professors and Adjuncts, who will be in charge of methods of teaching, supervision of the curriculum, and presentation of faculty problems to the Director.[30]

A comparison of the budgetary tables (see Appendix) reveals the enormous increase in funds allotted to the Main Pedagogical Institute in the period 1804-1816. The total budget of the institution rose from less than 45,000 rubles to more than 165,000 rubles, or nearly two and three-fourths times. In 1816 the money to be spent on faculty salaries and allowances alone exceeded by 10,000 rubles the total budget for 1804 and was nearly three and a half times the corresponding item for the earlier date. Thus, allotments for faculty salaries were more than keeping pace with appropriations for the entire Institute. However, a more minute examination of the budgets will reveal that the rise in instructional expenses was occasioned by additions to the staff rather than by increases in the salaries of the individual teachers. The pay of Ordinary Professors remained exactly the same over the twelve-year period: 2,500 rubles in salary and housing allowance. It is true that provision was made for many more teachers of all ranks, but the salary scale for these teachers had approximately the same range in 1804 as in 1816, 700-2,500 rubles in the former year and 800-2,500 rubles in the latter. On the other hand, the Director's salary was raised from 2,500 rubles to 3,000 rubles, plus a housing allowance of 1,200 rubles which was not mentioned in the 1804 budget; this gave him an actual increase of 1,700 rubles, or nearly 70 per cent, while the teachers got no raises at all aside from possible promotions in rank.

Moreover, this tendency to place more value upon administration than upon instruction is reflected throughout the 1816 decree, but especially in the budget. Although the supplementary salary for the Inspector (if already a member of the staff) rose only from 300 to 400 rubles, the 1804 regulations specified that he be chosen from among three acting Professors who received only 700 rubles in salary, plus either housing or an allowance for same. According to the 1816 regulations, however, the Inspector was intrusted with much greater responsibilities and consequently was probably selected from the higher-paid ranks of the faculty. (The fact that a salary of 1,500 rubles is allotted for this post in case the incumbent be appointed from outside is an indication of this probability.) But the most striking difference in the personnel lists of the two budgets is the increased number of administrative assistants, secretaries, counselors, and clerks. While it is expected that an expanding school program will require additional administrative officers, the following table shows that this category of allotments was the only one to show a *relative* increase over the period:

Total Funds Allotted, by Categories

CATEGORY	*1804*	*1816*	DIFFERENCE
Instruction only	36%	31%	−5%
Administrative Expenses	8	30	+22
Maintenance and Operation	14	12	−2
Assistance to Students	42	27	−15

The curriculum of the Higher Course, outlined earlier in this chapter, was not designed exclusively for the preparation of teachers for the elementary and secondary schools. The scope of instruction offered in Law, for example, was far beyond the needs of the ordinary prospective teacher, whether he elected the general course or one of the specialized fields. Nor did "pure and higher and theoretical" mathematics offer the proper training for a student expecting to teach simple arithmetic to the pupils of provincial schools. The admirably wide choice in languages might attract the would-be philologist or the prospective college teacher, but it had little practical value for the public schools in an era when the Holy Alliance was being used to encourage even further "Russification" of these same schools. Obviously, then, the Main Pedagogical Institute was veering away from its primary purpose as enunciated in both the 1804 and 1816 decrees, that purpose being the preparation of teachers for the public and private schools of the Empire. Very likely this tendency was apparent also to the officials of the Ministry of Public Education, but, having sponsored the policy and administered its application, these officials were naturally hesitant to condemn or even to alter basically their own work. The necessary changes had to await the emergence of a special opportunity. Nor was this opportunity long in making itself manifest in double form: a new Minister and a new Ministry.

In September 1816 Prince Alexander N. Golitsyn supplanted Count Razumovskii as head of the Ministry of Public Education, and in October 1817 this agency was renamed the Ministry of Spiritual Affairs and Public Education.[31] It is true that Prince Golitsyn had become Minister of the former agency nearly four months prior to his announcement of the new curriculum described just above, but these profound revisions had already been started under his predecessor and Golitsyn had to carry them out. In view of his own background of religious interests (he had long been Chief Procurator of the Holy Synod), the amalgamation of the Ministry with the Synod and the subsequent changes in the Main Pedagogical Institute appear much more consistent with Golitsyn's philosophy of education. As a matter of fact, the very first act of the Ministry of Spiritual Affairs and Public Education, taken the day after its inception, was the creation at the Institute of a Second Division which was to concentrate its entire attention upon "the training of teachers for the Public Schools." [32]

The most important difference between the Institute itself and the Second Division lay in the aims and organization of the respective curricula. As has been pointed out, the Institute had a six-year course offered by three sections and twenty-one departments. The new decree provided a four-year curriculum for the Second Division, reduced the number of courses to five, and modelled its structure on the order of the two-year Preliminary Course of the Institute. The details of these revisions are worth careful study, especially in view of subsequent shifts in governmental policy concerning teacher education in general and the Main Pedagogical Institute in particular.

First of all, the Second Division reduced the number of scholarships from one hundred to thirty, and announced that preference for these awards would be given to selected children of teachers in the district schools.[33] Pupils applying for general admission had to be between twelve and fourteen years of age, and even these had to be selected by a special committee appointed by the Curator of the St. Petersburg Educational Circuit. No pupil was to be admitted "without entrance examinations in (a) Divine Law, (b) reading and spelling, and (c) the first four rules of arithmetic." [34] The four-year course consisted of the following subjects: "(1) Divine Law, (2) Russian Language, (3) Mathematics and the first rules of Physics, (4) History and Geography, especially of Russia, (5) Spelling and Drawing." [35] If the 1816 curriculum of the Main Pedagogical Institute could be criticized for its tendency toward "overpreparation," certainly the Second Division was applying stringent countermeasures!

The decree states that "at the end of each year an examination is given the pupils in the presence of the Curator and the Council, [and] a report on the achievements and morality of the pupils is submitted by the Inspector for the perusal of the Council. . . . At the end of the four-year course, a public examination is given the pupils."[36] Those pupils who pass successfully this examination enter upon a period of practice work where they act "as assistants to teachers in the public schools; subsequently, they are confirmed in the title of Teacher at the discretion of the Curator. . . . Pupils who complete the four-year course with distinguished success, who possess high morals, and who are admitted to the teaching profession, also receive a certificate of civil rank of the XIV Class under the signature of the Curator, and acquire the privilege of not having to undergo examinations for further advancement of rank. These rights accrue to these persons only so long as they are employed in the profession under the jurisdiction of the Ministry of Education. . . . Pupils displaying only satisfactory success but good morals receive a certificate signed by the Inspector and the teachers, possess the title of Candidate, and advance toward the title of Teacher by the means provided by law. . . . Pupils confirmed in the title of Teacher are obligated to serve for at least six years under the jurisdiction of the Ministry of Public Education."[37]

The administration of the Second Division was, naturally, much less complex than that of the Institute. In fact, at the beginning the Division was not even a part of the Institute: the decree states that "the Second Division will be obliged at some time to merge with the Main Pedagogical Institute but, until then, it will exist under the administration of the Curator of the St. Petersburg Circuit and have its own Inspector . . . [who] is selected by the Curator and approved by the Ministry." The Inspector, who was permitted one assistant,[38] appears to have had little personal power in the administration of the Division, being particularly circumscribed in his authority by an Academic Council appointed by the Minister on the recommendation of the Curator. This Council consisted of five members, some of whom could be employed outside the teaching profession, "or not even employed at all." In the appointment of persons in the latter category, the Minister is ordered to consult the Tsar himself! [39]

Such serious attention seems somewhat out of place in the case of such a small institution, but evidently every effort was being made to ensure the "correct" leadership of the new Division. The importance of the Council is further highlighted in the decree: "above all, [its] membership . . . must be drawn from people experienced in public education, whom the Curator can entrust with the theoretical aspects of teaching methods, the reviewing of new systems, etc. The Council is the supervisor of all the activities of the academic section. . . . In cases where the Curator and the Council decide, with the approval of the academic section, to institute certain changes such as the addition of several subjects, the introduction of a new system of teaching, etc., the Minister of Public Education takes the necessary measures and grants the authority." [40] From the foregoing it appears that the entire plan for the Second Division was on a purely experimental basis, a suspicion further confirmed by the fact that the Curator was charged with the duty of approving a new schedule of courses each year.[41]

The status of the teacher in the new Division remains to be considered. Almost needless to say, with the great restriction in the number of students and the scope of instruction, there was a serious reduction in the budget. But this reduction was not simply appropriate: it was catastrophic. The total funds now were less than those allotted to the Teachers Gymnasium in 1804, and the amount to be expended on faculty salaries was considerably less than half of that provided for the original institution. Furthermore, of the 6,800 rubles assigned to this category, 3,200 rubles (or almost half) was for the salaries of the Inspector and his Assistant. While these administrative officials received much more than did their predecessors even in 1816 (2,000 instead of 1,500; 1,200 instead of 800), the teachers were reduced to well below the 1804 levels of pay.[42] The teaching staff itself was cut down to only five active instructors, and these were concerned largely with elementary or superficial subjects. While the decree itself states that "each of these subjects may be taught by a special teacher," it adds that "one teacher can give two subjects" if necessary.[43] One last clue is provided by the decree in the matter of whether the standing of the teachers of the Second Division was really that of university instructors: "Teachers having no special academic titles are granted equality with Senior Teachers in gymnasiums." [44]

Undoubtedly, much of the confusion in regard to the purpose of the Main Pedagogical Institute was engendered by the conflicting desires of several prominent Russian educational administrators. The Regulations for Educational Establishments Under the Jurisdiction of Universities, issued in 1804, had called for universities to be established immediately at Kharkov, Kazan, and St. Petersburg to supplement the work of the three which already existed (at Moscow, Vilna, and Dorpat).[45] This order was carried out that same year in regard to setting up universities at Kharkov and Kazan, but after much wrangling it was decided that St. Petersburg should convert its recently revived Teachers Gymnasium into a Pedagogical Institute, and to defer until later the creation there of a complete university. This solution seems to have sufficed until 1810, when Count Uvarov was appointed Curator of the St. Petersburg Educational Circuit.

Although only twenty-five years old at the time, Uvarov was already well known as a scholar with a deep respect for higher education. Therefore, it was natural that he should resent the fact that his native city, and now his own administrative district, was the only great center in Russia which had no university. Furthermore, since Uvarov was the son-in-law of Count Razumovskii (Minister of Public Education from 1810 to 1816) as well as Curator of the St. Petersburg Circuit, he was in a good position to do something about the matter.[46] On the other hand, he was opposed by similarly powerful forces which for nearly a decade prevented his achieving his aim. Evidently he had a good opportunity in 1816 when plans were under way for the reorganization of the Pedagogical Institute; but in April of that year Count Razumovskii was discredited and forced to resign because of his alleged favoritism toward the Jesuits. Nevertheless, "the University of St. Petersburg was finally established in 1819, owing to the exertions of Uvarov."[47]

But it was not Uvarov who got the credit. In a speech announcing the creation of the new institution, Prince Golitsyn, the Minister of Public Education, stated that "many years of experience have shown the necessity of establishing in this capital a university to replace the Main Pedagogical Institute," and he announced that Tsar Alexander I had given his blessing to the transformation. Although Golitsyn admitted that the Institute had done its work very well, he thought that "at this time" a real university would accomplish "a broader and more important purpose [by providing] a full Academy course in the highest sciences," which a mere pedagogical institute obviously could not do.[48] However, Golitsyn revealed that financial considerations also carried great weight in the decision, which statement was a veiled reference to the fact that the Napoleonic wars and the Holy Alliance were still having their effects upon the Tsar's treasury.

The new university was designated as the chief agency of the St. Petersburg Educational Circuit, and endowed with all the other rights and privileges formerly accruing to the Main Pedagogical Institute.[49] Its curriculum was greatly expanded, but essentially the same administration was retained. Also, all property of the former Institute was transferred to the new institution.[50] Preparation of teachers was continued, the Second Division remaining the same in substance but being renamed the Teachers Institute under the jurisdiction of the St. Petersburg University.[51] That the progress of the Teachers Institute was far from satisfactory is revealed by the fact that in 1822 it was completely abolished, and the teacher training program in the St. Petersburg circuit came to a standstill.[52]

That this state of affairs actually continued for six full years is an indication of the slough into which Russian education had fallen in the third decade of the nineteenth century. The abortive amalgamation of the Ministry with the Holy Synod, the Magnitskii inquiry into Kazan University and the subsequent repressions placed upon that institution, the withdrawal of Count Uvarov from all educational work in 1821, the decline of enrollments in all Russian universities except that at Moscow, and, finally, the appointment of Admiral A. S. Shishkov as Minister of Public Education—all these factors, and others like them, had brought Russian education, especially higher education, practically to an impasse. Previous commentary has been made on this period, and particularly on the policies of Admiral Shishkov. It will suffice to point out here that during his entire four-year administration, he made no attempt whatever to revive the teacher training program at St. Petersburg. All such moves were left to his successor, Prince K. A. Liven, one of the few administrators in Russia who fought to preserve the "ladder system," instituted by the reforms of 1804, by which all state schools in the Empire were opened to capable youths regardless of their social or economic backgrounds.[53] While Liven failed in his attempts to force retention of even the remnants of this system, he did win the battle for the re-establishment of the Main Pedagogical Institute which, by Imperial decree, began its new existence on September 30, 1828.[54]

On the same day, a new set of Regulations was issued for the Institute.[55] In nearly every respect, these two hundred rules were practically the duplicates of those issued for the original Main Pedagogical Institute in 1816 and described earlier in this chapter. The Regulations conferred upon the resuscitated agency the right to train teachers and professors for all educational establishments of the Ministry of Public Education, and placed the Institute directly under the orders of the Minister himself.[56] A budget was granted for one hundred students who had finished eight years of school before admission, and, in order to maintain serious standards of work, no auditors were permitted to attend the courses.[57] The curriculum again became six years in length: two years in the Preliminary Course; three years in the "Terminal," or Higher, Course; and one year in the Pedagogical Course, the latter to include some practice teaching.[58]

The three faculties (or sections) were also re-established: (1) Philosophical and Juridical Sciences, (2) Mathematical and Physical Sciences, and (3) Historical and Literary Sciences.[59] In the new organization, however, only eighteen departments were revived from the original twenty-one,[60] but those dropped were minor—Arabic, Persian, and Geography—and the last-named was probably incorporated into the departments of History and Statistics. Ranks assigned for the faculty were those of Ordinary Professor (17 posts) Extraordinary Professor (for specific subjects), Adjunct (6 posts) and Instructor, and special rules were laid down regarding the requirements for these positions.[61]

Although these rights, duties, departments, and courses were restored to approximately the status of 1816, the budget was not. Happily, though, the fiscal revisions were upward by a considerable margin: 207,400 rubles instead of 165,200, an increase of more than 25 per cent. Since the complete itemized budget is among the tables at the end of this volume,[62] only a few illustrative items need be considered here. The number of teaching positions in the upper ranks was slightly augmented, while those in the lower brackets were entirely abolished. The Regulations of 1816 call for twenty professors and adjuncts substituting for them, a Professor of Divine Law, and twelve more masters, lecturers and adjuncts to assist in miscellaneous duties. The budget for 1828 specifies seventeen Ordinary Professors, six Adjuncts, two highly paid teachers of Art and Divine Law, and no others. Thus in 1816 the teaching faculty consisted of thirty-three members, in 1828 of only twenty-five—in both counts the Director and Inspector being excluded. But the total salaries and allowances paid to the smaller group (nearly 94,000 rubles) is 70 per cent *more* than that paid the larger. In other words, the average teaching salary at the Institute rose from 1,667 rubles in 1816 to 3,760 rubles in 1828. Evidently the policy was to use fewer but better-trained personnel to instruct the carefully selected student body. It is interesting to note that greater monetary attraction was offered the students also, the subsistence allowance for each being increased from 300 rubles to 500, with more funds provided for foreign travel. Another encouraging note is that the allotment for administrative expenses, which constituted as large a share of the 1816 budget as did instructional expenses, fell to less than 30,000 rubles in 1828, with increased salaries to fewer officials, as elsewhere in the budget. However, the creation of the post of Room Supervisor (of which there were five at the Institute) is evidence of the greater emphasis on student discipline.[63] So began another period in the history of the Main Pedagogical Institute, a period which was to see many minor changes but, until the end, nothing as fundamental as had occurred before.

Despite the support given by the Government and the educational administration to the reforms of 1828, there was still a dearth of applicants for the Institute. Although the budget of that year had established a fund for the support of a hundred scholarship students,[64] it is unlikely that this number was actually provided for. Evidence for this conclusion is offered in an order of the Minister of Public Education in 1832 entitled "On Increasing the Number of Scholarship Pupils at the Main Pedagogical Institute," which "raised" the scholarships to sixty. The decree also set up two age-groups, with each group getting thirty scholarships. Recipients in the first group were to be graduates of the Theological Seminary who were recommended by the Holy Synod, while the second group was to be chosen from among the outstanding students, aged twelve to fourteen years, of the St. Petersburg Gymnasium. The students from the Seminary would take the regular six-year course at the Institute, but the Gymnasium pupils would take a nine-year course; thus both groups would graduate at the same age. The decree also expressed the hope of increasing the number of scholarships in each group to forty within the next few years.[65] However, even this figure is smaller than that proposed in the 1828 budget.

The next important innovation was the creation in 1837 of a Chair of Russian History at the Institute. The decree establishing this post notes that the History course had been divided into two parts by the Institute Administration in 1833. At that time, the part dealing with Russian History had been detached and placed under an Adjunct, while the General History course continued to be taught by a Professor. In confirming this decree, the Committee of the Ministry of Public Education recognized that under the Regulations of the Institute only one Professor could be assigned to a department. But the Committee went on to say that, "having in mind the fact that the teaching of the history of the Fatherland is becoming more important for pupils in all institutions for youth," it agreed that a Chair of Russian History should be established under a Professor (who for the time being might be only an Extraordinary Professor), with a salary of 2,800 rubles and 800 rubles for living quarters.[66] It will be noted that this figure, also, is much less than that assigned to Professors by the budget of 1828.[67]

In 1838 the Second Division, which had been abolished in 1822, was reorganized for the purpose of preparing teachers for district and parish schools. An indication of its real importance, however, is found in the fact that no teaching staff was supplied for the Division, all instruction being carried on by Institute students under the guidance of the Director and several special supervisors.[68] Certainly this practice did not augur well for the quality of training to be provided. A more hopeful sign came in 1840 when a special Chair of Pedagogy was created, with an Ordinary Professor assigned to teach all subjects in that field at a salary of a thousand silver rubles a year.[69] Although the salary given to the new post was low in comparison to that awarded teachers of other subjects, the move was important because it represented the first time in Russia that Pedagogy was recognized as a discipline in itself. There can be no doubt that the innovation fulfilled its purpose, for the reason that ten years later such chairs were established in all Russian universities, and the decree initiating this step refers specifically to the success of the experiment at the Main Pedagogical Institute.[70]

A major revision in the organization of the Institute occurred in 1847, when the Juridical Faculty was abolished, thus reducing the scope of the curriculum to two faculties: Historical-Philological and Physico-Mathematical. This change was evidently not the result of any failure on the part of the Institute, but rather to the fact that Law faculties had become firmly entrenched in the universities, where such instruction obviously could be carried on better than in a pedagogical establishment. However, a simultaneous change took place in the remaining faculties which did lower the standards of work: the curricula were reduced from six years to four. The preliminary course was retained at two years, but the higher course was reduced by a year and the sixth year was abolished.[71] Since the sixth year had been devoted entirely to the study of Pedagogy, this abbreviation of the curriculum meant a serious loss of time devoted both to professional and subject-matter courses. Two years later another blow fell: a decision of the Minister of Public Education, Count Uvarov, discontinued admissions to the preliminary course on the grounds that this stage of training was no longer necessary.[72] Thus the course of study provided prospective teachers by the highest pedagogical institution in Russia now consisted of only two years. In the period intervening between these two crippling decrees, another decision was promulgated which also seems designed to discourage the entrance of youths into the teaching profession. A ruling of 1848 authorized students of the Main Pedagogical Institute to apply for admission to the military schools,[73] a move stimulated, perhaps, by preparations for the Crimean War which was to break out five years later. On the other hand, the Regulations of the Institute were amended, also in 1848, to permit the preparation of private tutors; but very few candidates for such work presented themselves.[74]

Count Uvarov resigned as Minister of Public Education in 1849, and his successor, Prince P. A. Shirinskii-Shikhmatov, attempted to repair some of the damage done to the Main Pedagogical Institute in the previous decade. In 1850, Tsar Nicholas I approved a proposal of the new Minister that the twenty students then registered in the Pedagogical Institute of St. Petersburg University be transferred to the Main Pedagogical Institute, along with the monetary appropriation for their tuition.[75] The following year, the Minister expressed strong criticism of the work being done at the latter institution and issued a decree purporting to raise the quality of instruction in teacher training. However, as described in the previous chapter, the actual items of the decree were concerned much more with censorship than with academic standards.[76]

In 1852 and 1854, the two remaining faculties of the Institute were each subdivided in order to offer greater opportunity for specialization. The Physico-Mathematical Faculty was split into two departments—mathematical sciences and natural sciences—while the Historical-Philological Faculty was divided into the department of historical sciences and the department of philological sciences.[77] But the end was near, although it is likely that few of the people associated with these metamorphoses realized it. The Main Pedagogical Institute, during the half-century of its existence as an integer, had undergone almost constant alteration of structure, modification of curriculum, and revision of purpose. Three Tsars had taken part in shaping its various aspects, and ten Ministers of Public Education had molded its manifold features. The combined contribution of Tsar Alexander II (the Great Emancipator) and Minister A. S. Norov (the first commoner to hold this position) was expressed largely in a single decree: "His Imperial Majesty, on the recommendation of the Minister of Public Education, has authorized approval of a new design for the medal given as a prize to excellent students graduating from the Main Pedagogical Institute." [78] Only one more step remained to make the process of pedagogical dissolution complete, and this step was taken by Minister E. P. Kovalevskii. On November 15, 1858, the entire Main Pedagogical Institute was abolished by Imperial Decree, and all responsibility for teacher training in the St. Petersburg region was turned over to the pedagogical courses at the University.[79] Henceforth, the work of preparing teachers for the schools of Russia is carried on under various auspices, and therefore will be considered in connection with other institutions.

8

The Great Reforms
(1855–1894)

RUSSIA'S OWN "GREAT EMANCIPATOR" CAME to the throne in 1855 in the person of Alexander II, eldest son of Nicholas I. "Alexander at once relieved his people of some of the most oppressive burdens imposed on them in the previous reign, and raised their hopes for the future still higher. The censorship rules were so far relaxed that within moderate limits the press could discuss political questions [and] the prohibition of travel abroad was withdrawn. . . . During these early months Alexander had no definite program of reforms, though, in a manifesto published at the conclusion of peace [following the Crimean War, March 1856] he expressed a hope 'that the internal order of the State may be settled and brought to perfection; that justice and mercy may reign in our law-courts;

that the desire for education and all manner of useful activity may spread and grow stronger.' "[1]

With such views stemming from the very top, it would be only reasonable to expect a resurgence of liberalism in Russia in the next few decades. That such a resurgence occurred, however, is due not only to the attitude of the Tsar but also to the social forces already at work among the people. A Soviet educational historian has pointed out that, contrary to the popular belief outside Russia, the school reforms of Alexander II did not take place until eight years after his succession and then only as a result of the strong demands, on the one hand, of the peasantry for more elementary schools, and on the other, of the university students for an improved system of higher education.[2]

Since these two forces—peasants and students—seem to have been so powerful, it would be well to examine briefly the character of the educational movements they fostered. Chapter Six described some of the types of schools developed in the rural districts of Russia during the first half of the nineteenth century. Still another type—the Sunday school—began to make headway in the latter part of the 1850's. Between 1857 and 1860, there appeared in various parts of Russia about 500 such agencies (they can hardly be called institutions), created entirely by local and private initiative. "The distinguishing features of these schools were the following: the gratuitous and spontaneous labor of the teachers, the free lodgings and new pedagogical tasks provided the pupils, and the inclusion of the essentials of general development for adults and adolescents as well as the rudiments of literacy and mathematics."[3]

Although the Sunday schools were outlawed in 1861, they were revived in the 1870's and continued in some parts of the country even after 1917. These agencies, coupled with the "literacy schools" formed earlier in the century,[4] created and fostered a deep interest in education among the peasantry. As a matter of fact, the "literacy schools" served as the nuclei around which were woven the system of the *zemstvo* schools in the 1870's. But in the early years of the reign of Alexander these schools, though numbered in the thousands, were individually rather weak examples of institutions of learning. Supported entirely by the local peasants (or serfs, for the emancipation did not come until 1861), they lacked both funds and space. The teachers themselves were often barely literate, and as recompense for their services they were permitted to live in the huts of first one and then another of the pupils.[5]

The reactionary ministers of Nicholas I had been entirely right when they prophesied that a little education would only encourage the peasants to demand more freedom and still better education to go with it.[6] Alexander II himself respected the growing power of the peasantry to such an extent that he told a meeting of Moscow nobles that serfdom had best be abolished from the top rather than overthrown from below.[7] While it is impossible to ascertain whether the liberal sentiments of the Tsar and his court were actually more responsible for the Emancipation Proclamation of 1861 than was the revolutionary pressure of the peasantry, it cannot be denied that the latter exerted tremendous influence in bringing about the abolition of serfdom. Most historians of this period testify to the increasing number and violence of peasant revolts during the 1850's; at times these uprisings seem to have driven the courtiers and local landlords almost to the verge of hysteria.[8]

Nor was this force directed toward emancipation alone: a law of January 1864 created elective county councils, called *zemstvos*, which represented not only the wealthy nobles but the small landholders as well. Six years later, similar organizations were set up in the towns, and these two types of councils "from this time onward represented the cause of constructive reform in Russia." [9]

One of the reforms due directly to the work of the *zemstvos* was concerned with courts of law. "Hitherto the judiciary and police administration had been in the hands of officials chosen exclusively by the nobility. [Now], in place of ignorant magistrates, trained legal experts were elected to judicial positions, at the same time that the people were admitted, as jurors, to participation in the administration of justice." [10] This move constituted the introduction, for the first time in Russia, of the principle of trial by jury.[11] The *zemstvos* also had some influence in securing the innovation of a modern form of military conscription in 1873, which in years to come was to strengthen the authority of the laboring classes—both rural and urban—by supplying them with arms and the techniques of using them.[12]

In the matter of educational reform, however, the *zemstvos* were frequently limited by two factors, one internal and the other imposed from without. In the first place, these councils were not entirely democratic even though their members were elected. The wealthier landowners enjoyed the larger share of representation, and they were not always inclined to favor education for the peasants. Therefore, the attention given "elementary schools and the other local social services" usually depended upon "the varying quality of liberalism" among the members of a particular *zemstvo*. The second limitation lay in the fact that "Full freedom of the *zemstvos* in education was impossible . . . since its function was to provide and maintain, rather than control. These authorities could fix fees, but the curriculum of three R's, religion and church singing was decided for them." [13]

Since the educational work of the *zemstvos* attained its greatest scope in the last decade of the nineteenth century, a detailed account of this activity is postponed until a later chapter. It is sufficient to say here that in fulfilling their function to "provide and maintain," their annual expenditure for education in the period from their establishment to 1895 never reached ten million rubles nor constituted more than 16 per cent of their total outlay; the average yearly allotment to education by the *zemstvos* during these three decades was less than five million rubles, or just above 12 per cent of all money they expended.[14]

Nevertheless, whatever value their contributions to education were to have, it is no wonder that, in the light of the total reforms they accomplished, historians declare that their establishment marks one of the truly great reforms of Alexander II, that by this means "the former rule of the squires, or landed gentry, was abolished," that "the *zemstvos* . . . form the happiest exception to the general rule of reactionary absolutism which set in after 1812," and, finally, that the creation of these councils "was the most significant step towards local control taken by the ancient regime."[15]

In such manner did the influence of the peasant masses of Russia make itself felt through organized channels. The second disrupting force mentioned above, the university students, must be considered quite separately from the peasant efforts, for the two lanes of struggle seldom touched each other. Although they possessed the same large objective—better education—the peasants were almost wholly concerned with elementary schools, while the university students, naturally, sought improvement in the higher institutions of learning. Thus the two movements were parallel rather than integrated, even though both exerted great influence upon the remaining level of education—the secondary school.

Let us look first at the composition of the student body in the six universities of Russia in the year 1855. The total number of students was 3,659, representing 0.8 per 10,000 of population.[16] There are no complete statistics available to show the social origin of the students in that year, but in

1880 it was as follows: gentry and officials, 46.6 per cent; clergy, 23.4 per cent; merchants, etc., 14.3 per cent; workers and craftsmen, 12.4 per cent; and peasants, 3.3 per cent.[17] It is certain that these figures, which are for a date twenty-five years later than the period under review, do not give a true picture of the student bodies whose riotous activity resulted in the university reforms of 1863. An indication of this fact is found in a report that, of the 424 students at the St. Petersburg University in 1853, 299 (or 73 per cent) were of the nobility.[18] Even if allowance be made for the fact that St. Petersburg, being the seat of the Tsar's court, would logically tend toward a higher degree of aristocracy in its schools, it remains obvious that the mass of the peasantry could hardly have had much in common with the desires of the university students.

These were the types of students, then, who found themselves dissatisfied with the conditions of higher learning in Russia. Undoubtedly, they had much to complain about. "Since the middle of the preceding reign [1840], the universities had fallen even below the Russian standard, and in comparison with those of Western Europe they were quite evidently inferior. This condition was due to the lack of sufficient good teachers from Russian sources, the prohibition against inviting foreign instructors, the lowness of salaries, the difficulty of the examinations for the necessary higher degrees, the complexity and consequent superficiality with which the course of study was followed in the universities, the defective preparation afforded by the gymnasiums in Latin and modern languages, which were necessary for adequate work in the universities, and finally the poverty of the universities and the indifference of the public of the period preceding the reforms. Vacancies in some chairs, unsatisfactory incumbents in others, disorders on the part of the students were the outward signs of this unsatisfactory condition."[19]

Many of these student "disorders" took rather turbulent form. Inspired by the writings of the more radical philosophers, the university students took full advantage of the new liberties permitted by the early decrees of Tsar Alexander II. "They showed great interest in political affairs, and gave themselves up to violent criticism of the existing order." [20] The Minister of Public Education, E. P. Kovalevskii, was unable to deal with the recurrent crises, so he was supplanted by the reactionary Count E. V. Putiatin, who had been an admiral in the navy and was supposed to know how to deal with recalcitrant youth. The somewhat liberal Count T. D. Delianov (who was later to become Minister himself) was dismissed as Curator of the St. Petersburg educational circuit and his place was taken by a former Cossack general.

On May 31, 1861, a new series of university rules was announced, to take effect the following autumn. These rules abolished all student organizations and forbade any gathering of students without special permission of the authorities; they stopped the issuance of poverty-certificates and prohibited the exemption of indigent students from the payment of tuition fees; as a crowning insult, they outlawed the wearing of university uniforms.[21] Under these severe measures, the students became even more incensed than before. "Great demonstrations of protest in Moscow and Petersburg ended in conflict with the police and troops. In Moscow the police hounded the mob on to attack the students by spreading a rumor that they were dispossessed landowners agitating for the restoration of serfdom." [22] In St. Petersburg, three hundred students were imprisoned in the fortress; in Moscow, the students were mercilessly beaten, hundreds were arrested and many were expelled from the University.[23]

Evidently the Tsar was displeased with these rigorous tactics, for he began to make plans for Putiatin's dismissal.

He appointed A. V. Golovnin as Vice-Minister of Public Education in December 1861, and a year later made him Minister.[24] On June 18, 1863, the Tsar approved the new University Statutes, the first since 1835. Although these regulations appeared during Golovnin's administration, Alexander II had been interested in the matter as early as 1858. A preliminary plan had been drawn up, copies of which had been sent to all six universities and to many Russian scholars; translations had even been made and sent abroad for the comments of foreign educators. In addition, several Russian professors made observation tours to the outstanding European universities, and brought back further recommendations for the plan. "All suggestions were taken under consideration, and the university regulations were five times revised before [publication]. . . . The Russian university became a combination of the French and German systems. As in Germany, the Russian universities were granted administrative autonomy. . . . But as in France, the course of studies in each department was definitely prescribed, and yearly examinations in the course were required." [25]

In regard to autonomy, the 1863 Statutes restored that granted in 1804, and reduced the power of the Curator of the circuit to a level considerably below that accorded by the 1835 Regulations.[26] The offices of Rector, Dean, Vice-Dean, Inspector, and even Professor were to be assigned by faculty election, and all vacancies were to be filled in the same manner. A court of three professors was to conduct all student trials, thus placing more limitations upon the power of the Inspector. The "University Council" was created as the real governing board of the institution, to which even the Rector was subordinate. The Council was in charge of instruction, of the granting of degrees, and even of the censorship of all university publications. Chairs in constitutional law and philosophy were restored, and several new chairs created in other subjects. Faculty salaries were raised, even though the increase failed to cover the rising cost of living.[27]

Students also profited by the new regulations. Tuition fees were fixed at fifty rubles a year in the universities at Moscow and St. Petersburg, and at forty rubles in the other universities, but a number of fellowships (*stipendyi*) were provided, and indigent students were again exempted from fees. The limit of three hundred students imposed on each institution was lifted, and admissions were to be upon graduation certificates ("*attestat zrelosti*") rather than by entrance examinations. Only two major recommendations appear to have been ignored: it was decided not to admit women to the universities, and not to revive the student privilege of forming corporate organizations.[28]

Two more points raised in the Statutes had particular significance for teachers at the university level: academic rank was made dependent upon the type of degree held, and the rank of "Adjunct" was converted to that of "Docent." Both these regulations found implementation in decrees issued soon thereafter. In July 1863, it was announced that "His Imperial Highness, having noticed that many university professors do not possess the academic degrees required by His confirmation, on the 18th of June of this year, of the University Statutes regarding the occupancy of chairs, expresses His will that these circumstances be referred to the attention of the university councils in order that they might ask the persons mentioned to concern themselves with the acquisition of the required degrees." [29]

A year later, another decision put into effect the new rank of Docent. The decree of the State Council which established the Imperial Novorossisk University at Odessa ordered that institution to use the new rank in place of the old and, at the same time, it set up the scale for all academic ranks in all Russian universities except that at Dorpat. The ranks, in descending order of importance, were to be as follows: Rector, Dean, Ordinary Professor, Extraordinary Professor, Docent, and such other personnel permitted under the University Statutes currently in force. All ranking teachers were entitled to pensions and emergency aid to the extent codified in the staff regulations of the University of St. Vladimir at Kiev, and Docents were to assume the privileges awarded Adjuncts in those regulations.[30]

The university reforms described above constitute but the first of Alexander II's moves toward reorganizing the entire system of Russian education. In scope and depth, these reforms went almost as far as did the 1802-1804 programs which to a large extent they restored. Simultaneously with the University Statutes, a decree was issued concerning the organization of the Ministry of Public Education. Although this decree made no fundamental changes in the structure of the Ministry, it did expand its personnel, its services, and its budget. Six agencies now composed the Ministry: (1) Council of the Minister, (2) Department of Public Instruction, (3) Academic Committee, (4) Archeographic Commission, (5) Editorial Board for the Journal of the Ministry, and (6) Archives of the Ministry.[31] Thus was the Ministry stabilized in the form which it was to bear for several decades to come.

The next step in educational reform involved the elementary schools, a phase which the government seemed willing to leave largely to public initiative and the *zemstvos*.[32] The Elementary School Code, published on June 26, 1864, declared that "the elementary schools have the aim of strengthening the religious and moral understanding of the people, and of disseminating the essentials of useful knowledge." [33] All such schools were placed under the immediate jurisdiction of one of three administrative bureaus: the Ministry of Public Education, the Ministry of Public Domains and Internal Affairs, or the Holy Synod.[34]

The *zemstvos* were provided with special school boards in each district to supervise the educational agencies provided and maintained by the rural and town councils.

The mandated composition of these six-man boards affords a clue to the degree of freedom granted the schools. One of the landed gentry acted as chairman, another member was appointed by the hierarchy of the Office of Religious Affairs, a third represented the Ministry of Internal Affairs and was usually the chief of the district police, two members were appointed from the *zemstvo* itself, and the sixth was the Inspector of the district schools. "Control over the schools was placed in the hands of the Inspector, who was also responsible for the appointment of teachers and the discharge of 'unpromising' ones, such action being taken on the basis of accusation by the teacher of Religion or any outsider."[35] As mentioned earlier in this chapter, the *zemstvo* schools assumed much greater importance later in the century: even in 1868, four years after publication of the Code, the total expenditure on these schools amounted to only 738,000 rubles.[36]

Much more attention was paid to secondary education. According to the Secondary School Code, published on December 1, 1864, "the aim of the gymnasiums is to convey general education to the youth being trained in them, and at the same time to serve as preparatory institutions for entrance into universities and other specialized higher schools."[37] Two types of schools were recognized: the "classical gymnasium" and the "real gymnasium" (or progymnasium); the former was the traditional type of school fostered in Russia since the beginning of the century, while the latter was modeled on the German *Real-Schule* then becoming popular throughout Europe.[38] The classical gymnasiums were also separated into two forms, one requiring both Latin and Greek as well as a choice between French or German, the other offering only Latin but requiring both modern languages. The progymnasiums omitted the ancient languages entirely, and allotted this time to both French and German, to more work in Drawing and Design, and to great emphasis on Natural History.[39]

All this government activity in education could not fail to produce some tangible results, although historians of the period are not always agreed on their value. One consequence was that the number of students in all schools doubled (from 400,000 to 800,000) in the decade 1855-1865 while the total population rose only 5.5 per cent. Such an increase was a remarkable as well as an unusual accomplishment: a similar increase had occurred only once before in Russian history—during the time of Catherine II—and was not to happen again during the Tsarist regime. Most of the increase in enrollment, of course, was absorbed by the elementary schools, but the ratio at the secondary level also rose from 3.7 to 6.0 students per 10,000 of population. In the universities the growth was much less: from 0.8 in 1855 to 0.9 in 1865.[40]

In higher education as a whole, the achievements came somewhat later and must be measured in other ways. By 1870 there were eight universities in the Empire, that at Odessa having been established in 1864 and that at Warsaw brought under the jurisdiction of Moscow in 1869. "Amongst some 6,000 students, two-fifths received Government scholarships. . . . Modern schools had recently been founded to train boys for the less liberal professions." [41] A few comparative figures will indicate the progress made in this latter sphere. Between 1835 and 1862, no university and only one other type of institution of higher learning was founded in Russia. Between 1862 and 1870, Alexander II established the two universities mentioned above and, before his death in 1881, was to set up plans for another at Tomsk which opened seven years after the end of his reign. In the same nine-year period, he created five professional higher institutes, and added a sixth in 1879.[42] As to the quality of education to be gained in these institutions, we are assured by one historian that "in 1854 . . . the university instruction was below the average college instruction in the United States [but] in 1880 . . . the standard fully corresponded to that of the best American universities." [43]

It has already been pointed out that the school codes of 1863-64 made little provision for improved education of females. In 1858 two types of day schools for girls had been established, one with a six-year and the other with a three-year course, and both types were open to all social classes. The following year most of these schools were placed under the protection of the Empress Maria, wife of Alexander II, and for several years thereafter the founding of girls' schools was left to private enterprise. But in 1870 a large number of the six- and three-year schools were transformed into ten-year gymnasiums and progymnasiums for girls, modeled on the forms created for boys by the 1864 Secondary School Code described earlier in this chapter, with the addition of a supplementary one-year course in pedagogy for those desiring to become teachers.[44] One authority states that in 1870 the classical gymnasiums for girls outnumbered those for boys by 246 to 198 [45] but, even if this is true, the 50,000 enrollment in the latter type certainly exceeded that in the former.

Although women were excluded from universities by the Code of 1863, other higher institutions were open to them: "there were nearly 200 girl students of medicine and surgery at St. Petersburg" alone.[46] Nevertheless, many women from upper class families preferred to go abroad for their college educations. The situation aroused the ire of Madame Konradi, editor of the progressive journal *Nedelia* (The Weekly). As a result of her efforts, begun in 1867, a movement was started which five years later brought women the right to attend "advanced courses" given voluntarily in the evenings and on Sundays and holidays by members of the faculty of St. Petersburg University. In 1876 this practice was extended to other university towns, the only requirement for admission being graduation from a secondary school or the equivalent. By the time of Alexander II's death, these courses had assumed a four-year character which in most respects placed them on a par with the higher education of men.[47]

In all these achievements in secondary and higher education, however, one searches in vain for any really positive values accruing to the peasant masses of Russia. Figures given earlier in this chapter reveal that even in 1880 only 3.3 per cent of university students were of peasant origin, and only 12.4 per cent were from the other laboring classes.[48] After 1867 the only expenditure on elementary education was through the *zemstvos*, and in 1871 the sum amounted to a mere 1,600,000 rubles.[49] Thus there can be little doubt that "instruction in general remained more or less the monopoly of the upper and middle classes. Of these, the middle class now supplied the greater number of scholars and students, and this was precisely the class which was most cut off from all responsibilities. Schools and universities were chiefly recruited from that suspected population of the towns which had developed late in Russian history, and for which no regular place had been found by the government. The students would in many cases be the sons of poor officials; but that would not necessarily give them any great respect for the system of bureaucracy. Further, if Russia had already produced her greatest writers, the volume of literature was now definitely increased. Every subject of political, literary or scientific interest was now being dealt with by capable critics, and for the first time in Russia there was a really considerable reading public."[50]

This situation may have been satisfactory to Alexander II, but in the eyes of many of his cohorts it was fraught with peril to the stability of the regime. "From the very first there were apprehensions that this rising [*zemstvo*] school might become the nest of dangerous ideas, atheism, the soil for freethinking, etc. This was the reason for establishing such a complicated system of supervision over the schools from the very beginning." [51] Very soon the entire educational system of Russia was to feel again the force of reaction.

On April 16, 1866, an attempt was made to assassinate the Tsar. Although it was quickly determined that the would-be killer was prompted only by a very small group in Moscow, there were many people ready to blame the act on the alleged radical sentiments of the populace, and particularly of the younger elements. The Tsar was evidently so impressed by the threat against his life that he was ready to listen to his most bigoted advisers. On the day following the attack, Golovnin, the liberal and enlightened Minister of Public Education and the chief sponsor of many of the recent cultural reforms, was blamed in the Council of Ministers for laxity toward "the spread of revolutionary ideas among the students," and was forthwith removed from office.[52] His principal accuser—and successor—was Count D. A. Tolstoi, Chief Procurator of the Holy Synod. Tolstoi thus became the second person to hold both these offices simultaneously.[53] After half a century, history was to repeat itself in more ways than one. Reactionary forces had again triumphed over an initially progressive emperor, just as in the case of the Tsar's uncle, Alexander I.

Actually, repressive measures had been exercised in isolated cases even under Golovnin. An outstanding instance occurred in July 1862 when Government police raided the famous school of Count Leo Tolstoi at Yasnaia Poliana. According to the noted author's own report on the incident (based on information supplied by his students and relatives, for Tolstoi himself was not there at the time), the police arrived at midnight, demanded food and wine and the keys to all locks, rummaged through desks and closets, and even rifled Tolstoi's private diaries and correspondence after breaking the lock on his desk. Tolstoi was naturally very upset by the affair, and made a personal protest to the Tsar, who apologized. If the raid had the purpose of discouraging agencies of progressive education in Russia, it must be called successful. By the following winter Tolstoi had begun to lose interest in his school, paying more and more attention to his pedagogical and literary writing (it was in 1862 that he wrote "On Training and Education"). In the spring of 1863, he wrote a colleague that his school was falling to pieces, and his wife told friends that his teachers, infected by his own indifference, were leaving one by one.[54]

Such instances as the above, however, became the rule rather than the exception after D. A. Tolstoi became Minister. "The full force of reaction was immediately directed against the schools and universities, in which revolution was supposed to have its roots. Tolstoi held that the study of natural science had fostered the spirit of criticism and negation. . . . His new programme for secondary education . . . banished science altogether from the schools. . . . The teaching of the classics was made as lifeless as possible. . . . The teachers councils lost all their rights, which passed to 'directors' appointed by and responsible to the Ministry and virtually its agents, through whom it could exercise a close supervision over the whole course of school life. The spirit of the schools was distorted. Absolute, unquestioning obedience came to be demanded of the pupils, and though they were encouraged to be 'frank' with their teachers, 'frankness' took the form of spying on fellow pupils."[55]

Although the "Rules of Gymnasiums and Progymnasiums" issued in 1871 express precisely the same aim in the same words as those approved in 1864,[56] the actual conditions were drastically altered. The original progymnasiums had an eight-year course equivalent to that of the classical gymnasiums, but the new statutes reduced the former to a narrow technical course of only six years. Moreover, this course could not lead to the higher technical institutes, where the full gymnasium training was an entrance requirement. According to one authority, such sabotage of the 1864 reforms had a very specific aim: "The new secondary school system was intended to lower the general standard of knowledge, to deaden thought, and check the development of wide cultural interests, by providing a course of mere mental drill. It subjected the pupils to a severe process of selection; in the years 1872-90 only a very small proportion of them succeeded in finishing the school course in the proper time, while as many as 63 to 79 per cent were rejected at different stages." [57]

Minister Tolstoi was just as ruthless in dealing with personal enemies as with inimical ideas. When several newspapers and journals criticized his educational practices, he ordered them closed and then persuaded the Tsar to sign a decree making it unlawful for the press "to discuss the plans of the Government." [58] Again, when Tolstoi decided to extend his authority over the girls' schools, which were not within the jurisdiction of his Ministry, he forced the resignation of the person in charge even though the latter had the approval of the Empress. One of his first acts as Minister was an attempt to rescind the University Code of 1863 in its entirety, but the Code still had support in high places. Nevertheless, in 1867 Tolstoi succeeded in strengthening the police control over the students and in reducing the authority and autonomy of the University Councils. As a result, "serious student disturbances took place in 1869, 1874, and 1878." [59]

Elementary education, too, suffered from the very beginning of Dmitri Tolstoi's administration. The year after he became Minister, he withdrew all government financial support from this level of schools, and threw the entire responsibility of their creation and maintenance upon the *zemstvos*. At the same time, Tolstoi wanted to vest complete *control* of the schools in the Ministry and its agents. Toward this end, he began in 1869 to appoint more and more Inspectors to serve on the District School Boards as direct representatives of the Ministry responsible only to Tolstoi himself. In this effort he received the support even of the Tsar, who in 1873 addressed to him a statement that the elementary schools, "instead of serving the true enlightenment of the younger generation, may become converted into a weapon for the corruption of the people, and attempts of this kind have already been made." [60]

Thus encouraged, Tolstoi prepared a new Code for elementary schools which described their aims as being "to confirm religious and moral concepts in the people and to disseminate useful rudimentary knowledge." [61] All elementary schools were placed under the jurisdiction of the Holy Synod, the Ministry of Public Education, or the District School Boards.[62] Since the first two agencies were already under his complete control [63] it remained only for Tolstoi to capture control of the Boards. This he had already begun to do by the appointment of more Inspectors, and the new Code provided for a separate such official for each district who would in reality direct the activities of the Board: "Male and female Board members . . . , as well as the men and women Directors of private and Sunday schools, who superintend the affairs of the educational institutions entrusted to them, enter into the proper agreement with the Inspector of the public schools and are fully responsible for order in these institutions."[64] Lack of funds prevented Tolstoi from creating this large group of inspectorships; instead he had to compromise for two in each *guberniya* rather than one for each school district, or about one-fifth the number he wanted.[65] "The plan of subjecting elementary education to purely bureaucratic control thus failed, but Tolstoi led an active and unceasing campaign against the *zemstvos*, which became so difficult to bear that many of them in despair thought of abandoning the schools altogether."[66] That Tolstoi did not permit his defeat on the matter of inspectors to discourage him is indicated by the fact that he continued to increase the importance and authority of those he did have. In 1876 their police roles were emphasized "in view of the attempts made in several localities to carry on political and moral propaganda," against which the inspectors were directed to be on guard.[67] "Various phases of the activity of the *zemstvo* schools were regularly subjected to repression. At one time a campaign was conducted against textbooks used in the schools without proper approval by the higher authorities; at another time repression was directed against the use of the Ukrainian language. . . . The teachers were under constant investigation as to their mode of life, their acquaintances, whether they fasted [on holy days] or not, and so on."[68]

It should be borne in mind that all these acts occurred during the regime of a comparatively progressive Tsar, Alexander II. As such, they were but preparations for the really dark reaction which set in with the coronation of his son, Alexander III. It is true that the latter ascended the throne under unfortunate personal as well as political circumstances: his father had just been brutally assassinated by the bomb of a terrorist, and threats were being made against his own life also. In addition, the new Tsar was no match for his predecessor in intelligence, grasp of political affairs, or liberalism. The sole aim of Alexander III seems to have been the greater industrialization of Russia, even at the expense of the welfare of the people. He refused to put into effect the project for a constitutional monarchy which had been approved by his father the day before the latter's death, and dismissed in quick succession the two progressive Ministers of Public Education, A. A. Saburov and Baron A. P. Nikolai, who had followed Dmitri Tolstoi in office after that worthy had been promoted to the Ministry of Public Domains.

For the next fifteen years (1882-1897) the Education ministry was to be occupied by Count T. D. Delianov, who had been classed as a mild liberal during the 1850's when he had been Curator of the St. Petersburg educational circuit; in fact, he had been discharged from that post by Tolstoi himself. But the years had changed Delianov to such an extent that he now emerged as Tolstoi's protégé. When the latter was advanced to the really vital post of Minister of the Interior (which included the police), he saw to it that Delianov was put in charge of the educational system.[69] This pair, and others like them, made the remaining years of Alexander III's reign a period in which "reaction, as a theory of government and a practical policy, had never before been so clearly defined . . . [and] as in the previous reign, the schools and universities were the first to feel the effects of reaction."[70] Furthermore, education, along with the press and minority cultures, was the field in which the most vicious repressions took place.[71]

The year 1884 marks the complete downfall of autonomy and liberalism in the universities, the restoration of strong class distinctions at the secondary level, and a concerted attempt to restore the elementary schools to a sectarian basis. The University Code of that year abolished local control of higher educational institutions by removing all authority from the University Councils and stipulating that the Rectors and Inspectors must be appointed by the Ministry instead of being elected by the faculty as permitted by the Code of 1863. What little real academic freedom remained for the faculty was carefully nullified by stringent restrictions upon the activities of the students. Although the 1863 Code had refrained from sanctioning student organizations, a number of informal groups had flourished without severe recriminations; the new statutes made membership in such bodies a crime. In fact, expulsion was the mildest punishment for any sort of flagrant disobedience or protest, and this was frequently followed by conscription into the army or even exile to Siberia. In order to make surveillance of the students easier, they were required to wear special uniforms.[72] It will be recalled that the students protested in the summer and fall of 1861 when uniforms were forbidden. The apparent paradox between that reaction and the present one is that in the earlier period the uniform marked the student as a privileged person, while in this case it made him the prey of the police.

The Code of 1884 also increased tuition rates, while fellowships and scholarships were now to be awarded largely on the basis of political trustworthiness. Particular means, too, were employed to determine the quality of candidates for higher education: "The administration of the gymnasiums was ordered to report on the secret characteristics of each of its graduates, and in case these indicated tendencies in the student opposed to Autocracy or Church, they were refused admission to universities." [73]

But the gymnasiums themselves by no means escaped alteration. The 1871 Statutes for gymnasiums had greatly strengthened the classical curriculum; the 1884 Rules made it supreme and, as a result, practically insured the lower classes against the strains of obtaining a secondary education.[74] However, Delianov and Dmitri Tolstoi were not men who left such important matters to chance. A Circular of the Ministry of Public Education issued in 1887 declared that: "Gymnasiums and progymnasiums are freed from receiving the children of coachmen, servants, cooks, laundresses, small tradesmen, and the like, whose children, with the exception, perhaps, of those who are gifted with extraordinary capacities, ought by no means to be transferred from the sphere to which they belong, and thus [be] brought, as many years' experience has shown, to slight their parents, to feel dissatisfied with their lot, and to conceive an aversion to the existing inequality of fortune which is in the nature of things unavoidable." [75]

Nor did the reaction ignore the elementary schools. Although Dmitri Tolstoi had resigned as Chief Procurator of the Holy Synod at the time he left his post as Minister of Public Education in 1880, his successor, K. P. Pobedonostsev, was at least his equal in determination to bring the public schools under the sway of the Church. Pobedonostsev, like Delianov, had once been addicted to liberal ideas, and for this reason had been employed by Alexander II as a tutor for the son who was to become Alexander III. In later life, however, Pobedonostsev, again like Delianov, had become completely reactionary, and thus was now not only an acceptable colleague to Tolstoi but also one of his trusted disciples.[76] With the powerful triumvirate of Tolstoi, Delianov, and Pobedonostsev striving to sectarianize the schools, it is surprising to observe how successful the *zemstvos* were in repelling the attack. The failure to accomplish the aim envisioned by the three officials is explained by several authorities as due to the simple fact that the *zemstvos* refused to continue financial support of their schools if complete control were vested in the Holy Synod; neither the Government nor the Synod had the funds to take the schools by force and to maintain them; the result was that the *zemstvo* schools not only remained secular, but began a period of increased growth and influence.[77]

It must be pointed out, however, that the bureaucracy by

no means gave up the struggle because of this one setback. A plan was devised whereby the system of parish schools could be strengthened and thus compete with the *zemstvo* institutions; possibly the former could even "guide the latter along the proper pathway." [78] The plan was published in June 1884 under the title of "Rules of the Church-Parish Schools," and bore the following notation from Alexander III: "I hope that the parish clergy will prove itself worthy of its calling in this important matter." [79]

The Rules are rather brief, consisting of only twenty-three short articles; but they are quite dogmatic and specific as to their intentions. The aims are stated in much the same terms as in the 1874 Code for Elementary Schools in general: "to confirm Orthodox doctrines of faith and Christian morality in the people and to impart useful rudimentary knowledge." [80] It will be noted that the only differences in the two statements are that the present Rules use the words "Orthodox doctrines" and "Christian morality" instead of the broader "religious and moral concepts" of the earlier document, and that the term "impart" replaces the word "disseminate." These two verbal modifications provide a clue to the twin tendencies toward bigotry and seclusion then rampant in Russian education. Further evidence of the strength of these tendencies may be found in the curriculum of the two-year church-parish schools, which consisted of: "(1) Divine Law, consisting of (a) the learning of prayers, (b) sacred history and explanation of the divine service, (c) the short catechism; (2) church singing; (3) reading of church and lay journals and letters; (4) instruction in elementary arithmetic. In the four-year schools will be taught, in addition to the above, elementary instruction in the history of the Church and the Fatherland." [81]

All programs for these courses, as well as the manuals of instruction and other materials used, had to be approved by the Holy Synod.[82] Moreover, care was exercised to see that the teachers possessed the proper spiritual background: "Teaching posts in the church-parish schools will be filled preferably by persons who have received training in the ecclesiastical educational institutions and the women's schools of the Ecclesiastical Department." However, those teachers "who are secular persons possessing the rank of Teacher in the elementary public schools shall enjoy all the rights accorded to that rank." [83] Special efforts were also to be made to insure that the local trustees and board members were persons completely loyal to the Orthodox doctrines.[84]

Throughout the document, then, one may observe the great emphasis on religious instruction and the scant attention to any other type of knowledge. Had these schools been few in number and isolated in influence, no particular harm would have been done. But the situation was just the opposite: "The Government was by no means miserly in its appropriations for the parish school, which was thus subsidized from two sources since several *zemstvos* also supported such schools because they were less expensive [to maintain]. Due to these circumstances the parish school met with success for a considerable period of time, from the publication of the Rules until the close of the 1890's, when their number reached 46 per cent of the total number of rural elementary schools. But the prestige of the parish schools began to decline gradually, and after 1905 they disappeared completely, since popular sympathies had gone over entirely to the side of the *zemstvo* school. The artificially implanted parish school existed only so long as it enjoyed support from above." [85] Nevertheless, the schools existed over two decades, during which period they exerted a powerful influence over both children and adults; for the bureaucracy, though unsuccessful in its attempt to place all the *zemstvo* schools under the jurisdiction of the Holy

Synod, had been able to extend the authority of the Church over the numerous "literacy schools" for adults which had sprung up since the middle of the century.[86]

The 1884 educational revisions omitted only one important institution—the Real-School—although this type was included in the modifications imposed upon the gymnasiums. In 1888, however, it was separated from its classical brother and established as a distinct agency of semisecondary character. Its course became much more "practical" as well as much more "spiritual," and its graduates were permitted to enter only the higher technical institutes instead of the universities.[87] Segregation by social class, economic status, and religious creed was stronger than ever before in Russian education.

In other phases of life the same tendencies were apparent: educational practices, as usual, merely reflected the basic motives and principles inherent in the society itself. Those principles could again be summed up in the three-word formula devised by Count Uvarov half a century before—Orthodoxy, Autocracy, Nationalism. Many scholars bear witness to the thoroughness with which this doctrine was administered not only by Alexander III but also by his successor, Nicholas II. "It is to be borne in mind," says one of these authors, "that the law of Russia not only forbids the Orthodox from changing their religious faith—it punishes the offence with the loss of civil rights, and even permits an offender's property to be taken possession of by his relatives. No proselytism is allowed in any other interest than that of the Orthodox Church. Desertion of the church is a crime, and it becomes the duty of a father, of a mother, or of other relatives to inform against the deserter. It is under laws such as these that the government authorities, cooperating with the Holy Synod and its Chief Procurator Pobedonostsev, have inflicted upon the Roman Catholics of Poland, the Uniats of Russia and Poland, the Lutherans of the Baltic provinces, and the German Mennonites, various forms of persecution for religious opinions." [88]

Examples of this march of Orthodoxy are too numerous even to mention, but a few instances of its operation in the field of education can be shown. In 1886, the Lutheran schools in the Baltic provinces were removed from local control and placed directly under the central administration in St. Petersburg. Between 1884 and 1894 Russian supplanted German as the language of instruction in the secondary and higher schools of the Dorpat educational circuit, and became a required subject in the elementary schools. Russification of Poland had begun in the 1860's, but was made complete in 1885 by a law imposing Russian as the language of instruction, even in elementary schools, for all subjects except religion and the Polish language itself.[89] In all these cases, "the professors were ordered within a given period to read their lectures in Russian; half of them resigned, and were replaced by men who were practically Russian officials. To Dorpat, as to Warsaw, were sent those Russian students who were considered not trustworthy, and were therefore thought to need a closer system of supervision." [90]

But the Jews suffered most of all, for they bore the brunt of both religious and nationalistic persecution. "The treatment of the Jews, carried out not only unofficially by anti-Semitic mobs but also officially . . . was such as to call forth the condemnation of the civilized world." [91] From 1881 to 1888, and even later, a stream of regulations, edicts, and decrees placed more and more restrictions on the Jews. "Taxes were imposed upon the Jewish dress, candles, and meat; it was made very difficult for Jews to travel into the interior of the Empire, even for the collection of just debts; Jews were forbidden to own land [or to hold public office]; Jews were herded together in the towns of certain areas; they were forbidden to live within a certain distance of the frontier. As it was they who made the best use of educational opportunities, the percentage of Jewish scholars was cut down, even in the schools which were built inside the pale of Jewish settlement and chiefly out of Jewish money. Naturally enough, many Jews saw their only safety in leaving the country." [92] Another historian estimates that "between April of 1881 and June of 1882 no fewer than 225,000 Jewish families, comprising over a million souls, were forced to leave Russia under circumstances for the most part of inconceivable hardship." [93]

The prophecy allegedly made by Pobedonostsev was at least in part coming true: he is said to have predicted that, as a result of the Government's policy toward the Jews, "a third of them would be converted, a third would emigrate, while the rest would die of hunger." [94] In addition to these general controls imposed upon Jews, there were specific quotas established for them in educational institutions. In 1886 a regulation limited the number of Jews in the universities as follows: 10 per cent in those universities within the Jewish Pale (Poland and southwestern Russia); 5 per cent in other provincial universities; 2 per cent in Moscow and St. Petersburg. The following year, corresponding quotas were set up for Jews in the secondary schools. "One result of this legislation has been to increase greatly the number of Russian Jews seeking education in foreign universities, especially in those of Germany and Switzerland." [95]

Persecution of minorities frequently results in the persecutors themselves coming to bear somewhat the same scars as their victims. The hatreds aroused, the suspicions implanted, the doubts fostered ultimately surge out of the channels originally prescribed for them, and engulf the instigators as well. So it was in Russia during the last quarter of the nineteenth century. "The same policy which penalized the aliens for being aliens also penalized the Russian

Intelligents for being intelligent. The Russian universities had been founded with the object of producing well-informed officials. During the first reaction of Nicholas I they had been kept under the closest supervision; but the students of all Russia were like a kind of republican corporation which stood solid for the principles of liberty; and with the rare generosity of Russian character, instead of using their special opportunities exclusively for their personal advantage, they devoted themselves to sowing the seed of intelligence all over the country.

"During this period [1870-1895] they were more suspect than ever to the Government. The Rectors named by the Minister were expected to be instruments of repression; the inspectors, whose only duty was to forbid and to punish, became more important than the professors themselves; police agents assumed the dress of students and sat with them in their classes; all association and intercommunication of the students was carefully watched; clubs and societies could only exist by defying the police. The students, infected with Nihilism, were certainly revolutionary in spirit, and needed watching; but this regime taught each successive generation to take up an attitude hostile to the Government, and to government in general. As yet most of the professors confined themselves to teaching their subjects and obeying regulations; and many of the students, when they had to set about making a livelihood, were ready to give up their young ideals; but the universities as a whole were already fortresses of the spirit of opposition. It was the same even with secondary schools, the gymnasia and the real-schools. The government did not found any more universities during this period with the significant exception of Tomsk, in Siberia [fn. Significant because of Russia's current expansion toward the East]. It preferred to found technical institutes as being more practically useful and not so likely to foster abstract thoughts; but all these new higher schools became as revolutionary as the universities."[96]

That a number of restrictions mentioned in previous pages also applied to teachers has already been pointed out. As a matter of fact, however, teachers' organizations had been banned even before student societies. In 1860, a group of tutors and teachers of the St. Petersburg schools began holding private meetings at the Second St. Petersburg Gymnasium for the purpose of "collectively discussing and deciding various pedagogical questions." These meetings grew in popularity and frequency, and in 1862 the group addressed to the Ministry of Public Education a petition requesting formal recognition under the title of the St. Petersburg Pedagogical Society. On July 4, 1862, the Council of Ministers replied that, after due and proper consideration, "the majority of the members of the Council of Ministers has decided not to establish, at the present time, the St. Petersburg Pedagogical Society." Instead, the question was referred to the entire management of the Ministry of Public Education, with directions to decide the propriety of permitting even the informal meetings to continue.[97]

On the other hand, some attempts were being made, before the reaction set in, to obtain better teachers. A new "Projected Budget for Gymnasiums and District Schools," approved by Tsar Alexander II in 1859, called for considerable increases in staff salaries over those of 1828. For example, gymnasium directors received increases averaging 28 per cent, inspectors 36 per cent, and senior teachers 33 per cent; in the district schools, principals' raises averaged 58 per cent, and teachers' 64 per cent. Considered thus, the increases appear generous and correctly graduated to encourage better personnel in the weakest link, the district schools. But when it is realized that nearly three decades elapsed between the two salary scales, all semblance of generosity disappears. And, when a closer examination of the data[98] is made, the abject poverty of Russian teachers is revealed. The highest paid employees of the secondary school system (the directors of Moscow and St. Petersburg gymnasiums) received only a thousand rubles a year, and the highest paid teachers only 750. In the district schools salary conditions were, of course, much worse, with the top principals getting only five hundred rubles and teachers a maximum of four hundred. Even after the increases, the huge majority of district school teachers received only from 300 to 350 rubles a year!

The abolition of the Main Pedagogical Institute at St. Petersburg in 1858 had also set back the progress of teacher education in Russia. It will be recalled that at that time all such training had been transferred to the Pedagogical Courses at the universities. But only five of the universities offered such courses, and each of these prepared teachers only for its own educational circuit: thus several large and important areas had no direct means of supplying teachers for their own schools. This situation was remedied somewhat in 1860 when a decree ordered the establishment of Pedagogical Courses in all towns and cities possessing universities.[99] The decree stated further that "the immediate aim of the pedagogical courses is the preparation of worthy teachers particularly for the secondary schools of the Ministry of Public Education as well as for other ministries and administrations."[100]

The courses were charged with training teachers not only for the local circuit but also for those circuits which possessed no university. For example, St. Petersburg was to furnish teachers for Vilna and Warsaw, Moscow for Vilna, Kiev for Odessa, Kharkov for Transcaucasia, and Kazan for Siberia.[101] Sufficient funds were allotted to provide stipends for sixty students at the rate of 350 rubles a year in St. Petersburg and Moscow, and 300 rubles for the other three cities.[102] Several months later this arrangement was extended to include Dorpat: seven thousand rubles was appropriated for the first year of work, half of this sum being assigned for instruction and half for student stipends.[103] The courses were designed to prepare teachers for the gymnasiums, progymnasiums, and district schools.[104] Foreigners were permitted only as teachers of foreign languages.[105] The course consisted of two years' instruction,[106] and the students could select any one of the following fields in which to qualify themselves as teachers: (1) Divine Law with Greek and Hebrew languages; (2) Latin and Greek; (3) German and Latin; (4) Russian language, literature and history; (5) historical sciences; (6) mathematical sciences; (7) those subjects demanded from junior teachers of sciences in the gymnasiums and progymnasiums; and (8) those subjects demanded from teachers of sciences in the district schools.[107]

That these efforts were by no means adequate to overcome the shortage of teachers is revealed in a Circular of the Chief Administration of Schools sent to the Minister of Public Education in the summer of 1863. This circular declared that the sixty stipends for the Pedagogical Courses created by the decree of March 20, 1860, were "insufficient for the preparation of the number of teachers required," and recommended the transfer of enough funds to the budgets of these Courses to provide for an additional 150 stipends. The Circular noted that such a transfer had been made during the previous year at St. Petersburg University, and urged that the practice be followed at the universities of Moscow, Kazan, and Kharkov. According to this proposal, the stipends would be limited exclusively to those students who obligated themselves in two ways: (1) to finish either the historical-philological or the physico-mathematical course at the university before starting on the pedagogical course, and then (2) to qualify themselves as teachers in the schools of the Ministry of Public Education. Competitive examinations would be given as the basis for selection of recipients of the stipends, but excellent university or gymnasium records in the given subject were to be prerequisite even to admission to the examinations.[108]

A week later, the Minister of Public Education A. V. Golovnin, replied to these recommendations. Although he found much fault with the details of the proposals, the Minister admitted that "the aims set in establishing the pedagogical courses have not been achieved up to the present time." He acknowledged that the sixty-seven stipends currently in force (the extra seven had been assigned to Dorpat in 1861), were by no means sufficient to prepare enough teachers to supply the schools of the whole Empire, and therefore he approved in principle the creation of 150 new stipends. Nevertheless, he said, such a move was impossible at the time, due to the fact that the funds to pay for them did not exist. In closing, the Minister urged the university councils at Moscow, Kazan and Kharkov to do all within their power to encourage more young people to enter the teaching profession.[109]

Although Minister Golovnin's reply gave very little hope for the improvement of the situation, the Minister had not been idle regarding the serious matter of training-schools for teachers. Observing that the Orthodox Church had for two centuries been supplying its parish schools with teachers from its several theological seminaries, Golovnin had fostered the growth of such institutions on a secular plane. In January 1863, the Tsar acted upon one of his Minister's recommendations by ordering the establishment of two new teachers seminaries, one at Kiev and the other at Vilna, "for the preparation of capable and completely reliable teachers for the public schools" of these two educational circuits. For this purpose, each circuit was granted a little over three thousand rubles from the state educational surplus of the preceding year.[110]

The following year another teachers seminary for the Vilna circuit was founded at Molodechno, and 11,280 rubles was assigned as its annual budget for the first four years.[111] Because so much care went into the planning of this latter institution, and because it served as a model for the establishment of many subsequent teachers seminaries, some space will be devoted here to a description of its character. First, its course of study: a comparison of the curriculum with that of the pedagogical institutes indicates clearly that it ranks far below the latter in scope and depth of instruction.[112] Its two-year course admitted persons who were themselves barely graduates of the district schools in which they were preparing to teach. The subjects number only eleven altogether, as against the thirty-odd comprising the curriculum of the former autonomous pedagogical institutes and the usual twenty offered by the pedagogical courses. Moreover, the curriculum practically duplicated that of the district schools, and attempted no background or "cultural" preparation. Only one brief course in Methods was included, and that only in the second (or senior) year. In short, the teachers seminaries purported to be no more than what they actually were: agencies of pedagogical training, with an abbreviated course of study, to supplement low-grade secondary education sufficiently to permit their graduates to serve as sorely needed teachers in the provincial elementary schools. The salaries of the small teaching staff were low, but in many cases they were supplemented by living quarters and food allowances which made them superior to the 1859 scale described earlier. Furthermore, sixty student stipends, constituting nearly half the entire budget, was a generous number for such a small institution.[113]

The standards required of teachers in urban elementary

schools remained somewhat higher. A new Code for City Schools was published in 1872, one of the articles of which outlined the training necessary for applicants for teaching posts at this level: "Persons who have successfully completed the full course of study in a teachers institute, or who have passed complete examinations at such an institute in theoretical scientific subjects as well as ability to teach in city schools, may become teachers or assistant teachers in city schools. Upon recommendation by an Inspector of public schools, such persons are confirmed in their employment by the Curator of the educational circuit." [114] Sixteen years later this same statement of qualifications became one of the foundations of the attempt to raise the standards of instruction in several types of industrial schools. In the Basic Code for these latter institutions, published in 1888, the following regulations are set forth: "Teachers and job-instructors in the *technical schools* are chosen from among persons possessing, because of their education, the right to hold corresponding posts in the Real-School. In *trade schools*, however, teachers of general educational subjects are chosen from among persons holding the status of Teacher in district or city schools under the decree of May 31, 1872 [described above]. Teachers of geometric (linear) drawing and design are selected from among persons who have received technical or art education, but teachers of technical subjects and technical drawing, and instructors in practical work, must have received not less than a secondary technical education." [115]

Significantly, this Code makes it clear that the industrial schools did not have full autonomy in the appointment of teachers. "Teachers of religion, of the sciences, of applied subjects, of drawing and design, instructors in practical work, laboratory technicians, and masters having the status of technicians—all these categories are considered as government employees" and therefore must be appointed by one or another Ministry. "Masters not having such definite status, as well as teachers of modeling, gymnastics, music and dancing" can be hired by any industrial school where these subjects are taught. However, "upon application of the school administration, and approval by the Curator of the educational circuit, instruction in all general subjects in the industrial school may be intrusted to the teachers employed." [116]

It might legitimately be asked: What *did* the four decades under the two Alexanders accomplish in the area of public enlightenment? The answer, unfortunately, reveals almost as much loss as gain so far as any results of direct efforts on the part of the State or the Church are concerned. It is true that this era brought some progress in the education of females, in that several girls' gymnasiums were established and women were at last admitted to certain university courses. The *zemstvo* schools increased in number, but they were still in disadvantageous competition with the schools under the Holy Synod, and the latter, well supplied with both funds and moral support from above, dispensed a type of instruction which was by no means calculated to stimulate social progress. In like manner, the great increase in the number and influence of technical institutes and vocational schools appears, on the surface, to reflect an urge toward modernization and progress; but closer examination reveals the superficiality and even hypocrisy of their efforts. One historian states categorically that the growth of both professional and church-parish schools was fostered as part of the reactionary plan of the Government and the Holy Synod to crush the lay schools of the *zemstvos* and the municipalities.[117]

Possibly the worst single act in the entire period, however, was the adoption of the University Code of 1884, for its evil results soon permeated every level of education, and some of them remained in effect until the end of Tsardom itself. From this Code stemmed renewed State control of higher education, abolition of academic freedom for both teachers and students, greater discrimination against the poorer classes, more blatant and vicious chauvinism in nationality and religion, increased persecution of even the slightest political unorthodoxy, and finally, the widening of the chasm between State and Church on the one hand and the people of Russia on the other.

For it must not be assumed that these moves on the part of the ruling hierarchy were popular just because they met with no strong, widespread, and organized opposition. Russia in the latter part of the nineteenth century was by no means a cultural wilderness, even though many of its voices could not be heard afar. Great gains had been made in literacy in spite of the multitude of restrictions and difficulties, and these gains had produced a much larger reading public. As the next chapters will reveal, many new publications, both popular and professional, sprang up to disseminate ideas ranging from the mildly critical to the violently revolutionary. The efforts of the State to discourage enlightenment served both to popularize the concept of public education and to undermine faith in the concept of autocracy.

In addition, the economic results of the Great Reforms must not be overlooked. "Numbers of the poorer gentry found their material position seriously affected for the worse by the emancipation of their serfs, and were confronted with the necessity of finding careers for their sons and daughters, by which they could earn their own livings; and to such careers education formed the only avenue. Hence arose an unprecedented demand on the part of the lesser nobility for opportunities of higher education for both men and women. At the same time, the reforms in the judicature and the institution of the *zemstvos*, and of the organs of municipal government, actually opened out careers in a number of new directions; careers, too, which were apparently open to noble and simple alike, provided only the aspirant for employment could obtain the necessary educational equipment. The result was a great influx of students from all ranks of the population into the gymnasia and the universities; and this influx speedily increased the supply of candidates for administrative posts to a point exceeding the demand. The fact that between the years 1854 and 1885 the number of university students rose from 3,551 to 12,939, and that of boys attending gymnasia or real-schools from 17,809 to 93,109, whilst the number of girls receiving secondary education had grown in even greater proportion, may serve as a measure of the increased desire for education in this reign. Finally, as soon as the abolition of serfdom made it easy to move labour from place to place in response to economic requirements, the great natural resources of Russia began to be exploited; an era of unprecedented industrial expansion set in; and this created a demand for special and professional instruction." [118]

Thus, Russian education undoubtedly grew in size, if not in character, during the period under review. Even the *quantitative* expansion of a school system, however, cannot be accomplished without additional teachers, and this chapter has described how the entire system of teacher education in Russia was disrupted by constant shifting of State policy in regard to preparation for the profession. As early as 1865, Minister Golovnin had set up pedagogical courses in an effort to compensate for the closing of the pedagogical institutes, and soon afterward he began to experiment with the teachers seminary. Such makeshift arrangements proved insufficient both in scope and in quality: "In 1870 there were in Russia only three teachers seminaries, twelve pedagogical courses, and two *zemstvo* schools for teachers, and the total number of teachers leaving these institutions did not exceed 700 a year." [119] In 1871 Golovnin's successor, Count Dmitri Tolstoi, expressed his own preference for the seminary method of training; he abolished all the pedagogical courses and opened five new seminaries.[120] After that, "every year six or seven new seminaries were added. In 1875 there were 34 seminaries with 1,847 pupils and 12 *zemstvo* schools [for teachers] with 959 pupils, and in 1881, 39 seminaries with 2,527 pupils and 11 *zemstvo* schools (one had been closed) with 930 pupils. More than 1,000 efficient teachers graduated yearly from these institutions." [121] Such expansion in the field of teacher education soon created an active and well trained body of teachers, who began to insist on a higher status for themselves and for their profession.

Some of the gains described in the preceding few pages are material, some are cultural, some are psychological. But according to one contemporary Russian teacher, "the most valuable contributions of the educational movement [of 1860-1890] were its idealism and its deep faith in man and his essential goodness. As it was also a period in which theoretical propositions were given definite form, it fully deserves to be known as the classical period in the development of education in Russia. . . . The movement . . . should be recognized as the period in the history of Russian education in which were developed the ideas which inspired all later movements, not only down to the time of the Revolution, but also under the Soviet Union." [122] In view of this statement, a later chapter will offer an account of these ideas and theoretical propositions, after completion of the review of the more concrete aspects of Russian educational history.

9

The Beginning of the End (1894–1917)

GENERAL CONDITIONS

THE PERIOD CONSTITUTING THE LAST QUARTER-century of Tsardom is so complex in its educational ramifications and implications that it cannot be handled adequately in the same chronological manner as most of the previous periods have been. One of the outstanding authorities on Russian history has been explicit in his views on this subject: in 1916, he stated that "the history of the last twenty-five years [in Russia] cannot be written from the same point of view or with the same perspective as the history of the previous seventy-five years." [1] The twilight of the Romanov regime blends light and dark through so many shades that it is often impossible to distinguish one from the other. Expansion of elementary education, for example, was accompanied by a ruthless campaign of Russification, nationalism, and clericalism. The great increase in secondary school enrollment paralleled as deep a descent into mysticism and superstition as Russian education had known since the time of Ivan IV. State allotments for schools trebled in per cent of total expenditure, but education still ranked next to last in the budget. Institutions of higher learning grew both in number and in enrollment, but their moral and intellectual standards fell far below those maintained in past decades. Before beginning an analysis of these various complex aspects of the period, it would be well to examine closely the educational status of the Russian Empire as depicted in the famous census of 1897, the only national census ever taken in Tsarist Russia.[2]

The total population of Russia in 1897 was 125,680,682. Of this number, 25,569,585 were classed as literate, or at least able to read, giving the nation a literacy rate of 21.1 per cent. The following table arranged by age and sex presents an interesting picture: [3]

	PER CENT LITERATE	
AGE GROUP	MALES	FEMALES
4-9 years	8.4	4.9
10-19 "	45.5	21.8
20-29 "	44.9	19.5
30-39 "	39.5	16.7
40-49 "	33.2	12.6
50-59 "	26.5	11.1
60-69 "	22.4	10.2
70-79 "	18.6	9.6
80-89 "	13.0	7.6
90-99 "	8.6	5.1
100-109 "	5.9	3.4
110 and over	5.9	3.3
All ages	29.3	13.1

The achievements of the increasing educational expansion that occurred during the latter part of the nineteenth century are reflected in the fact that the only groups above the national average for both sexes are the groups from ten to forty years of age. Beyond these ages, the rate declines steadily, although the rate for males is above the national average up to fifty years of age. Further indication of the paucity of female education even in the 1890's is found in the fact that males between the ages of seven and fourteen years show a literacy rate of 31 per cent, while females in the same age group possess a rate only a little more than half as great. The total picture reveals clearly the need for compulsory elementary education: of the nearly 23 million school-age children, only one-fourth were literate in 1897.[4]

Striking as is the disparity between the literacy of males and females, and between younger and older persons, the inequities of the system are demonstrated even better if the several geographic areas of the Empire are compared. The brief table on the preceding page has already shown the general literacy figures on a nationwide basis: 29.3 per cent for males, 13.1 per cent for females, 21.1 per cent for all. But these figures conceal the fact that the Caucasus and Siberia fell far below these averages in all respects, and that Central Asia had a literacy rate of only 5.3 per cent for its entire population.[5]

Great cultural differences existed also between rural and urban areas: 45.3 per cent of all people in cities were literate, as against the figure of 21.1 per cent for the nation.[6] More than half of all urban males were literate, while only slightly more than one-fourth of all rural males possessed that advantage; nearly a third of all urban females could read, while less than one-tenth of all rural females had this skill. Wide chasms existed between the opportunities provided the different classes: from any point of view, both males and females of the nobility and clergy enjoyed a high degree of literacy for that period, but these powers extended to no other groups in the population. Discounting the fact that higher education in an autocratic society would naturally be reserved for the upper levels, the practice of furnishing general secondary training to 23.4 per cent of noble girls and to only 0.1 per cent of females in rural areas can be classed only as barbaric. The corresponding figures for men reveal almost as deplorable a situation.[7]

In succeeding pages it will be pointed out that the Ministry of Public Education under Nicholas II (1894-1917) several times considered the introduction of laws making universal elementary education compulsory throughout the Empire. How great was the need for such a reform can be seen better if the problem is approached in terms of *illiteracy*. The best section from this point of view was Tsarist Poland, and even there 65.8 per cent of males and 73.2 per cent of females were illiterate. More discouraging still is the realization that, while the rate of increase in female literacy did show acceleration in some areas of the Empire, the average rate among males in every part of Russia was less during the period 1860-1897 than in the nineteenth century as a whole! [8] Even allowing for the unreliability of such statistical implications, it can be seen that the Russian Government faced serious social, as well as educational, problems at the turn of the century. The manner in which the Government approached these problems, the means it adopted to deal with them, and the end results of its efforts—these are the themes for consideration in the succeeding passages of this chapter.

The Universities

In the conclusion of Chapter Eight it was pointed out that the reigns of the two last Alexanders had widened the breach between the people and the State, and Chapter Eleven will deal with the ideological reactions of the more enlightened groups to this ever-broadening gulf. Although a unique combination of the forces set in motion by these phenomena was soon to make itself felt in a cataclysmic eruption, there were few tangible evidences of this latent power visible when the son of Alexander III ascended the throne in 1894. "From the beginning . . . an imminent conflict between the two forces, government and public, cast its shadow over the reign of Nicholas II. But the struggle did not begin immediately. . . . The first few years of the new reign did not differ much from the previous period as far as internal administration and public opinion were concerned. To all appearances the political machinery of the country experienced no alteration; the first sign of the impending sharp change was manifested in the younger generation, among the students in the country's higher institutions of learning."[9]

Since the universities experienced the first effects of this tension, it is well to begin with an examination of these institutions. However, such a review must be undertaken with an outlook much broader than that which has characterized previous chapters. Emphasis must be more upon concepts than upon courses, more upon moral principles than upon methods of teaching, more upon the relations of the student to his society than upon his academic progress. For, as a renowned Russian historian has said, there was no normal academic life in Russia after 1896.[10] The student disturbances of this period might appear, on the surface, to be mere repetitions of those which occurred so frequently throughout the nineteenth century, particularly during the decades 1860-1880. But it will soon be seen, in retrospect, that several factors made these disorders different from their predecessors, even though such perception was rarely within the capacities of the contemporary Tsarist officials.

In the first place, student disturbances were a major characteristic of the reign of Nicholas II.[11] The first important one occurred only two years after his coronation, when students of the University of St. Petersburg were denied the right to hold their annual celebration. That such a restriction would annoy the local studentry is not at all surprising. But the issue became larger than that. The students of Moscow University decided to protest this insult to their sister institution by marching to a mass memorial service at the cemetery where several victims of a recent Tsarist punitive expedition were buried. But the demonstrators never reached their objective: they "were driven by Cossacks back to the University, their names were taken by the police, and thirty-six of them who seemed to be leaders were arrested. On the next day the students gathered at the University, and asked the Rector to obtain the release of the prisoners; he refused and ordered them to disperse. As they disobeyed, 403 students were imprisoned . . . , 105 of their number were subsequently banished to Siberia, and 26 were expelled from the University. Thus was inaugurated the policy of the new reign towards the youth of the country."[12]

Thenceforward, such revolts and suppressions occurred with increasing frequency. In 1899 the chief of the St. Petersburg police was rewarded by the government for breaking up a student demonstration with knouts. Students throughout the country were enraged both at the police action and the official sanction, and 13,000 of them went on strike—an astonishing number when it is considered that there were less than 16,000 students that year in all the Russian universities.[13] The Tsar's reaction to this widespread discontent was to order all the strikers inducted into the army. At the same time, many liberal professors were dismissed from the universities, especially in Moscow and St. Petersburg.[14]

The following year a great disturbance took place in Kiev when over a thousand students assembled and denounced the Ministry of Public Education for its reactionary policies. The Rector of the University called in the police, who surrounded the demonstrators while Cossack troops beat them with whips and knouts. Several students were killed in the affray, 500 were arrested, about 200 inducted into the army, and 300 expelled. One result of this violence was still more student revolts in Moscow, Kharkov and St. Petersburg, and "in every case the Cossacks attacked the protesting students and flogged them mercilessly." In 1901, St. Petersburg police killed seven students, one a woman, and wounded an untold number.[15] That same year, the Ministry tripled the number of Inspectors in the universities, making their ratio to students 1 to 150, and also ruled that students had to attend the particular university which served the educational circuit wherein they had graduated secondary school.[16] This latter move, of course, permitted a more thorough investigation of applicants, and prevented expellees from moving from one institution to another, as Lenin himself had done a decade earlier.

The reply of the students to these measures was most direct: N. P. Bogolepov, Minister of Public Education since 1898, was shot by a former university student on February 14, 1901 and died two weeks later. The public had been so outraged by the extreme measures taken by the government against the students that this act of terrorism was actually approved in many circles. Instead of condemning the assassination, many mothers, authors, high officials, and persons of all ranks and professions showered protests upon the government itself for bringing about such a situation.[17] When Sipiagin, Minister of the Interior, was killed by a university student the following year, the masses of people "accepted [it] with silent approbation. The opposition press strove, as much as conditions of censorship permitted, to prove that these acts were a natural and even inevitable product of the existing regime."[18] Another sign of the new times was that in many of these university demonstrations, the local workers joined with the students.

The masses of people throughout Russia were beginning to make it clear that they were tired of Absolutism.[19]

During the next four years the situation became still more aggravated, both on the cultural and the even broader social fronts. For it must be borne in mind that these conflicts in university affairs were but one manifestation of the profound dissatisfactions convulsing the entire political and economic system. In many sections of the Empire, groups were demanding governmental reforms ranging from mere relaxation of autocratic power to outright abolition of the monarchy. In the industrial cities, strikes were growing in frequency and in scope. These acts placed simultaneous strains upon both the decrepit productive organization and the archaic administrative apparatus. Moreover, the Tsar's ministers had maneuvered the country into a war with Japan which, after only a few months, revealed the inherent deficiencies of the system and foreshadowed ignominious military and naval defeat. Upon the fall of Port Arthur early in January 1905, the various protesting groups intensified their efforts to bring about changes. Professional organizations, learned societies, labor unions, *zemstvo* leaders, and the numerous political parties—all reopened their campaigns for reform and in many cases began for the first time to co-ordinate their moves toward common ends. The government, plagued thus from all sides and realizing to a certain extent its own weakness, once more took up its most formidable weapon, violent suppression.

On January 9, 1905 occurred one of the most shocking incidents of modern Russian history—the infamous "Bloody Sunday." Several thousand workingmen, led by the Government priest Father Gapon, marched toward the Imperial Palace in St. Petersburg to present to the Tsar a most moderate and respectful petition. The marchers were mowed down by the guns of the Palace troops: 1500 men, women, and children were killed or wounded.[20] During the next two months, street riots took place in Tomsk, martial law had to be instituted in parts of the Caucasus, and *zemstvo* members were beaten on their way to a meeting in Tambov.[21]

These events indicate how widespread was public vexation. But "the universities and higher schools, in which the professors and the students were now acting in concert, took the same step." Several St. Petersburg students were wounded in a street demonstration in late January, and on February 17 the same fate befell a number of students in Moscow. On February 19, police chased a group of students down the streets of Kazan. On February 20 in Pskov and February 25 in Kursk—neither town possessing a university—the police vented their anger on bands of mere schoolboys.[22] One authority states that the frequency and violence of such demonstrations became so great that several universities were temporarily closed.[23] Another, after pointing out that the experiences "of the past year had brought the students into much closer contact with the workingmen of the towns," declares that these town-and-gown strikes continued all through the summer of 1905.[24]

Ultimately the government was forced to grant some of the reforms demanded. Those changes concerned directly with such institutions as the *zemstvos*, the press, the Ministry of Public Education, and the secondary and teacher-training establishments will be discussed later in this volume. But the problem of university regulations, under serious consideration since 1901, was dealt with by Nicholas II in a series of revisions in 1905, 1906, and 1911. The first of these decrees, approved by the Tsar on August 27 and published by the Ministry of Public Education on September 8, abolished the most oppressive articles of the University Code of 1884 and restored several of the rights granted by the Code of 1863. The universities were now declared to be autonomous institutions, with the privilege of choosing their own Rectors and of holding meetings within their own buildings. The dreaded Inspectors, though remaining numerous, were subordinated to the Rectors and thus lost much of their power. Students benefited indirectly from these reforms and in addition were granted the right to hold meetings of their own, theoretically without the presence of police spies.[25]

The results of such a policy would probably have been very good had they been allowed to work themselves out. But the government seems to have distrusted even its own feeble attempts at liberalism, for on another ill-chosen occasion some of its recent reforms were retracted. That occasion was the funeral of Prince S. N. Trubetskoi, who had just been elected Rector of Moscow University under the privileges accorded in the decree of September 1905. Trubetskoi had long been a tireless worker for the cause of academic freedom, and even at the time of his death was in St. Petersburg to plead with the Ministry of Public Education for extensions of such freedom. Naturally, such a man was beloved by most Russian students, and several thousand of these assembled in Moscow to attend his funeral. So far as can be learned, these students were there for reasons of reverence, not revolt. Nevertheless, the lawful assemblage was huge, and the Moscow police could not abide it: they charged the mourners in old-style manner, and many casualties resulted.[26] One of these casualties was certainly public faith in the sincerity of the Tsar and his government. And not without reason, for in a few months "the school autonomy won in the fall of 1905 was nullified in a series of 'modifications.'"[27]

From this time on, each repressive act of the government was countered by an illegal move on the part of the students (who were often supported by other elements of the populace), and these moves in turn met with further governmental restrictions. It was indeed a vicious—and usually violent—circle. Student demonstrations and strikes were resorted to again, causing the Ministry to make several attempts to reintroduce the Code of 1884. Although such attempts failed of legal passage, the educational policy of the government was daily bent more in the reactionary direction of that pursued by Count Dmitri Tolstoi from 1866 to 1880.[28]

When Count Leo Tolstoi, noted author and educator, died in 1910 the government, anticipating nation-wide demonstrations of grief, published a decree outlawing "public mourning." The result was that many students defied the law and again ran into police stupidity and brutality. Other student meetings also became suspect, so in January 1911 the Ministry of Public Education forbade all assemblages of students not approved by the provincial governors, even those which the 1905 laws had permitted within the grounds of institutions. In addition, the Ministry set up more stringent penalties for "violations of order." Again the students went on strike. Members of the several University Councils, realizing that the situation was extremely tense, attempted to persuade the students to obey the law; but police pushed aside the professors and proceeded to beat up the students. Police officials demanded and got the resignation of the Rector of Moscow University. In protest, more than a hundred of his faculty also resigned their posts. "The oldest Russian university was thus outraged."[29]

Similar events were taking place elsewhere, notably in Kiev. In the theological academies professors could belong only to "approved" political parties. "Spies and provocateurs were so common that no one felt safe."[30] The Government followed up its attacks by appointing professors and administrators on whom it could rely. Thus, "public instruction was once more forced by the boot of the policeman into 'politically safe' ruts. The same policy, needless to say, was carried on in secondary and primary schools." [31]

Just what did such restrictions accomplish? In the view of one witness to the events of these years, the Government was sealing its own doom: "The universities were hotbeds of socialism and revolution. The students were expelled from the universities, they were imprisoned, they were exiled to Siberia; but the spirit lived on and constantly gathered force." [32] It was neither the first nor the last time in history that such a phenomenon took place.

MINISTRY OF PUBLIC EDUCATION

The Russian universities have been shown as centers of radicalism during the period 1894-1914. For the sake of contrast, it is advisable to take up a brief account of the activities of that seat of conservatism, the Ministry of Public Education. The accession of Nicholas II did not disturb the ministerial position of Count T. D. Delianov, the incumbent since 1882, for Nicholas had no idea of revising either the aims or the methods of public education which had so well satisfied his father. But Delianov's death in 1898 forced the Tsar to cast about for a new appointee, and at last he settled on Nikolai Pavlovich Bogolepov. The new Minister's background made him appear unusually well qualified: a graduate of Moscow University in 1872, he had later served that institution as Professor of Roman Law and, from 1883-1895, as Rector. Moreover, his next three years had been spent as Curator of the Moscow educational circuit.[33]

It must be recalled, however, that Bogolepov had risen to prominence under the sponsorship of that almost fanatical bigot, K. P. Pobedonostsev, who, as Chief Procurator of the Holy Synod, dominated cultural affairs in Russia from 1880 right up to the Revolution of 1905.[34] Bogolepov's attitude toward such issues as academic freedom, student liberties, and the role of higher education in society is indicated in the foregoing pages devoted to the status of Russian universities during his administration. His views on other educational matters deserve more minute scrutiny. But first it is advisable to describe the situation in regard to the jurisdiction of the Ministry in the first year of Bogolepov's administration. The following tables reveal the high degree of decentralization in effect, and give a hint regarding the status of the historic struggle between Ministry and Synod for the control of the Russian school system.

Administration of Elementary Schools, 1898[35]

CONTROLLING AGENCY	NUMBER OF SCHOOLS	NUMBER OF TEACHERS	NUMBER OF PUPILS
Ministry of Public Education	37,046	84,121	2,650,058
Holy Synod	40,028	67,907	1,476,124
Ministry of War	848	1,058	46,420
Ministry of the Interior	553	1,102	20,510
Department of the Institutions of the Empress Maria	153	210	5,097
Imperial Philanthropic Society	40	179	2,822
Ministry of the Court and Domains	23	63	1,599
Ministry of Finance	4	12	237
Ministry of Marine	4	?	379
TOTAL	78,699	154,652	4,203,246

(included above are 1,785 adult schools with enrollments of 89,045)

A recapitulation of the figures in this table shows the apportionment of authority between the two major agencies:

CONTROLLING AGENCY	SCHOOLS	TEACHERS	PUPILS
Ministry of Public Education	47.1%	54.4%	63.0%
Holy Synod	50.9	43.9	35.1
All others	2.0	1.7	1.9

Although the Holy Synod had succeeded in capturing the majority of the schools, it is clear that it did not exert direct control over most of the teachers or pupils. On the other hand, there were definite advantages accruing to the Synod schools because of their lower pupil-school and pupil-teacher ratio: [36]

	MPE SCHOOLS	SYNOD SCHOOLS	OTHER SCHOOLS	AVERAGE FOR ALL
Pupils per teacher	31.5	22.0	29.4	27.2
Pupils per school	71.5	36.9	47.4	53.4

Bogolepov was determined to bring these ratios down in the schools operated by the Ministry, and ultimately he found ways to achieve this aim to a marked degree. In his three years in office, he increased the number of schools in his system by more than 25 per cent.[37]

Bogolepov was even more deeply interested in the affairs of secondary education. In 1899 he addressed to the Curator of each educational circuit a message reviewing various complaints against the secondary schools and requesting that each Curator nominate several delegates to a Commission of Inquiry which would meet to study the system and recommend improvements. The message cautioned that the personnel selected should be most capable, that the conclusions should be based on actual experience and worked out in detail, and that the scope of the study should include structure, aims, and curriculum.[38] The proposed Commission was actually formed and met for thirty-two full sessions in St. Petersburg from January 7 to March 6, 1900. Its suggestions were then submitted to a smaller commission which met in the fall of 1900 and continued in session until February 1901 when Bogolepov was assassinated. There is evidence that this commission was ready to recommend important curricular revisions but no profound structural changes; however, the report itself was buried so far as practical results are concerned.[39]

Bogolepov's successor, General P. S. Vannovskii, was one of Russia's "elder statesmen," and had been Minister of War during the entire reign of Alexander III. At the age of 79, "he was dug out of the archives and appointed Minister of Public Education."[40] Vannovskii had no knowledge of pedagogical theories, but he had worked in the field of military education and had taken a leading part in the attempts to ferret out the roots of the university disorders of the preceding five years. In addition, he was a good administrator: immediately after his appointment, he sent questionnaires to all the universities asking for data and opinions on student rights, instructional methods, adequacy of salaries, system of control, etc. Moreover, he proved willing to act upon the replies by inaugurating certain revisions which would have been considered liberal a decade before. But it was too late for mild reforms: the students and faculty were demanding revolutionary changes, and so the Minister's programs accomplished little.[41]

In the area of secondary education, Vannovskii achieved a greater degree of success, but only temporarily. Throwing out the findings of Bogolepov's commissions, he started an entirely new investigation which brought forth quite different conclusions. The results of the new survey indicated that fundamental changes were necessary in secondary school administration and structure as well as in curriculum. Vannovskii courageously acted upon these proposals and actually got the Tsar's permission to try them out experimentally for a year. But during that period Nicholas II withdrew his support, the Minister resigned his post after a little more than a year in office, and matters dragged along as before.[42]

The next incumbent of the Ministership was G. E. Sänger, a professional educator who had been a professor at the University of Warsaw, and whose chief interest naturally was directed toward the improvement of higher education. Again the State's educational policy underwent change, this time in the direction of encouraging reorganization of both secondary schools and universities. Although Sänger remained at his post for two years, he accomplished almost nothing, largely because the tasks laid upon him by a series of Imperial Rescripts proved far too heavy for any mortal to bear in those trying times.[43]

In 1904 Sänger was succeeded by General V. G. Glazov, who evidently felt that enough time had been wasted on "frills" such as courses of study, articulation between grades, and student self-government. At any rate, Glazov called a meeting of Curators in August 1904 and informed them that thereafter the schools were to emphasize patriotic and religious education above all else. Armed with this directive, the Curators came forward with one of the most reactionary educational plans ever to be devised even in Russia. Fortunately for all concerned, the Revolution of 1905 prevented the project from escaping the archives.[44] Glazov resigned, Pobedonostsev resigned, the Tsar issued a manifesto on civil rights, the Duma was established and given the power of veto, and the Council of Ministers seemed open at last to many able men who had risen to prominence in the already long struggle for an enlightened government in Russia.

The new Minister of Public Education, despite his scholarly background, was not of these men. He was Count

Ivan Ivanovich Tolstoi, a member of the nobility and a graduate of St. Petersburg University. Tolstoi's chief interest was archeology, and he had served the State Archeological Commission both as secretary and as vice-president. In addition, he had been vice-president of the Imperial Art Academy and chairman of the Russian Society of the Art of Printing.[45] Although not in the least familiar with the rapidly growing radical movements, Tolstoi was much more liberal in his thinking than his immediate predecessors had been. Since his own career had been spent almost entirely in the realm of higher learning, Tolstoi welcomed as his first task the organization of a new University Code based upon the series of Imperial edicts of the preceding summer.

Early in 1906 he called a meeting of all university rectors to discuss this problem. At the same time, the matter was considered by the Academic Union of Professors which had been established the year before for the purpose of guarding and furthering the rights of college teachers. It is an indication of the tenor of the times that both these groups, meeting independently, arrived at practically the same conclusions. Tolstoi then incorporated these recommendations into a Ministry project which promised significant reforms in just the opposite direction from those proposed by Minister Delianov in the preceding decade. Autonomy was to be restored to the universities, the university councils were to become once more the real directing agencies of the institutions even to the point of electing the staffs, all social and religious barriers to student enrollment were to be cancelled, and the student right to form societies was to be re-established. But again the vacillation of Nicholas II prevented what would have been a major achievement in Russian education: the Tsar dismissed Tolstoi at the end of the latter's first year in office, thus conveniently shelving the projected new Code.[46]

The next appointee to the Ministership of Public Education was a confirmed bureaucrat of the conservative school. Peter Mikhailovich Kaufmann was a graduate of the Imperial Alexander Lycée and had held several rather important posts in the Council of Ministers during the past quarter century. He had been in charge of Red Cross work in Russia in the Russo-Japanese War, and was to be reappointed to the same post in 1915. Almost none of his experience had been connected even indirectly with education.[47] One of his colleagues in the Council of Ministers says that Kaufmann was "hardly noticeable" and that his opinions "had no effect" upon that body.[48] Yet it was under the two-year administration of this man that laudable—though largely futile—attempts were made to expand higher education (especially for females), to re-establish a democratic "ladder system" in the secondary schools, and to make elementary education compulsory for all. In the first endeavor, Kaufmann was signally successful. Although he did not bring forth a new University Code, three new institutions were opened, enrollments continued to expand, and higher courses for women were attached to every university in Russia.[49]

The ladder system was not given serious consideration at this time outside the Ministry itself, and so failed to excite attention. But the principle of compulsory education had been advanced repeatedly ever since the 1860's, and had received the unqualified support of the Duma. Nevertheless, it too was squelched by the Council of Ministers, although this by no means settled the question, for succeeding Dumas continued to press for the reform.[50] In order to appreciate fully the lukewarm attitude of the government toward this extremely important problem, it might be well to consult the opinions of a man who was present at the meeting of the Council of Ministers which considered the original recommendation in 1906. Mr. V. I. Gurko, then Assistant Minister of the Interior, says that after the Tsar had been persuaded to transfer certain state and Imperial lands to the peasantry, Prime Minister Stolypin opened meetings of the Council to discussion of other needed reforms. One of the first of these taken up, says Gurko, was the matter of compulsory elementary education. The plan "was presented and defended, not by the Minister of Education, Kaufmann, who seemed to be not too well acquainted with it, but by his assistant, Gerasimov. . . . The project was really childish. It proclaimed the principle of general compulsory education but provided no program for putting it into effect. . . . I [Gurko] pointed out to the Council of Ministers this lack of necessary preparation, and that the Ministry of Education would have done much better to busy itself preparing teachers for primary and secondary schools. Kokovtsov [then Minister of Finance and later Chairman of the Council of Ministers as well] also opposed the project because of the expenditures it would entail. In the end it was suggested that the Minister of Education alter the project—a suggestion which amounted to rejecting it altogether." [51] Thus most of Kaufmann's major projects came to naught, and early in 1908 he was removed from office.

Kaufmann's successor represented the now prevalent tendency in the Government toward deep reaction. In a series of sweeping decrees on higher education, Minister of Public Education A. N. Schwarz restricted student liberties, expelled all women from university courses, and reintroduced the restrictions on Jewish students which had been cancelled four years before. Schwarz was finally forced to permit the women to finish their courses, but before leaving office in 1910 he drafted a new University Code which almost completely abolished the autonomy granted by Count I. I. Tolstoi. However it was left for the next incumbent actually to put the new Code into effect, an act which Minister Lev Aristidovich Kasso probably found much to his liking.[52]

Educated at Paris, Berlin and Heidelberg, Kasso had been on the faculties of three Russian universities–Dorpat, Kharkov and Moscow–before taking over his new post.[53] Whether his foreign education had permitted Kasso to escape the influence of the Russian reform movement, or whether he consciously rejected all its principles is not important to the purposes of this study. One conclusion is certain: he was one of the most reactionary and heavy-handed of all Russian ministers of education. As one writer puts it, "this Minister became famous for his constant disregard of law. Among students a new proverb came into vogue: 'Kasso has made a wholesale cassation.' And so it was." [54]

Kasso assisted in the suppression of the student demonstration at the funeral of Leo Tolstoi, described earlier in this chapter, and it was he who ordered the wholesale expulsions which followed the demonstration. During the month of February 1911 alone, Kasso expelled or countenanced the expulsion of 6,000 students, and the following summer he personally expelled nearly all the 1,400 enrollees at the Medical Institute for Women in St. Petersburg. While many of these students were later readmitted to their studies, violence and repression continued throughout Kasso's administration. The system of espionage which he introduced in all the universities and many other schools became a characteristic feature of Russian education for years to come.[55]

Kasso took little interest in secondary education and was the only Minister of Public Education who prepared no plan whatever for this level.[56] But, despite the frequent changes of executives, the campaign of the Ministry of Public Education to increase the number of elementary schools under its jurisdiction was showing fairly rapid progress. The situation at the opening of the twentieth century was described earlier in this chapter, and the following table recapitulates enough of that information to reveal the trend:

Administration of Elementary Schools, 1898–1911[57]

CONTROLLING AGENCY	*Number of Schools* 1898	1911	*Number of Teachers* 1898	1911	*Number of Pupils* 1898	1911
Min. Pub. Ed.	37,046	59,682	84,121	130,019	2,650,058	4,186,078
Holy Synod	40,028	37,922	67,907	66,525	1,476,124	1,793,429
All others	1,625	2,691	2,624	6,729	77,064	201,003
TOTALS	78,699	100,295	154,652	203,273	4,203,246	6,180,510

The total figures themselves show a rather remarkable achievement, consisting as they do of a 27 per cent rise in the number of schools, a 31 per cent increase in the number of teachers, and a 47 per cent boost in enrollment—all this in the relatively short space of thirteen years! Close examination of the table will reveal the fact that nearly all of these increases were to the credit of the schools under the Ministry of Public Education: although the Synod achieved a slightly increased enrollment, both its schools and its teachers actually declined in number. It should also be noted that the great expansion in Ministry schools was accomplished without adding significantly (only 0.7) to the number of pupils per teacher, and that the ratio of pupils to school was considerably reduced (by 8.5).

Thus school construction and teacher supply were, at long last, keeping pace with the growing elementary school enrollment. That this progress was not achieved without a tremendous rise in expenditures by the government is indicated by the fact that the funds allotted to elementary schools nearly tripled in the same period, as indicated by the following table:

Government Expenditures on Elementary Education[58]
(in rubles)

YEAR	AMOUNT
1871	1,600,000
1890	7,225,800
1900	15,970,900
1911	42,882,000

In addition to these funds, of course, there were *zemstvo* and private expenditures which will be considered later in this chapter.

Kasso resigned as Minister of Public Education at the end of 1914, and was succeeded by Count Pavel Nikolaevich Ignatiev, one of the most enlightened men ever to hold that post. Ignatiev had graduated from the University of Kiev, and almost immediately afterward, in 1892, he entered government service in the Ministry of the Interior. In 1904 he became chairman of the board of the Kiev *guberniya zemstvo*, and in 1907-1908 served as Governor of that *guberniya*. He was made Director of the Department of Agriculture in the Chief Administration of Land Organizations and Agriculture in 1909 and advanced to Assistant Chief of the entire Administration three years later.[59] Thus Ignatiev possessed first-hand knowledge of the three most important administrative channels of the Russian governmental apparatus: ministerial, *zemstvo*, and provincial. In addition, he was a man of liberal and democratic sentiments, as was demonstrated in 1913 when, as a government official, he presided over an agricultural conference in St. Petersburg. At the end of the conference the *zemstvo* agricultural experts in attendance addressed to Ignatiev "a warm speech expressing their gratitude for having been given an opportunity freely to express their opinions and desires."[60]

It is no wonder that such a man created "something of a sensation" in the bureaucratic circles of St. Petersburg, or that he considered himself an outsider even after years of civil service there.[61] Influenced by the educational philosophy of John Dewey, Ignatiev strove to re-establish the "ladder system" in the schools. It will be recalled that P. M. Kaufmann had attempted to do the same thing during his administration (1906-1908); and in 1911 a bill supporting this objective had been introduced in the Duma, but Minister Kasso ignored the matter. Ignatiev took this bill as the basis of his own project, but he, too, failed to obtain official approval for it.[62] With other features of his reform plan Ignatiev was more successful.[63] His new curriculum for secondary schools was adopted in 1915 and began to be put into practice the following year. Distinguished particularly for its concentration upon modern languages and history, this curriculum represented a great advance in Russian pedagogical thought.[64]

But events of a more significant nature had moved forward even faster, and demanded nearly all the attention of the Tsarist government. With its very existence threatened by war and impending revolution, the government again resorted to measures which could not help but offend those officials who retained some semblance of genuine interest in the welfare of the Russian people. Being one of these, Ignatiev had no choice but to resign his post, after only two years in office. His successor, N. K. Kulchitskii, became the last Minister of Public Education in the dying Imperial government, and so was able to accomplish almost nothing.[65]

The wording of Ignatiev's resignation offers such an excellent view both of the man himself and of the conditions prevailing at the time that it is worth quoting at length. Dated January 9, 1917 and addressed to "Your Imperial Majesty, Most Gracious Monarch," the letter reads as follows:

"At Your Majesty's Imperial Headquarters on December 2 [1916] I felt bound by my duty, oath and conscience to sound the alarm over the part played by certain persons and the political situation of the country. I pray Your Imperial Majesty not to oblige me to be an accomplice of these persons whose acts I regard as ruinous to the throne and the State.

"I am firmly convinced that the only kind of government that could be useful to Your Imperial Majesty and the country is one that is united in its conception of the state, in its understanding of the fundamental objects of government and in the manner of realizing them. It is my duty as a loyal subject to beg most humbly Your Imperial Majesty to relieve me of the unbearable burden of serving against the dictates of my conscience. Believe me, my Sovereign, that in making this petition I am guided by the traditions of my ancestors who were from old devoted to the ancient [monarchic] principle. It is in this principle and the union of Tsar and people that the Russian State was created and grew strong. . . ." [66]

Ignatiev had devoted himself to all his responsibilities, and particularly those in the field of public education, "with remarkable enthusiasm and great ability. If under the conditions prevailing during the War only a few of his proposals were carried out, this was certainly not due to his lack of courage or vision." [67] The former was demonstrated by his resignation, and the latter by his understanding of the yawning gulf between the autocracy and the people.

Despite the adverse conditions, however, indisputable marks of progress in these years are discernible. According to a report of the Ministry of Public Education covering the years 1911-1915, the number of elementary schools under the jurisdiction of the Ministry alone on January 1, 1915 was 80,801, an increase of 32.3 per cent over the number for 1911. Enrollment of pupils had increased 35.7 per cent in the same period, standing at 5,942,000; the number of teachers rose to 146,000, or 38.6 per cent, making a national average of 40.7 pupils per teacher. An interesting shift is revealed in the ratio of male to female teachers, the former dropping from 43.5 per cent in 1911 to 37 per cent in 1915. While the advances indicated by these figures were undoubtedly encouraging, it should be noted that rural Russia still suffered from inadequate cultural opportunities: of the 80,801 existing schools, 71,795 were in towns and only 9,006 in the villages.[68] Secondary schools also shared in this progress, although by no means to the same extent as did the elementary institutions. During the last two decades of Tsarist rule, enrollment in secondary schools almost tripled in relation to the entire population, rising from 13.3 per 10,000 in 1895 to 36.0 per 10,000 in 1914.[69] The following table shows the enrollments in the several types of schools on this level in January 1914 (except where other dates are specified): [70]

TYPE OF SECONDARY SCHOOL	NUMBER	ENROLLMENT
Gymnasiums	441	147,751
Progymnasiums	29	4,359
Real-Schools	284	80,800
Normal Schools	33	1,249
Normal Seminaries	122	19,190
Girls Gymnasiums	837	341,637
Girls Progymnasiums	92	11,940
Cadet Corps Schools	29	29,646
Gymnasiums of Empress Maria (1912)	35	17,166
Institutions of Empress Maria (1912)	34	9,562
Seminaries (1913)	57	22,311
TOTAL OF ALL TYPES	1993	685,611

Since some of the above figures are based on 1912 and 1913 records, it is probably safe to assume that upon the outbreak of World War I Russia possessed 2,000 secondary schools attended by 700,000 students. It has been estimated that enrollment in the elementary schools was about 8 million in 1914 and that about 150,000 students were then in institutions of higher education.[71] Thus, in that year the Russian Empire had close to 9 million students of all ages attending educational institutions.

Commendable as was this progress, it was both too little and too late. "In spite of the very real efforts made by the *zemstvos* and even by the Government for the promotion of education, it must be admitted that the percentage of illiteracy on the eve of the War was still extraordinarily high. We know that only a small percentage of Russian children went to school. A still smaller portion had received any scholastic training in the past, with the result that it seems doubtful whether the general average of literacy was more than 20 or 25 per cent. One should remember that even among those children who went to school many never saw a newspaper or book in later years, and their knowledge of even the rudiments of reading and writing therefore was purely nominal." [72]

Although the author just quoted gives some praise to the Tsarist government for the educational progress of the two last decades of the regime, the Ministry of Public Education, according to other authorities, was not entitled to share this credit. In 1908 a Duma leader, who had himself been Curator of an educational circuit, declared that the Ministry "has never satisfied the crying needs of the country; it has never anticipated the requirements of the country in education; it has never stimulated the thirst for knowledge. Its procedure has always been prompted by pushes from the outside: society and the country by pushing have compelled the Ministry to make certain concessions and from time to time to satisfy the needs of the country, but certainly in proportions immensely inferior to those demanded." [73]

An English author writing at about the same time points out that "the Minister of the department—the post has more than once been filled by a general—has far too often acted as a kind of police officer. It is not without reason that he has been styled 'the Minister for the prevention of public instruction.'" [74] Count Witte is quoted as having said that "every successive Minister of Public Instruction has been worse than his predecessor," and, with the possible exception of Count I. I. Tolstoi and Count P. N. Ignatiev, this statement might apply to the entire roster of the ten such officials who served during the reign of Nicholas II.[75]

Lest the statements quoted above appear to be more captious than correct, it is well to consider a careful evaluation of the Ministry of Public Education made by one of Tsarist Russia's outstanding schoolmen, formerly a professor of economics in the University of Moscow. Writing of the decade immediately preceding World War I, this authority states that "the extremely rapid growth [of Russian higher education] met with no encouragement on the part of the principal organ that had charge of the schools in Russia, namely, the Ministry of Education, and was even hampered by it. . . . [Other ministries] did much more for higher education during the period in question than the Ministry of Education. The reason for this most unusual development was that the Ministry, still fearing revolutionary outbursts, continued to follow the path of reprisals and to view with great suspicion the growth of the universities. . . . At the same time, in the general policy of the Government the line of narrow conservatism was becoming more and more pronounced. . . . Even moderate elements were looked upon with suspicion. . . .

"This tragic split between the Government and the public serves to explain the sad and amazing fact in the prewar history of Russian education which cannot be described otherwise than as the war of the Government against the universities. . . . In the last years preceding the War, the Ministry of Education took most drastic measures in order to destroy the last remnants of independence of the faculties and of their members."[76] In view of this remarkable unanimity of opinion regarding the role of the Ministry itself in the educational programs of the period, it is necessary to turn now to a brief consideration of two other public agencies whose influence in this field was considerable, the Duma and the *Zemstvos*.

THE DUMA

The Duma was originally created by an Imperial decree of October 17, 1905, as a result of the popular dissatisfaction growing out of the miserable failure of the Tsarist government in the Russo-Japanese War. It was intended to be chiefly a deliberative and advisory body to the various Ministers, who continued to be responsible only to the Tsar. On the other hand, the fact that it possessed veto powers and that its membership was elected on a broad franchise made its establishment Russia's first successful attempt to introduce an elective legislative assembly.

The First Duma was convened in May 1906 but dissolved in July of the same year; the Second Duma followed the same course in March-June 1907. On June 3, 1907, the electoral law was changed in such a way as to narrow the franchise, with the result that the Third Duma (1907-1912) was much less representative than its ill-fated predecessors. The Fourth Duma, elected on the same basis as the Third, also stayed in session for its full term of five years, being disbanded by the first revolution of 1917. Thus the two popularly elected Dumas were dissolved before they could accomplish anything, while the two restricted-membership Dumas became, in turn, the "lower chamber of the Russian parliament," with a reorganized State Council as the upper chamber.[77]

Although the Third Duma, meeting for the first time in November 1907, was most intent upon such practical matters as national defense, it soon got around to the question of education.[78] At the sessions of this body early in 1908, a program was launched which was "designed to provide ultimately a free, primary education for all the children of

Russia." [79] Toward this end, the Duma voted Government expenditures far above those recommended by the Ministry of Public Education, and was directly responsible for the founding of the university at Saratov in 1909 and the establishment of commercial institutes at Kharkov and Moscow. [80]

But the government, despite a greatly increased allotment to education during the period of the Third Duma, did not provide sufficient funds for the accomplishments envisioned in the 1908 plan.[81] Therefore, in June 1912, the Duma went a step further and specified an *annual* increase of twenty million rubles until the program of universal elementary education would be achieved.[82] The power of the Duma is best illustrated by the fact that such an increase was not only effected but actually exceeded the very next year, although the approach of war prevented any continuation of such large appropriations.[83]

THE ZEMSTVOS

As has already been indicated, the role of the *zemstvos* in Russian education was much more important than that of the Duma, if for no other reason than that the former had a considerably longer history. *Zemstvos* had existed as units of local government in Russia since the middle of the sixteenth century, but their real power began to assert itself only after their reorganization in 1864 as part of the reform program of Alexander II.

At that time, *zemstvos* were set up in thirty-four central *guberniyas*, each of which had one *zemstvo* for each *uyezd* as well as one for the entire *guberniya*. Each *zemstvo* had an assembly (*sobranie*) and a board, or executive organ (*uprava*). The *uyezd* assemblies were elected by the local citizenry which voted as three separate groups (*kuria*): the nobility, the urban bourgeoisie, and the peasants. The *uyezd* assemblies then elected delegates from their member-

courage the maintenance of *zemstvo* schools. Unsuccessful in this indirect attempt, Witte later suggested openly that all *zemstvo* schools be placed under the authority of the Holy Synod.[101] Although this plan, too, was defeated, there was no longer any doubt that the Government and the Synod had joined hands to stamp out the challenge to orthodoxy, autocracy, and nationalism provided by the *zemstvo* organizations.

For the roots of this conflict lay much deeper than is indicated by mere rivalry in the field of education, health or other public services. As one contemporary official viewed the matter: "The public was little interested in the economic activity of local government, particularly that of the *zemstvos*. It saw in the *zemstvo* workers the vanguard of those who were fighting to win for the masses of the population a share in the deciding of state problems. It was for these reasons that the public valued and cherished the *zemstvos*." [102] Had Nicholas II permitted the representative First or Second Dumas to survive, had he filled his cabinet after 1905 with real men-of-the-people, had he given the Ministry of Public Education in 1898 over to such a popular leader as Prince S. N. Trubetskoi, rather than to the inept Bogolepov, the rising tide of revolt might have been diverted into a broad channel of reform.

That such representation was desired by the people is shown by the fact that the first man chosen to head the Provisional Government after the revolution of February-March 1917 was Prince George E. Lvov, president of the Union of Zemstvos.[103] But by that time it was too late: the awful chasm between government and people had widened to such an extent that all governments were distrusted by most citizens.[104] The essential weakness of the Provisional Government of Russia probably lay in just the fact that by 1917 even a government which trusted the people could no longer count upon the reciprocity necessary for survival.

10

The Status of Teachers During the Last Two Decades of Tsardom (1897–1917)

THE IMPORTANCE OF THE FINAL ATTEMPTS of the Tsarist government and various public agencies toward refurbishing the Russian educational system to meet the needs of the time is subordinate in the end to the effects which those efforts had upon the Russian people. As one historian of the period has clearly stated, it would be unjust to blame the peasant "for his lack of stamina, his low sense of duty, his inability to grasp anything outside the field of his immediate interests. All these [faults] were probably the inevitable results of the historical conditions under which he had lived since time immemorial. The progress of education since the Emancipation had been far too slow to bring any real results. The apathy and ignorance of the masses bore their evil fruit, and the historian who disregards or minimizes the effects of this fundamental factor is hardly doing service to the Russian people."[1]

Despite such progressive achievements as the emancipation of the serfs, the growth of the *zemstvos*, the great industrialization of the country, the increase in literacy, the rise of serious publications, and the extension of the school system, Russia nonetheless entered the twentieth century as a backward nation in political, economic, religious, social, and cultural affairs. This view is supported by Andrew D. White, an American who first resided in Russia in 1854-55 as an attache of the U. S. Legation in St. Petersburg. In 1892 he was appointed U. S. Minister to Russia. During the interim of 37 years White had heard much about the reforms and progress under Alexander II and Alexander III and he looked forward to observing the new conditions. He found some technical advances, particularly in the field of railway transportation, but no change in the life of the ordinary people. White reported that "the *muzhik* remained, to all appearances, what he was before. . . . The old impressions [returned] so vividly that I seemed not to have been absent a week. The old atmosphere of repression was evident everywhere." Later experiences served only to strengthen these opinions: "I stayed long in Russia before and after the emancipation of the peasants. I do not want to question the noble intentions of Alexander II and his collaborators, but I must say that if there is at all any difference in the peasants' situation before the reform and after it, it is hardly noticeable."[2]

Since this chapter will be concerned primarily with the status of school teachers during the reign of the last Tsar, it will deal chiefly with the material and psychological conditions in which the teacher lived and worked. But the fact must always be borne in mind that the laws, the customs, and the relationships which governed the teacher also in a large part were the concern of his fellow-citizens in factory, farm, and marketplace. Moreover, as an intellectual the teacher shared the lot of all others who worked with brain instead of hand. The role of the teacher has significance beyond that of other citizens only because it is through the teacher more than through any other channel that society deliberately attempts to instill in the youth the ideals, habits, and outlooks which seem most essential to social and personal survival. Therefore, an examination of the status of the teacher in Russia in the closing years of Tsardom can provide a key both to the efforts made to sustain the regime and to the reasons why those efforts so miserably failed.

Unfortunately, the conditions under which the teachers of Russia lived had become no more attractive as the need for their services grew with the expanding school system. One authority states that teachers "had always been lacking in Russia, due, of course, to the fundamental poverty of institutions for training them, as well as to the restrictions which hedged them round, and the very poor pay granted for their services." [3] Thus, no matter how hard the government and other agencies strove to select and train good teachers, those persons who entered the profession soon found themselves disillusioned regarding its prospects. The report of the Chief Procurator of the Holy Synod in 1899, for example, pointed out that only 5 per cent of school teachers served more than ten years, 20 per cent more than five years, and 37 per cent more than three years; moreover, nearly one-fourth of the new teachers failed to complete even their first year. The report concludes that the only ideal common to all members of the teaching profession is the hope of finding a better post in some other line of work.[4] The author who cites this report states that thousands of school teachers quit their jobs and became saloonkeepers when the government took over the sale of liquor, and he inquires: "Why should they not? They are subjected to all sorts of ill treatment and abuse on the part of petty officers, and their average remuneration for their hard work is less than that of a skilled factory hand. In 1900 their salaries did not exceed 250 rubles a year; 45.6 per cent of the school teachers received less than 200 rubles, and 26.6 per cent less than 100 rubles," the ruble at that time being worth fifty cents in United States money.[5]

Salaries in *zemstvo* elementary schools varied considerably, since outlying districts usually paid more than metropolitan areas, except for Moscow. In 1912, a teacher in Tula might receive 195 rubles a year while another in Ekaterinaslav would get 430 rubles for the same services. The average for all *zemstvo* teachers was still from 200 to 300 rubles a year. Some *zemstvos* had a stable salary scale with increments, others paid according to the education of the teacher, still others paid men more than women.[6] Despite the fact that *zemstvo* teachers often enjoyed greater authority, prestige, and freedom than did the urban teachers, such low salaries forced many of them to seek other fields of employment.[7] The material conditions of secondary school teachers were no better, except that they could be promoted to inspectorships after serving 20-25 years.[8]

The government made several attempts to offer greater inducements to candidates for the profession. In 1900, Minister of Public Education Bogolepov created a pension fund for teachers, established temporary pedagogical courses in many localities, and relaxed the restrictions on pedagogical conferences.[9] But the pensions were small, the courses inadequate both in quality and in number, and government officials continued to discourage collective action on the part of the teachers. Early in 1904, for example, the third congress of representatives of professional and technical education met in St. Petersburg, and almost immediately shared the same fate as many *zemstvo* and student meetings described in the preceding chapter. The day after the congress opened, the governor of the city ordered it adjourned on the grounds that some of the delegates had made "revolutionary" speeches. Several of the delegates were banished from the city, an act which aroused great indignation among teachers throughout the country.[10]

In 1907 a bill sought to remedy the situations wherein many teachers had to deal with large groups of pupils, segregated by sexes, all day and night during the school week, since many pupils did not return to their distant homes except on Sundays. This bill would have erected more local schools, allowed groups of boys and girls to study together, and limited classes to fifty pupils per teacher. But the bill was never passed, and these conditions continued as before.[11] Again, in 1912, a bill was introduced in the Duma to provide salary increments to teachers with five or more years of service; this, too, failed to get the approval of the government.[12]

It must also be remembered that many persons experiencing the material hardships of the teaching profession had undergone similar experiences as students. One authority states categorically that "of all European students, the Russian students were certainly the most impecunious. . . . Poverty was something quite normal" in their lives; he also mentions that other observers have named "their impecunious condition as one of the main causes of discontent and disturbance." [13]

The same author declares that "of all this pre-revolutionary period [up to 1917] the most trying years for the Russian universities were the last decade before the War." In the year 1913, he says, 53 per cent of all Russian university students were impecunious. At Dorpat, the figure was 83 per cent; at St. Petersburg, 72 per cent of men students and 82 per cent of women students were in this category. "The

University of Kiev, with only 45 per cent of its students poverty-stricken, had the best record in this connection of all universities in Russia." [14] Teaching as a career probably did not frighten such students so far as income was concerned, but neither did it attract those who desired to improve their circumstances.

Low salaries, however, were only one of the many disadvantages suffered by teachers. One traveller in Russia in 1910-1912 summed up the situation as follows: "The Russian village teacher has a poor and miserable existence. His surroundings are wretched, his home one room, his salary a minimum, [on which it is] absolutely impossible to keep a family. A friendship with any 'suspected' person is sufficient to make him lose his post, and it often happens that a master is discharged on the evidence offered by 'well-meaning' persons who have some petty spite against him. Once discharged, no inspector will give him a post elsewhere." [15] The effect that such repressions can have upon a sensitive teacher is well illustrated in the case of one who ran the gamut of experiences from sincerity and love of her fellowmen to murder and death on the gallows. Although certainly too extreme to be classed as typical, this case reveals that teachers endured much the same psychological tortures as did the students described in the preceding chapter, and that some teachers reacted in the same way.

Zinaida Konopliannikova was born of moderately poor parents in St. Petersburg in 1879. After leaving elementary school, she graduated with honors from a six-year vocational school and then completed a three-year course in teacher training at St. Petersburg. Her education being well above that of the average applicant, she had no difficulty in obtaining a position, finally selecting a small town in one of the Baltic provinces. Here she became disgusted with the strong program of Russification and with the obsolete course of study, and after one year obtained a transfer to a school in Peterhoff, near St. Petersburg. Her own words best describe her reaction to conditions there:

"In front of the school lived a gendarme, behind the school lived a police official, on the mountain nearby lived a priest, next to him a clergyman, and all of them were constantly reporting me to my superiors. If I arranged popular readings or discussions of the most innocent nature, the clergyman reported to the inspector that 'the school teacher was engaged in discussions and readings which had nothing to do with regular school work,' the priest kept busy writing to his superiors that the teacher was founding sects, spreading [Leo] Tolstoy's doctrines, and demoralizing the younger generation. If I arranged theatrical performances, the police official and the gendarme would immediately get busy. As a consequence, the inspector, the school board, and the Governor were constantly calling on me for explanations. Two and a half years I taught in that village, until the school board finally dismissed me. I gave up my profession without regret. . . . I saw that under such circumstances one could not even dream about the harmonious development of the spirit and intellect of the individual. I saw the necessity for first creating the conditions under which the development of what is best in human nature will be possible. I saw the prime necessity for the struggle with the autocratic and despotic Government. I became a revolutionist."

Thereafter, Zinaida began to do propaganda work among the employees in St. Petersburg factories. Arrested several times, persecuted often, she fled abroad for a brief time. She returned because she had decided that there was no way of bringing about peaceful reform in Russia. Again her own words: "Life itself has taught me as follows—you cannot create anything new without first destroying the old; if you cannot pierce an idea with a bayonet, neither can you resist the power of a bayonet with ideas only. I became a terrorist." In the summer of 1906, Zinaida shot General Mien, head of the notorious Semionovsky Guards, and was herself executed in August of that year at the age of twenty-seven.[16] From student to teacher to revolutionist to terrorist—more than a few intellectuals of the period followed this same deadly progression.

Yet such acts of terrorism do not account for the lack of influence which the teachers of Russia had over the people in the last few years before the downfall of the regime. Rather was it that so many of the teachers themselves failed to keep pace with the growing radical sentiment. For example, in the spring of 1917 a report on conditions in twenty-eight provinces of Russia was made for the Provisional Committee of the Fourth Duma. This report revealed that the peasants had lost all interest in the War and were preoccupied with their own affairs, just as the author quoted in the first part of this chapter has stated.

According to the report, the peasants were particularly desirous of the abolition of private property in land, saying that "land must belong to the people as a whole." They also wanted more education, especially through the means of books written in terms they could understand. On the subject of schools and teachers the report says that "the attitude of the peasants toward the schools differs a great deal. Some of them ask for an extension of the curricula of the elementary schools which would make it possible for students to enter secondary schools. On the other hand, the peasants of . . . a number of provinces declare: 'We don't want these school teachers, they are too costly. The ex-service men will soon get home from the army and they will teach the children free of charge.' An illiterate peasant, who never went to school himself, is extremely reluctant to contribute for the maintenance of schools. He wants free schools, free books, and free teachers." [17]

Such an attitude on the part of the peasants indicates that they had not lost faith in education itself but in the representatives and purveyors of education which the government and the *zemstvos* had produced. This conclusion is confirmed in later passages of the same report which point out that the peasants "are decidedly unwilling to elect educated people to their institutions. The attitude gaining ground among them says virtually: 'There is no room for the intelligentsia among us. We shall ourselves look after our own affairs'. . . . It is true that school teachers are occasionally elected chairmen of the *volost* [local] committees; but such are exclusively men who follow the peasants' wishes, owe their success to this policy, and exercise no restraining influence. . . . School teachers, especially women teachers, . . . have nothing in common with the peasants and enjoy no authority. Even those representatives of the intelligentsia in whom the peasants have always seen a friendly interest and whom, in the early days of the [February] Revolution, they themselves unanimously elected chairmen of their committees, are now being removed." [18]

In view of this wholesale popular contempt for the professional and civic value of the teacher, it is well to inquire into the type of preparation through which candidates for the profession passed. Conditions of pedagogical work, already described, obviously could not inspire reciprocal respect between teachers and the public. But what about the problem of training teachers which had so often occupied the attention of Russian officials and philosophers since the days of Catherine II? Had efforts to solve this problem ceased entirely under Tsar Nicholas II? The answer is, of course, in the negative, for the period 1894-1917 witnessed several attempts to improve the system of teacher training; furthermore, some of these attempts came from sources which were either nonexistent or largely unknown during earlier periods.

Before analyzing the methods utilized to prepare teachers, it is advisable to consider the physical facilities devoted to this purpose. As mentioned before, such facilities in Russia had never been adequate, but astounding progress was made in the last years of the regime. In 1910, for example, there were in all Russia only 102 institutions devoted to the training of teachers, with only 9,295 trainees enrolled. Of this number, 15 of the agencies were teachers institutes preparing 1,041 students for secondary school work, while 87 were teachers seminaries attended by 8,254 candidates for posts in elementary schools.[19] Two years later, the number of institutes had increased to 20, and of seminaries to 98. Then, in the brief period 1912-1916, 28 new institutes and 91 seminaries were opened, bringing the total numbers, respectively, to 48 and 126. In addition to these formal agencies, there were also, in 1915, about 150 pedagogical courses with curricula covering from one to three years of study.[20] It should also be remembered that many graduates of the universities entered the teaching profession with no special training at all outside their chosen subjects.[21]

One astute observer, Professor Bernard Pares, makes an interesting comparison between the methods employed in a teachers seminary operating directly under the Ministry of Public Education and those followed in a similar institution run by the Tver *zemstvo*.[22] Although his visits to these schools took place in 1904-05, when only five *zemstvos* had teachers seminaries, the major portion of his report possesses validity for the succeeding decade also.[23] Pares visited the Ministry seminary first, and found the physical plant quite adequate for the 90 students, who ranged in age from fifteen to twenty-two years. The four-year curriculum included the subjects which the graduates expected to teach, plus courses in history, geometry, arithmetic, algebra, Russian literature, natural history, and physics. No foreign language was offered. In addition to teaching his own subject, each teacher acted as tutor or preceptor for one of the classes all the time and took turns in charge of all the students at recess periods. The Director was solely responsible for the practice work in teaching, which was confined to the two last years. In the third year the students wrote essays on how to teach and these were corrected by the Director; in the fourth year they were assigned practice teaching in the model elementary school which was attached to the seminary. The seminary staff did not supervise this practice (until 1911), but left this matter to the principal of the elementary school. As one student taught, the others observed, and in the evening the whole class discussed the merits and demerits of the lesson with the Director, who offered his own opinions and summation. No examinations were held in any subject. Upon graduation, the candidate selected the school in which he wished to teach, and the Director wrote in his behalf to the Curator of the proper educational circuit.[24]

Professor Pares found the *zemstvo* seminary much less formal and more democratic than the Ministry institution. All such *zemstvo* agencies were required to have a governing board, and this one consisted of the Director of the seminary, his assistant in charge of studies, several representatives of the *zemstvo* itself, and one representative of the Ministry of Public Education. The last-named official had only one vote, like the others, but his opinion was final on such matters as admission of students with criminal records. In some cases, says Pares, the Ministry representative went so far as to close a *zemstvo* school because of some minor infraction on the part of the students.

The seminary at Tver had twenty teachers, and a fine comradely spirit existed among them. The 160 students were divided into five classes of equal size; all were girls and half were of peasant origin. No individual punishments were inflicted: when an offense was committed, the offender's entire class was lectured and reprimanded. The course of study and program of activity were similar to those of the Ministry seminary, but Pares considered the *zemstvo* school superior because it had better teachers and better supervision of work. Of the 600 graduates of the seminary up to 1905, however, only half had remained in the teaching profession, most of the others having married.[25] In later years, the *zemstvos* not only established more teachers seminaries but also organized courses to improve the qualifications of teachers in service.[26]

Thus the machinery for the training of teachers, though still too small in scope to meet the needs of a growing school system, was at least attempting to live up to its quantitative requirements. Although there was no established system of methodology common to all types of training institutions, many disparate efforts were being made to find the methods which suited the particular situation. But what about the *aims* of teacher education? Was there a more or less universal goal toward which these agencies were supposed to strive? Was there a set pattern indicating what sort of person the Russian school teacher should be? And if such a goal or pattern existed, who defined its character?

The answers to these questions will furnish a better evaluation of Russian teacher education than will statistics on physical capacity or analyses of method. One might expect that in an autocratic society the aims of all types of education would be clearly specified, and that the deciding factor in this delineation would be the will and judgment of the ruling authorities. So it was in Russia: in a series of rescripts and decrees the Tsar and the Ministry of Public Education stated patently their desires in regard to the purposes of teacher education. But Russia, even in the early part of the twentieth century, was ruled not only by Crown and Council, but also by the hierarchy of the established Church. In its attempt to satisfy all three branches of this trinity, the Ministry of Public Education was forced to reiterate the time-worn formula: Orthodoxy, Autocracy, and Nationalism.

In the preceding chapter, mention was made of the Commission of Inquiry called in session early in 1900 by Minister Bogolepov. The Circular which set forth the tasks of this Commission outlined very clearly the aims of public education in Russia, and it was of further importance to teachers because the Commission itself was composed almost entirely of educators. Article 5 of this Circular is devoted to the "moral aims" of education: "The question of moral training in the wide sense deserves still greater attention [than does physical training]. Though it is precisely in regard to this side of life that the school finds itself most dependent on the moral standard of the family and society in general, it is nevertheless bound to do all that lies in its power to develop in those who come under its influence a will directed by moral and religious principle. The Commission will therefore have to consider what means can be adopted to assist the development in scholars of genuine religious feeling, of sincere attachment and devotion to their Emperor and country, of the sense of duty, honour, truthfulness, respect for authority, and the like, having in view not a mere system of formal precepts, but also measures which shall permeate the every-day life of the school." [27] A few years later, in 1907, a new set of Regulations for Teachers Seminaries stated categorically that "your chief duty is to instill religion and inspire your pupils with a love for attendance on God's worship." [28]

In order that such aims might govern every school and teacher training establishment in Russia, the government took great care to center in its hands the control of as much of the educational system as possible. By 1914 the entire country had been divided into thirteen educational circuits, and in charge of each circuit was a Curator appointed by the Minister of Public Education. The powers of these curators had ebbed and flowed at various periods, but toward the end of the regime their authority was stronger than ever before. The Curator was head of all the educational institutions in his district, and he appointed the teachers of all the secondary schools and the principals of the elementary schools. His power in the smaller towns was almost unlimited, extending even to the right to introduce any new method of teaching for which he could gain the approval of the Ministry.[29] Nor did most curators fail to exercise these privileges: "the dismissal of teachers, reported to be radical or opposed to the autocracy, was a common matter. Thinking men and women were looked upon as enemies."[30]

Although the *zemstvo* schools did enjoy somewhat more autonomy, they were technically under the jurisdiction of the Ministry, and it has been pointed out earlier in this chapter that cases had occurred where one Ministry representative was able to close an entire school because of his disapproval on even a minor issue.[31] The schools under the jurisdiction of the Holy Synod were, of course, even more tightly controlled at the center. Thus, of the approximately 100,000 schools in Russia in 1911, two agencies—the Ministry of Public Education and the Holy Synod—ruled all but about 2,700.[32] "Not a country school or church could be built which was not planned in St. Petersburg."[33]

Anton Chekhov, in his story entitled "A Lot of Paper," uses the device of letters supposed to be exchanged between bureaucrats attempting to deal with an epidemic in a village school. The initial report of the outbreak is sent "through channels" on November 19, and the wheels of bureaucracy commence to grind. By the time the order for the closing of the school is delivered on February 22, the epidemic has long since passed.[34] There is no record of whether this incident actually occurred, and if so, whether its results were disastrous or simply amusing. But there are many other records which reveal how strong was the arm of the government during the reign of Nicholas II, and how this bureaucracy was made to work most efficiently in some respects. The censorship of publications, being closely connected with education and particularly with the interests of teachers, will serve to illustrate the effectiveness of the government's methods in matters considered vital to the welfare of the nation.

Writing in 1907, one historian points out that "no book can be printed in Russia that is not previously approved by the government censor. From the beginning of printing in Russia up to 1895 something over 75,000 works were printed with the permission of the Government. But the man who will assume that the common people may read these books is mistaken. Only such of the printed books as are especially approved by the department [Ministry] of public education may be kept in elementary or secondary school libraries or in libraries established for the use of teachers of the primary schools and gymnasiums, and of the 75,000 titles but 5,635 books are admitted in such libraries, i.e., but eight per cent of the books which the censor allowed to be printed. The percentage is actually much smaller, because many of these books were published in numerous editions, and every edition was newly registered. Out of these 5,635 books, 3,288 are school textbooks. There are, therefore, but 2,347 books and pamphlets which the workingman, the schoolboy, and the teacher are permitted to read and to use for their intellectual and moral advancement." [35]

Rather than relax its grip upon the press in later years, the government chose to impose even greater restrictions. "The press was hampered in many ways: heavy fines were laid for 'false news' about the Government or for anything that might be declared anti-governmental instigation; and, as a measure of 'extraordinary protection,' a paper could be suppressed."[36] The following table shows the year-by-year increase in penalties imposed by the government for violations of censorship regulations (amount of fines are minimal estimates):[37]

YEAR	NUMBER OF PENALTIES	FINES IN RUBLES
1906	16	15,525
1907	148	65,000
1908	120	82,200
1909	182	87,375
1910	243	60,150
1911	268	73,450
1912	317	96,800
1913	340	129,000
Totals for 8 years	1,634	609,500

Nor were dismissals and censorship the favorite means employed by the autocracy to mold the populace to its will. In the same years noted above, 1906-1913, "there took place 3,282 executions by trial."[38] In other words, for each censorship fine imposed, two persons met death for their antagonism to the regime. Alexander Hertzen is quoted as saying in the 1860's that "the history of Russian thinkers is a long list of martyrs and a register of convicts."[39] A number of later writers bear witness to the fact that the remaining six decades of Tsardom made these lists too long to measure.[40] "Thus, by strictly controlled agencies of schools, universities, Church, press and assemblies, an effort was made to form an official collective mind, loyal to autocracy, Orthodoxy, national destiny, caste-society; and filled with hatred and distrust of individual freedom, self-government, dissent in religion, and nationalities."[41]

Lest it be thought that the Church schools made some attempt to counteract these tendencies, another author declares unequivocally that "it would be rash to say that the principal object of these schools is to save people from ignorance; they seem to be chiefly the outcome of government tactics—to have been established as bulwarks against Liberalism rather than as a help for the poor. They are eminently religious: every teaching is subordinate to the religious teaching; and to the maxims of loyalty to be instilled into the children. The development of their intelligence is of small importance provided they can praise God according to the rites of the Church, and pay the Tsar the respect and gratitude to which he is entitled. Such is a dispassionate account of the religious and parochial schools." [42] That religious dogma was given not only lip service but actually put seriously to work is indicated by the fact that of a total of about 200,000 teachers in Russia in 1911, nearly 50,000—or one-fourth—were "ordained teacher-priests." With a national average of only 1.5 lay teachers per school in 1911, both the Ministry and the Synod insisted upon one teacher of religion for every two schools.[43] The following year, a new set of regulations for Advanced Elementary Schools required that there be a teacher of religion in *each* school of this type.[44]

Did this concentration upon religion, allegiance, and stern moral character find support among the people of Russia? Did it result in greater piety, loyalty, and morality? Several answers have already been given in this chapter: the apathy of most peasants toward cultural questions, the growing contempt for educated persons, the ever rising number of assassinations and retributive executions, and the great increase in anti-government sentiment in the press. But there were still other effects, less spectacular, perhaps, but no less insidious.

Note, for example, the findings of a *zemstvo* statistician regarding the total expenditures during the year 1909 of 107 representative families in the Kostroma *guberniya*, just two hundred miles northeast of Moscow. The report itemizes *in part* the expenditures of all 107 families as follows: [45]

Education	
schools	12 rubles
books	34 rubles
Religion	
payments to the clergy	589 rubles
oil, incense, etc.	505 rubles
gifts to the poor	89 rubles
Funerals and weddings	693 rubles
Vodka	1,671 rubles

Obviously, although the peasants continued to give money to the Church when it was demanded, the surcease provided by intoxication was deemed more valuable.

Intellectuals suffered increasingly from neurasthenia, and sexuality and mysticism became excessive in artistic circles. In the five-year period immediately following the Revolution of 1905, more than 45,000 persons committed suicide. In St. Petersburg alone, the number of suicides doubled between 1905 and 1907, and doubled again in 1909; the five-year total for this capital city was 10 percent of all the cases in the nation. That most of the suicides were young is shown by 1,000 cases in Moscow in 1908-09: 73 were in their forties, 117 in their thirties, 313 in their twenties, and 426 under twenty years of age.[46] At a congress of Russian physicians early in 1910, one of the doctors read the following suicide note from a 20-year-old student in Odessa: "To live as I would is impossible now, and live as it is possible I cannot. . . . I cannot witness atrocities and suffering, cannot bear the complaints and sobs of the oppressed, and at the same time feel my impotence to solace, however little, this horror that is life. And I am going out of life, for there is nothing to live for." [47]

These conditions, then, were the end product of the Russian system of education. One may well ask what was the fatal weakness in the system, why so many high motives resulted in such low morality. The whole answer, of course, may never be found, but one scholar with an interest in Russia covering half a century offers at least a partial explanation. Writing in 1907, this author declares that "the Russian Government hampers the intellectual development of the student in the name of morality, but it does not provide for him any moral training at all. In England the education of character is considered to be more important than the informing of the mind. In Russia it is the moral control that is absent. . . . Nowhere is the incompleteness of Russia's moral education more clear than in the life of the students. . . . These will usually have discovered for themselves some special reason for dissenting from the ordinary view. . . . There is no cultivation of discipline, no conscious control. . . . Spies dressed in their [student] uniform sit with them at their lectures; attempts have even been made to use the professors for the purposes of police work. . . . Every effort is made to dissolve any grouping of the students, to morally confine them in separate cells." [48]

Despite all the efforts to change this situation in the last decade of the regime, it remained in 1917 much as pictured above. A much later observer has realized in retrospect that what was most needed in Russia was the formation of "a numerous, strong, and materially independent teachers' class that would be capable of educating the young generation to take pride in belonging to the great Russian people and to love their country instead of holding it in contempt. For teachers of all classes of the population had for many years indulged in wholesale criticism of everything Russian—Russian system of government, Russian social order, and even Russian history. The result had been to breed contempt for everything Russian." [49] The unbiased witness might be justified in concluding that some of this contempt was deserved. For many voices were lifted, from the 1860's onward, in demand for the type of government and social order—yes, and system of education too—which would have warranted less criticism and might even have changed the course of Russian history. It is time now to turn to a review of some of the reforms outlined in these expressions of discontent, especially as they applied to education and the training of teachers.

11

Pioneers in Russian Educational Philosophy

THE PREVIOUS CHAPTERS OF THIS VOLUME have described some of the more important personalities and ideas concerned with education which appeared in Russia in the seventeenth, eighteenth, and nineteenth centuries. The early church fathers—Peter Mogila, Simeon Polotskii, and the leaders of the Lutsk Brotherhood—had clear concepts both of the role of education in society and of the means necessary to make this role an active one. Tsar Peter I was no philosopher, but he realized that sectarian domination of the schools meant sectarian domination of the nation, and, with the sympathetic assistance of V. N. Tatishchev and Feofan Prokopovich, he sought throughout his reign to establish state control of education. Peter's wholesale importation of foreign scholars and students was a shrewd move in his plan to wrest monopoly of education from the Church without facing the danger of having it pass to another organized group in Russia such as the military or the boyars.

Mikhail Lomonosov, whose grasp of many branches of science was amazing for the eighteenth century, reorganized the infant Russian Academy of Sciences into a powerful cultural instrument, albeit that its influence was long confined to the upper classes.[1] As is well known, the wide acquaintance which Catherine II had with foreign philosophers—Voltaire, Diderot, von Grimm, de Mirievo, and others—influenced her mind if not her heart, and certainly injected into Russian philosophy the concept of an education based upon broad social principles. Moreover, Catherine and her advisers were able to put some of their ideals into practice through the founding of many state schools.

The beginning of the nineteenth century witnessed the creation of the Ministry of Public Education and the subsidiary provincial administrative organs. Although the reactionary Holy Synod opposed nearly every step in the establishment of a state system of education, such a system had become a reality by 1825, due largely to the wisdom and energy of such men as Count P. V. Zavadovskii, Mikhail Muraviev, and for a time even Prince A. N. Golitsyn. After the next three decades of stern reaction, during most of which the educational system was dominated by the learned and able, but extremely conservative, Count S. S. Uvarov, Russia entered upon the period of the Great Reforms. Not only did the Empire have for nearly forty years a most enlightened monarch, but it was also blessed with a number of capable civil officials, among whom might be listed four Ministers of Public Education—Golovnin, Dmitri Tolstoi, Saburov, and Delianov—if one neglects to raise the question of social philosophy. For it can be noted that all the persons mentioned in the preceding few paragraphs had one quality in common: regardless of certain variations in social attitudes and methods of work, they were invariably complete supporters of the Imperial regime and thus enjoyed, for a time at least, the favor of the current Government.

But it was also during this period, which has been called Russia's "Age of Enlightenment," that a great many individuals, publications, and institutions arose to expound other ideas than those which the Autocracy held acceptable. Among the institutions, the *zemstvos* were by far the most important, and they have been described adequately for present purposes in previous chapters. Since behind each radical publication there was at least one insurgent individual, it is best to consider both these elements together. Even though such elements sometimes varied considerably in aims, approach and methods, they, like the loyal officials, had one possession shared by all: in this case, however, the common denominator was deep-seated dissatisfaction with the *status quo*.

Some of the dissident writings simply preached idealistic principles unwelcome to the government, while others urged specific reforms. Still others called for a complete regeneration of the social system, and a few sounded the clarion for the forceful overthrow of the regime. But, regardless of the degree of violence or the areas of change recommended, these rebellious voices almost invariably had something to say about education. And in this interest they had enough precedent to constitute almost a heritage, for countless earlier dissenters had brought this matter within the compass of both their invective and their aspirations.

For example, Nikolai Novikov (1744-1818) had incurred the undying enmity of Catherine II because he insisted that her budding system of education bring teachers and pupils into closer contact with their own communities through such radical devices as excursions, field trips, and local sociological projects. Discharged from his civil service post, Novikov continued to expound his ideas through the organs of his own publishing company and the channels provided by his Friendly Learning Society, until Catherine finally sent him to prison.[2] Alexander Radishchev (c.1750-1802) suffered a like fate at the hands of this "liberal" Empress: the sentence of death imposed for his authorship of a book demanding constitutional government and a free press in Russia was commuted to exile in Siberia, but soon after his release Radishchev committed suicide.[3]

The writer Ryleev (1795-1826) "atoned on the gallows for his endeavor to be a poet and citizen." He edited an opposition journal called *Polar Star* (a name later chosen by Alexander Hertzen for a similar publication) and took part in the Decembrist uprising of 1825.[4] Peter Y. Chaadaev (1793-1856) was author of the famous *Philosophical Letters* which stressed the desirability of the unity of Russian and European culture as against the isolation imposed upon the former by its autocratic rulers. For this act he was considered so dangerous a revolutionary that, by personal order of Nicholas I, he was declared insane and forbidden to write even in his home.[5]

It was also during the reign of Nicholas I that the great Russian literary critic, Vissarion G. Belinskii (1811-1848), flourished without encountering any greater punishment than mere expulsion from Moscow University for having written a drama protesting against serfdom. Strongly influenced by the German philosophers Hegel and Feuerbach, Belinskii later became converted to the doctrines of the French socialists. But his was a highly individualistic socialism, wherein the criminal would find his own punishment without any move on the part of the State, couples in love would live together without holy wedlock and separate when they wished, and no one would be either poor or rich.[6] Yet Belinskii, who was often inconsistent, held that the state was responsible for the education of its citizens; this education should be for everyone and should inculcate "respect for the name of man, . . . without any reference to him as an individual or to his nationality, religion or rank, or even to his personal dignity; in a word, unbounded love and unbounded respect for mankind even as represented by the least of its members. . . ." [7] To prove that his ideas were practical, Belinskii for years carried on an active campaign for better textbooks in the schools, and wrote specifications for their form and content.[8] While Belinskii was able to continue his writing and still remain a free man (although under surveillance) in Russia, his colleague Alexander Hertzen (1812-1870) was twice exiled by Nicholas I before fleeing abroad in 1847, there to reside for the remainder of his life. Hertzen, too, was preoccupied with the problem of individualism in an organized society, but he attempted to reconcile the apparent conflicts between personal liberty and collective action. Although greatly concerned with systems of ethics, Hertzen ultimately decided that there were no fixed moral laws to govern this reconciliation, and that each society and each age had to work out the solution for itself. He favored socialism as a political-economic system, but wanted to see it extended internationally as a "confraternity of nations" rather than as a "confraternity of men." Thus he appears to trust governments more than people, although he states categorically that the latter must control the former. While most of his colleagues deplored the "backwardness" of Russia and the practice of the peasant commune, Hertzen prophesied that these very factors would make it easier to introduce socialism because of the lack of strong ties with Western capitalism. He was also a keen student of Russian psychology, and often spoke of the Russian inability to temporize: everything must be adjudged as either good or bad.[9]

Hertzen was too concerned with the broad elements of social philosophy to pay more than passing attention to education, but he did characterize the educational system under Nicholas I as "one of the most frightful infringements" of human rights because back of every school, every teacher, stood the gendarmes of the Tsar. He also spoke vigorously against the factor of nationalism in education, and for better teaching of literature, history and physical science.[10]

Of the writers, educators, and philosophers mentioned above, Belinskii and Hertzen did most to usher in the "Golden Age" of Russian pedagogical thought. In the words of a prominent Soviet educational historian, "at the beginning of the 19th century in the works of A. Hertzen and V. Belinskii, and in the 60's in the works of N. Chernyshevskii and N. Dobroliubov, a new pedagogical tendency arose, 'the pedagogy of revolutionary democracy,' which was quite original and, at that time, the most progressive in the world. . . . The 60's of the 19th century saw the flourishing of Russian pedagogical thought. During this decade the great Russian pedagogues K. Ushinskii, N. Pirogov, L. Tolstoi, N. Chernyshevskii, N. Dobroliubov and a number of specialists in teaching methods . . . wrote books which brought much which was new and valuable to the science of pedagogy. . . . Belinskii, Chernyshevskii and Dobroliubov fought against the suppression of the child's personality, demanded the development of his creative powers, and regarded education as the training of a citizen, of a fighter for democracy." [11]

While the above quotation serves as a fair summary of the educational ideas of these writers, each of them deserves at least brief individual attention here. Nikolai G. Chernyshevskii (1828-1889), like Alexander Hertzen, was interested in many other matters than education and, although he deals with this problem in more than fifty articles and letters, his activity centered upon political economy. According to one historian, his "ideas of socialism and his plans for the solution of the agrarian question were the starting point of all revolutionary programs of the 'sixties onwards." [12] Chernyshevskii was an outright revolutionary socialist who, again like Hertzen, condoned the existence of communal property in Russia because it meant there would be fewer private-property customs to be overthrown by socialism. He agreed with Belinskii that Feuerbach's materialism constituted a better philosophical basis than did Hegel's idealism, and also that such French socialists as Fourier and St. Simon offered the best plan for the new society to come.[13] On the way toward this new society, the masses must be educated to fight for the overthrow of the old regime; once socialism is established, the masses must have general education in order that they can improve their conditions of life. The role of the teacher is of great importance, says Chernyshevskii, for he must not only lead the pupils into self-activity but also stand as a model for them to emulate.[14]

In most of these views, Nikolai A. Dobroliubov (1836-1861) concurred. He, too, was a Feuerbachian, but he believed that ideas govern the world. With Chernyshevskii he was co-editor of *Sovremennik* (The Contemporary), a magazine which had wide influence in the radical movements of the time. Dobroliubov's educational writings far outnumber those of his main colleague, and he was far more interested in the practical details of the problem. Strongly influenced by Pestalozzi, he adopted the principle of self-activity and urged all teachers to pay close attention to the child's natural development. While Chernyshevskii asked that the teacher be a model of action, Dobroliubov believed it more important that he be a model of morality and ethical conduct, particularly in his relations with his pupils. In addition to a good general education and firm grasp of his own subject, the teacher, according to Dobroliubov, must assist in rearing a generation of free men who will resist autocratic authority.[15]

One of the many school practices which Dobroliubov attacked ferociously was the use of corporal punishment. Despite the fact that several Ministerial decrees and circulars had attempted to discourage this practice, Dobroliubov found by examining reports of the individual educational circuits that it had by no means been discontinued. In a widely read article he publicized the fact that among 4,109 pupils in ten urban gymnasiums there were 308 thrashings administered in the year 1858 alone.[16]

Another educational writer who took a great interest in the abolition of corporal punishment was N. I. Pirogov (1810-1881), a surgeon whose article entitled "Questions of Life" in 1856 brought so much acclaim that he was noticed by the Ministry of Public Education. As Curator of the Odessa, and later the Kiev, educational circuit, Pirogov found it impossible to stop the thrashings by outright administrative order, so he discouraged them by the subtle use of persuasion and mild regulations. But his chief ire was reserved for bureaucratic methods of administration, and he constantly proposed that local school boards be given greater authority. Believing that work should be done for its own sake, he opposed the system of marks, examinations, and rewards, and introduced extra-curricular discussion periods which were a complete novelty in Russia. At the university level, Pirogov observed that the lectures of the professors merely repeated orally the material in the textbooks; thereupon, he proposed that the lectures be utilized to clarify the obscure points of the text and to develop new concepts. Finally, he recommended that higher education be free to all, and that university staffs be chosen by public competition rather than by either appointment or election. With such radical ideas as these, it is no wonder that one historian says that Pirogov "brought fresh life into all grades of the schools." [17]

Although all the men whose educational ideas are described above wanted fundamental reforms in the Russian system of education, all of them except Belinskii wished to preserve a considerable amount of teacher authority in the schools, and even he thought education should be compulsory. But there was another great writer of the period whose educational views came much closer to the "free school" ideas of the later decades of the nineteenth century: this was Leo Nikolaevich Tolstoi (1828-1910), famous author of *War and Peace*, *Anna Karenina*, and other novels. Mention has already been made in Chapter Eight of Tolstoi's school at Yasnaia Poliana, where pupils and teachers were encouraged to work together in complete harmony and independence.

Tolstoi had no higher respect for the Russian schools than did his more politically radical contemporaries, but he opposed all efforts toward further systemization of administration, increase of academic requirements for teachers, modernization of curriculum, etc. His solution was for all schools to allow the child free expression of its individuality, instead of crushing such a universal urge by concentration upon methods. Education, he said, should be attractive but not compulsory: children should be enticed into the school rather than forced to attend. Each lesson must be planned to suit the needs and abilities of each child, and its completion must represent to him a concrete step forward in his education. The first quality required in the teacher is a love of his pupils, the second is a love of his work; if he possesses these two attributes it does not matter greatly whether he has book-knowledge. Thus the teacher's role becomes one of establishing such relations with the pupil as will bring about the latter's desire to learn, and then to share as much of the former's knowledge as seems advisable.[18] Although Tolstoi's ideas were practiced only in very limited educational circles in Russia, they had profound influence in Europe and America.

It was just the opposite in the cases of the other Russian philosophers: although the Tsarist Government actively tried to suppress their ideas and publications, even going so far as to imprison and exile Chernyshevskii for twenty-seven years on faked evidence,[19] many Russians read their works avidly. But abroad all except Hertzen remained almost unknown until the end of the nineteenth century. This situation was particularly odd because, in every case, the genesis of their radicalism had come from western Europe. Even under the despotic Nicholas I, socialistic ideas had crept into Russia from the West, and when the press got more freedom under Alexander II a great many foreign authors were translated: Spencer, Darwin, Mill, Buckle, Fourier, St. Simon and others. "The ideas and theories elaborated by these authors were the starting points for Russian writers and publicists." [20] The influence of these writers, both Russian and foreign, was particularly strong in the universities, which "from the 'sixties on . . . became the most sensitive barometer of public feeling" [21] and in the 'seventies "the chief homesteads of revolt." [22] Many professors as well as students took part in the movements fostered by the radical writers, and such pedagogical journals as *Uchitel* (The Teacher), *Pedagogicheskii Sbornik* (Pedagogical Collection) and *Zhurnal dlia Vospitaniia* (Journal of Education) had their origins in the activities of these writers or their disciples.[23]

This is all the more remarkable when it is realized that not one of the men described was an active teacher, and only two, Pirogov and Tolstoi, had direct contact with the school system. Not that educators remained aloof from these movements—many, in fact, were extremely active either in political or academic circles, or both. But their names were not so well known nor was their influence so great as to command national attention at the time: Korf, Stoiunin, Bunakov, Vodovozov, Ostrogorskii, Lesgaft, Redkin—all were great educators but all are of secondary importance in the history of Russian education.

Only one professionally trained and progressively inclined teacher of this period devoted a large part of his energy to the philosophy and organization of education: this teacher was Konstantin Dmitrievich Ushinskii (1824-1870) who was "in the fullest sense of the word, the founder of the Russian primary school and of pedagogical training for teachers." [24] An analysis of the ideas, activities, and influence of this man will perhaps explain why he is held in such high esteem in Russia even today.

Born in 1824 in Chernigov *guberniya*, Ushinskii grew up during the early part of the long period of reaction under Tsar Nicholas I. His father, a moderately well-to-do landowner, seems to have had little influence upon him, but his mother's deep religiousness made a lasting impression on the serious child. Ushinskii learned very early to apply himself independently to his studies and, after making a fine record in the gymnasium, he enrolled at Moscow University at the age of sixteen and graduated at twenty with high honors. Thus his years at the University coincided with one of the most brilliant periods in the history of that institution.[25]

Two years later, despite his youth, Ushinskii was appointed as Professor of Jurisprudence at the Demidov Lycée in Yaroslavl. His lectures were an immediate success, for they were based upon his already considerable erudition and delivered with all the fervor of his fresh and attractive personality. Although the ideas he expressed were by no means hostile to the Tsarist regime (he remained throughout his life a monarchist), Ushinskii did criticize the growing gulf between institutionalized law and the will of the people. When a series of Ministerial decrees in 1848 drastically curtailed whatever academic freedom had previously existed,[26] Ushinskii resigned his post rather than bear what he felt to be humiliation of his professional rights. In retaliation for this show of independence, he was forbidden by the Ministry of Public Education to engage in further teaching at any level, even in elementary schools. Since he had no private income, Ushinskii was forced to take a niggling civil service position which paid only 400 rubles a year, about one-tenth his professorial salary. In order to supplement this meager income, he did hack work as a translator of English pedagogical articles, and in 1852 began to contribute his own writings to *Sovremennik* (The Contemporary) and *Bibliotek dlia Chteniia* (The Reading Library).[27]

When Alexander II became Tsar in 1855 there was an immediate relaxation of some of the more odious civil restrictions imposed by his predecessor, and many teachers discharged during the previous reign now found jobs again. That year Ushinskii accepted a double post as Inspector and teacher of literature and jurisprudence at Gatchinsk Institute. During the four years he occupied this post, he reorganized the entire program of the Institute along the lines of his progressive theories. At the same time, he continued his contributions to the professional periodicals *Pedagogicheskii Sbornik* (Pedagogical Collection) and *Zhurnal dlia vospitaniia* (Journal of Education). Three of his best known articles, "On the Uses of Pedagogical Literature," "On Nationalism in Public Education," and "The Three Elements of the School" appeared in 1857-58 and brought his name to the attention of educational leaders in the capital.

In 1859 Ushinskii was appointed to one of the most responsible school jobs in Russia—Inspector at Smolny Institute in St. Petersburg. Smolny was a good example of the European "finishing" school for girls of noble birth, so Ushinskii found much need of improvement. He employed several of the best teachers in the country, reduced the general course from nine to seven years, and converted the two years thus saved into an advanced pedagogical course for those students who wished to become teachers. In addition, he reorganized the entire curriculum, abolishing the obsolete courses and setting up more work in science, as well as shifting the language emphasis from French to Russian.

In 1860 Ushinskii became editor of the *Zhurnal Ministerstva Narodnogo Prosveshcheniia* (Journal of the Ministry of Public Education) and in two years completely changed its character. Under his editorship its focus was centered upon real problems of teaching, theories of pedagogy and psychology, accounts of educational activities, and criticism of current pedagogical literature.[28] His apartment in the Institute was a meeting place for students, teachers, writers, and others interested in new pedagogical ideas. "Smolny Institute became a laboratory to which were directed the eyes of everyone interested in education. Ushinskii's name became popularly known throughout Russia and at the end of his three years of work there he was already firmly established as one of the foremost teachers and guides of the educational movement in Russia, and as a teacher of teachers." [29]

Despite his personal popularity, enormous professional prestige, and even high standing with the Government, Ushinskii's progressive measures had created for him a number of enemies who in 1862 "initiated against [him] a campaign of slander and accusation." [30] He was discharged from his post at Smolny and also from the editorship of the *Journal*. Although the Empress Maria Alexandrovna herself came to his support, she was able only to mitigate some of his disgrace by arranging for him a long trip abroad. "This fact goes to show how powerful were the forces of opposition to all that was new and fresh in the life of the society." [31]

During the next five years, Ushinskii lived in Switzerland but made trips to Germany, Italy, and France in order to observe the school systems in these countries. In addition, he wrote reports on his travels, carried on several literary battles with his enemies in Russia, and did much research for his later books. He returned home in 1867 but still could find no teaching position in any Russian school. For the remaining three years of his life he devoted his waning energies to the St. Petersburg Pedagogical Society, an organization which he had helped establish in 1862 as an outgrowth of the meetings held in his Smolny apartment. He travelled, lectured, held conferences and interviews, and continued his research and writing. Such a program was too much for a man who, though still in early middle age, had been already weakened by worry, overwork, and poor health. His death in 1870 "was mourned not only by the teachers of Russia, who had lost their teacher, but by all people of public spirit in Russia, not merely in the capital but in the most distant corners of the country to which his ideas and the lofty example of his life had penetrated." [32]

The above cursory account of Ushinskii's life by no means reflects the full stature of his career as an educational philosopher. Although his major writings took three general forms—(1) articles in which he outlined his views on Russian education and expounded his own theories of what should be done, (2) handbooks and guides for teachers which put these theories on a practical plane, and (3) school texts for children which were based upon his conceptions of learning [33]—a true estimate of his philosophy can be gained only through examination of the specific basic ideas which he sought to disseminate throughout the teaching profession in Russia and, even beyond that, to Russian society as a whole. One authority has listed as follows the main themes which drew Ushinskii's attention: "the definition of the aim of education and of instruction; the significance and limits of the field of education; the whole people as the cornerstone of education and of school life; the native language as the basis of teaching; the educational significance of work; the close relationship between teaching and science; the role of the university in education; the role and significance of pedagogical literature; and, as the crowning thought, the future of the Russian school developing in an era of awakening public life in Russia." [34] With this list as a topical guide, it is necessary now to examine briefly the content of Ushinskii's views on these subjects.

The aims of education, said Ushinskii, must be mental, physical, social, and moral—but moral, most of all. Education should devote itself primarily to the formation of character. "Education must illuminate the conscience of man and show him clearly the road to the good." [35] Thus, every act and function of the school has to be examined in the light of how it affects first of all the character of the child and, secondly, the character of the society. Since the public will be deeply affected by the type of education practiced in the schools, the public must identify itself closely with all educational institutions and help to guide their work. For Ushinskii, unlike some of the other thinkers of the period, was no revolutionary—he was not even a mild socialist. He wanted education to produce a better society, but he wanted this transformation to occur gradually and peacefully, with the public and the teachers cooperating toward a common goal. As one Soviet educational historian puts it, "Ushinskii is only a liberal, and for him a revolution in the future is no less dreadful than was Pugachev's rebellion in the past." [36]

Nourished on the writings of the liberal western philosophers such as Bacon, Locke, Mill, Spencer, Kant, and Descartes,[37] Ushinskii was far removed from those of his contemporaries who drew their radical inspiration from Feuerbach, Marx, Bakunin, and Hertzen. Whereas these latter philosophers and their disciples were internationalists in their political outlooks, Ushinskii was not only preoccupied with Russian affairs but was a devout patriot and even strongly nationalist in his educational views. One of the basic principles of his system of pedagogy is the inculcation of a feeling of nationalism in the young. In his early articles in 1857-58 he expounded this view, and he never changed his basic concept that "love for the fatherland, present in every person, provides a true key to the heart of man, and education must accordingly rest upon nationalism." [38] It was Ushinskii's conviction that nationalism could best be fostered by means of strong emphasis on the native language throughout the school system. One of his most famous works, *Rodnoe Slovo* (The Native Word) was a series of readers for Russian school children designed to give them greater love and respect for their national literature.[39]

Another device which Ushinskii regarded as most useful in the development of character was the actual doing of work. Influenced by both Pestalozzi and Wundt, he believed that self-activity is an innate urge in all humans, and that the materialist-idealist duality in our natures can be bridged to a certain extent by devoting some of our energies to physical labor. In his article on "*Trudi ego psikhicheskom i vospitatel'nom znachenii*" (Labor and Its Psychological and Educational Significance), Ushinskii points out that mental work also constitutes labor and, in fact, is the highest form of labor. Therefore, the type of work done is not as important as the habit of working. "Education must develop in the pupil a habit of work and must make it possible for him to find for himself a life work. The school must not only provide intellectual development and a definite fund of knowledge, but must arouse in the youth a thirst for serious work, without which life can be neither worthy nor happy." [40] Ushinskii also believed that the family, as well as the school, should follow these educational precepts by instilling in the child sound qualities of moral character, love of the Fatherland, and respect for work.[41]

These ideas, then, constitute the major facets of Ushinskii's views on the public school. Great as was his contribution to that level of education in Russia, there was another where his influence was even greater—the field of teacher education. His long article entitled "*Proekt uchitel'skoi seminarii*" (Plan for a Teachers Seminary), written in 1861, is the most important of his writings on this subject, but the figure of the teacher was constantly in his mind in all his writings. He saw the personal influence of the teacher as an educational force for which there is no adequate substitute: not textbooks, nor moral precepts, nor punishments and rewards. "The personality of the teacher means everything in education." [42] With so much responsibility resting upon him, the teacher must bring to his work the utmost enthusiasm. Even in small village schools, he must keep in mind the fact that his work has great importance to his society. "The teacher feels that he is an active member of a great organism, which struggles against the ignorance and vices of humanity, a mediator between his own generation and everything noble and sublime in the past history of mankind, a keeper of the sacred legacy of the people who have struggled for truth and virtue. He feels that he is a living link between the past and the future . . . and understands that . . . kingdoms rest upon his work and that whole generations live by it." [43]

Thus, despite his concern for a scientific basis of pedagogy, Ushinskii saw teaching as more of an art than a science, since he placed so much reliance upon subjective factors. But he would not ignore science in the training of teachers. He thought that the art of teaching requires knowledge of the basic elements of anthropology, physiology, and especially psychology. The teacher should be aware that he is teaching a young human being, and therefore learn to know each pupil's abilities and peculiarities. A current Soviet writer states that "this acknowledgment of the enormous role of psychology in education was made in Russian pedagogy for the first time by Ushinskii." [44]

The "Plan for a Teachers Seminary" first appeared in the *Journal of the Ministry of Public Education*, Nos. 2-3, in 1861, during the period of Ushinskii's editorship of that periodical. Realizing that the Emancipation Act of that year would result in the opening of thousands of elementary schools, Ushinskii drew upon his knowledge of the type of institution then popular in Europe, and particularly in Germany, which supplied the moderate amount of training he thought requisite in a teacher of these lower schools. Although the essay presents a synthesis of this European practice and the program of reorganization carried out by Ushinskii himself at Gatchinsk Institute, it is replete with his views on teacher education in general.[45]

Opening with the statement that "the most serious defect in Russian public education is the inadequacy of good teachers specially prepared for the carrying out of their responsibilities," the article proceeds to outline in detail the program recommended by the author to deal with this situation.[46] Very early in the work, Ushinskii states that the training of elementary school teachers is a different problem than that of preparing instructors for the higher levels, including even the gymnasium. He thinks that too much study for the former can actually be harmful, in that it might lead to radical ideas concerning politics, morals, or religion which would be unbecoming in a village teacher. For, in addition to a devout belief in Christianity, "it is only fair to require of the public school teacher . . . that his life not only offer no grounds for scandal, not only not subvert respect for him on the part of parents and children, but, on the contrary, that [his life] serve as an example to them as well as to others, and not contradict his school precepts. Only under such conditions can he have an ethical influence on the children, and his school work be truly educative. That is why young people in teachers seminaries who have chosen the modest career of public school teacher should get used to a simple, even austere and poor life, without worldly diversions. . . ." [47]

But the knowledge required for teaching in such schools, although neither broad nor deep, should be "as clear as possible, exact and well defined." It should include, of course, all the subjects taught in the school as well as a high degree of certain communicative skills such as reading, writing, drawing, and even singing; for the teacher at this level must often resort to varied means of presenting the material so that even the youngest child can understand. The mastery of these accomplishments requires more self-practice than instruction, so the seminary must provide much opportunity for the trainee to drill himself in the actual atmosphere of teaching. Referring to the methods in the German seminaries, Ushinskii recommends that "pedagogical practice" (practice teaching) be initiated by having the trainee observe the lessons of a good teacher and then attempt a practice lesson himself in the presence of his comrades and the teacher responsible for his work. After the lesson, the practice teacher listens to the criticisms of this group and applies them to the preparation of a new lesson. Ushinskii admits that "such preparation is very slow and difficult in the beginning . . . [but] after two or three years of such study, the practice teacher will be turned into a good teacher with excellent teaching methods and habits and with the subject itself clearly and definitely fixed in his mind." [48]

The article also describes the administrative and curricular structure of the ideal seminary. Since the plan adopted by Ushinskii at Gatchinsk Institute included the incorporation of the local orphanage instead of a public school as an adjunct institution, he recommends that the Director of the seminary be *ex officio* the head of the orphanage. The faculty of the seminary should consist of five or six instructors "who are not only well acquainted with pedagogical theory but are also experienced teachers." The supplementary staff would consist of all the teachers at the adjunct school as well as the trainees. Since the program of the seminary requires a great deal of discussion, conference, and extra hours of preparation, it is well to have most, if not all, the trainees housed in a dormitory near the school, in charge of a steward or housekeeper. The instructors "should live together with the trainees so that the latter can always turn to them for advice and be completely under their moral and mental influence." All members of the seminary staff should be full members of the Pedagogical Council and take part in managing the institution; in addition, the most promising trainees can also be elected to the Council as full members. In order to give individual attention to the resident trainees, their number should be limited to forty or fifty, but a few others may be permitted to attend the day sessions. Because of the rather ascetic life demanded by the program, expenses for each student (tuition, board, room, clothing) should not exceed 100 rubles a year. Those persons who wish to lead a less frugal existence have no place in the seminary, and "persons whose conduct does not measure up to the duties they have taken upon themselves should be immediately expelled." [49]

Ushinskii goes into some detail regarding the curriculum of the seminary, particularly those courses not usually offered in such institutions. It is his idea that, in addition to the regular study in pedagogy and the subjects to be taught in the schools, every trainee should have thorough grounding in the rudiments of botany, zoology, physiology, and psychology. More specifically, the graduate of the seminary must know simple hygiene, the symptoms of the most prevalent children's diseases, and the uses of first-aid devices and reliable medicaments—such knowledge to be gained by periodic visits to the local hospital. For those who expect to teach in rural areas, an understanding of basic agricultural processes is necessary, as well as skill in handicrafts, such as carpentry and basket weaving.

Nor was the study of civics to be neglected: the trainee can be much more useful to his peasant community if he knows elementary civil and criminal law, the local system of taxation and finance, and the organization of the police agencies. The history and geography courses were to concentrate upon the native land, with the inclusion of only "those few most important events of universal history necessary either for an understanding of the Holy Scripture and church history or for a better grasp of the history" of Russia. For the same reasons, the Church-Slavonic language must be learned sufficiently to make clear the ritual and dogma of the Church. No formal examinations are deemed necessary: the contact between faculty and trainee is so close that written and oral reports will suffice to provide evidence of the latter's progress through each stage of the curriculum. Similarly, each trainee will proceed at his own rate of accomplishment, with no exact length of time set for the course; "but under no circumstances should it be less than two years or more than four years." [50]

In line with his conception that the teachers seminary should be not only a training institution for its young students but also "the pedagogical center of the community," Ushinskii advises that advanced courses be set up for the older teachers and periodic lectures on education be opened to the public. The seminary teachers and students can assist the public school teachers in the preparation of textbooks, courses of study, lesson plans, and teaching aids, the latter particularly to include drawings, diagrams, pictures and other visual devices. Such assistance would be automatically given to recent graduates of the seminary, who would also be entitled to receive some temporary financial support if needed, advice on practical teaching problems, issues of current pedagogical publications, and "legal protection in cases where the graduate is not guilty" of the charges against him.[51]

Honor graduates, said Ushinskii, might even be selected through competition to pursue their pedagogical studies abroad in German or Swiss teachers seminaries. It is obvious that Ushinskii had given these ideas much thought, and it should also be remembered that most of them had already been tried out in practice at the Gatchinsk Institute and Orphanage. More important still, however, is the question of how these ideas have been regarded by Ushinskii's contemporaries, by Russian educators in the later nineteenth and early twentieth centuries, and by Soviet educators today. Since Ushinskii undoubtedly represents the broadest and also the most profound expression of pedagogical thought which the Tsarist regime achieved, such estimates of his worth will in themselves provide keys to the educational philosophies current in each period.

Some indication has already been given in this chapter regarding Ushinskii's importance during his own lifetime, and his influence on current Soviet pedagogy. Despite the honors and acclaim which came to him before his death, these accolades were largely counterbalanced by the persecutions which he suffered. After all, it must be recalled that his entire pedagogical career covered only fifteen years, seven of these spent in administration and teaching, and eight in writing and lecturing. Moreover, the other progressive and radical movements of the 'sixties, from which Ushinskii himself drew much stimulation, required more than a decade to disseminate their influence throughout the huge Russian Empire.

As early as the 'seventies, however, many of Ushinskii's proposals had rather wide application. "On the basis of his 'Plan [for a Teachers Seminary]' the best pedagogical establishments of the 1870's were opened in the form of the *zemstvo* schools for teachers." [52] His two-volume masterpiece, *Man As the Subject of Education*, "became the standard reference book of teachers and of professors of education, and was used as a textbook in teachers seminaries. A generation of teachers of education was brought up on this book and in the spirit of Ushinskii. They became teachers of teachers who cherished his instructions and passed them on to their successors." [53] Long after his death, many of his works were still popular: in the late 1880's, for example, *Man As the Subject of Education* received its thirteenth printing, *The Child's World* (a sequel to *The Native Word*) its twenty-seventh, and *The Native Word* its ninety-ninth. "Altogether the writings of Ushinskii were distributed by the millions of copies and were used in the instruction of many school generations of pupils and teachers." [54]

In regard to specific ideas, the record can hardly be as clear, nor the judgments as affirmative. As early as 1861, in the journal *Sovremennik* (The Contemporary), an article attacked several of his theories in regard to the aims of elementary teacher education, particularly his points that breadth of knowledge was more of a hindrance than a help and that only the meek, patient, and self-sacrificing persons should attempt to bear the rigors of the teaching profession.[55] On the other hand, a Soviet critic willingly admits that "Ushinskii was the first Russian educator and one of the earliest in history to promote the theory that the teacher requires a deep understanding of empirical psychology and who gave a detailed exposition of the questions of memory, attention, imagination, etc." [56] Certainly in the direction of encouraging the concept that education, and especially teacher education, be taken very seriously, Ushinskii has been a great force and probably will be for some time to come. "His basic idea, that of the recognition of pedagogy . . . as an art on a scientific basis, still awaits its fulfillment, which will mark a new era in the development of pedagogy." [57] When that era arrives, perhaps the whole world will give more attention than in the past to the theories of Ushinskii, and to the course of Russian educational history in general.

12

The Educational Heritage of the U.S.S.R.

THE RUSSIAN REVOLUTIONS OF 1917, whatever their intent, did not establish a complete break with the Russian past. Throughout its relatively brief history to the present moment, the Soviet Union has been haunted by the mistakes, the failures, and the omissions of three hundred years of Tsardom. Just as the Soviet forms of politics, economy, and general social welfare have had to be built in the main upon the heritage bequeathed by the Imperial regime, so the educational system since 1917 has borrowed now here, now there, from the pedagogical theory and practice of Tsarist Russia. In this realm, however, the Soviets have had several firm pillars on which to build. The seventeenth century witnessed the arousal of popular interest in education, the eighteenth century brought the Government into the struggle for educational reform, and the nineteenth century saw a real system of schools established. These tangible contributions cannot be ignored in assessing the value of Soviet progress in the cultural field.

The present volume attempts to reveal some of the roots which have fed—and will probably long continue to feed—the Soviet system of education, particularly in relation to the education of teachers for Soviet schools and colleges. Those readers familiar with recent Russian history will have seen in the preceding chapters many examples of similarity between Tsarist and Soviet educational procedures. Some of the more important connections are pointed out in the text itself; others are indicated in the Reference Notes. However, since the study is concerned chiefly with Russian education only up to the revolutions of 1917, additional instances should be mentioned here, even though the selection of such examples must necessarily be random and uncoordinated.

It will be noted that the Soviets consciously and deliberately emulate many Tsarist practices and laud many historical figures. For example, the letter written by Prince Vladimir Monomakh to his children in 1096 (mentioned on the first page of this volume) is praised in the Soviet Union today as "the most ancient Russian pedagogical document," valuable because its author "advises his children to be solicitous towards all, to protect widows and orphans, to be hospitable. Profound humanism prompts [his] instruction to his children that when they become soldiers they should not allow the civil population to be insulted and plundered during a campaign, even on enemy territory. He persistently advises the children to study, urging them to emulate his father, who knew five languages. He admonishes his children to be brave, to defend their country, always to lead active, strenuous lives."[1] One may be sure from the foregoing that these principles expounded by an eleventh-century Russian nobleman are approved in substance by the Soviet Government today.

Several Tsars are also included in the growing list of historical characters deemed important by the Soviets. Russian emperors were condemned wholesale in the early Soviet textbooks, but in the last decade this point of view has shifted. Ivan IV ("the Terrible") is now described as the first unifier of the Russian Empire, and is praised particularly for his expansionist tendencies. An excellent Soviet film extolls Peter the Great, and he is also given many plaudits in Soviet history textbooks.[2] It is interesting to note that the present "Suvorov" and "Nakhimov" schools of Soviet Russia, created primarily for children of soldiers who served in World War II, not only bear the names of two famous Tsarist officers but are similar in many ways to the "garrison schools" established by Peter in 1732. The garrison schools soon served their announced purpose and disappeared two decades later—no one can yet know whether the same fate will overtake their Soviet counterparts. Another of Peter's creations, the Academy of Sciences, has had an unbroken existence since its establishment in 1725. Although greatly expanded both in scope and in membership and somewhat modified in structure, its essential function as the co-ordinating and directing agency of scientific research in Russia remains intact. Each year the Soviet Union celebrates the anniversary of its founding, and hundreds of Soviet volumes describe or indicate its influence.[3] Also in connection with the Academy, the work of the great Russian scientist and writer, Mikhail V. Lomonosov, attracts the highest acclaim of present-day Soviet publicists and historians.[4]

Although Empress Catherine II is not personally included on the current Soviet roll of honor, her influence on present-day education in Russia is great indeed. She was a pioneer in such fields as the education of women, the concentration on the Russian language, the establishment of a network of military schools, the indoctrination of rules of courtesy and deportment, the training of teachers in special institutions, and the creation of a system of state schools. All of these principles except two—concentration upon the Russian language and the indoctrination of standards of conduct—were accepted and put into practice in the early years of the Soviet regime. The two exceptions, though spurned until recently, are now also approved procedure. The "Rules for School Children" adopted by the Soviet Government in 1943 bear a striking similarity to the ideas of Catherine II.[5] And for the past decade, Soviet pedagogical literature has stressed the need for more study of the Russian language, which is now a required course in all Soviet elementary and secondary schools even though the local language remains the basic vehicle of instruction.

Some of Catherine's organizational practices in education have also either survived to the present day or been reincarnated under the Soviets. Many readers will see points of similarity between her plans for a nation-wide system of schools and recent Russian efforts in the same direction, even though the present Soviet system owes much more to the project of Alexander I. In military education, however, current practice strongly resembles the network of schools centering around the Corpus Cadet: today it is the Frunze Academy in Moscow which serves as the fountainhead of a system of at least sixty higher institutions of military training. Thus Soviet Russia has not followed the American or British plan of a single Government military academy at the college level—a West Point or a Sandhurst—but has reached back a hundred and fifty years into its own history for its models.

Strangely enough, the eighteenth-century concept of separate higher schools for the upper and lower classes also has found acceptance in the Soviet Union, but on an ideological rather than a socio-economic basis. The Communist Party of the Soviet Union maintains its own system of higher education, entirely separate from the networks operated by the various Government agencies. There are Communist institutes of engineering, agriculture, industrial administration, banking, pedagogy, and several other fields of study; and no noble establishment of the past was ever more exclusive or more careful in its selection of teachers and students. It is these Party schools, moreover, which train the persons who will become the real leaders in the most important professions and occupations. The old criterion of birth and social position has been swept away; in its stead has come Party membership as the gateway to power and prestige.

Several of the passages and tables in this volume reveal the great degree of decentralization in the administration of higher education which evolved during the nineteenth century despite all efforts to establish a unified system. Although the conditions of a century ago no longer bear influence today, the Soviets have chosen to follow much the same pattern. There have been several important changes in the organization of the system of higher education since 1917, and each change has resulted in more higher schools being placed within the jurisdiction of the various educational administrative organs. Nevertheless, when the Ministry of Higher Education of the U.S.S.R. was created in 1946 the decree establishing this office assigned to its authority less than half of the institutions of higher learning then operating in the Soviet Union.[6] In elementary and secondary education, the fact is well known that responsibility is divided among sixteen separate ministries of public education, one for each constituent republic. But there is still greater dispersion of control, for the same ministries and industries which operate higher schools also have their own secondary institutions, just as in the nineteenth century. On the question of private schools, however, the Soviet Union has carried to complete success the aim of several Tsarist rulers and officials. No private institution of learning is permitted to exist in Russia today; all such agencies are operated by one branch or another of the government, except a few quasi-autonomous schools used by religious bodies for the training of church officials.

The traditional Russian attitude toward foreign specialists in general, and foreign teachers in particular, has had interesting applications in the three decades since the Bolshevik Revolution. In several places the pages of this volume reveal how both Peter I and Catherine II welcomed specialists from abroad, but it should always be noted that such importations were for one major purpose: the training of Russians to become self-sufficient. Peter never lost faith in the value of the foreign teacher, but Catherine and all the other monarchs ultimately regarded such visitors with extreme suspicion. Over a period of three hundred years of Tsarist history, foreigners in Russia held a very tenuous position: in one decade they would be welcomed, admired, and heeded as experts; in the next, they would be spurned, excluded or even expelled from the country. Much the same oscillation has characterized the Soviet attitude toward foreigners, and the pendulum has swung from the proffer of enormous salaries and unusual privileges during the 1930's to the present reaction bordering upon xenophobia.

From its own citizens the Soviet Government now demands a degree of political loyalty which is astonishingly similar to the religious orthodoxy required in previous ages. The Soviet teacher today must subscribe as devotedly to the aims and practices of the State as did the instructor at the Moscow Academy in the seventeenth century. The directions to teachers published in 1804 find their equivalents, not greatly modified, in the Soviet press today, and some statements of Soviet educational aims bear marked resemblance to the fulminations of the notorious Leonti Magnitskii! Just as Tsar Alexander I used his educational system as a device to support the Holy Alliance of 1815, Prime Minister Stalin has utilized the schools for the indoctrination of the concept of Soviet infallibility. There has frequently appeared a strong suspicion of teachers who have studied abroad, and as many professors probably have lost their jobs through political heresy in three decades of Soviet rule as ever in a comparable period of Tsardom.

Yet it should not be assumed that all of the adaptations from the past have been of a theoretical nature. The Soviet Union has based the organizational aspects of its educational system on the finest example provided by the Empire—the "ladder system" set up in the early years of the reign of Alexander I. In administration, it has wisely emulated the best features of the old chain of command of the *zemstvo* schools.[7] The institution of stipends to students has not only been preserved but enormously expanded.[8] The standardization of academic degrees which took place in 1819 has been adopted, with proper modifications, and has provided an excellent means of stabilizing the decentralized system of higher education. Three of the best elements expressed even in the early Rules of the Lutsk Brotherhood are today integral parts of the Soviet system of teacher education: strict standards of personal character, the necessity for cooperation between parents and teachers, and the value of the teacher as an example to children.

Catherine's idea that education must prepare a person for social existence is one of the strongest motivating factors in the Soviet schools.[9] Peter I stressed the authority of the teacher and, although this view was spurned in the early years of the Soviet regime, it has now achieved complete acceptance, as has also the traditional Russian "lecture method" of instruction.[10] In at least one case, the present Soviet leaders have favored the terminology of Alexander I even over that preferred by Vladimir Ilich Lenin. It has been stated on excellent authority that Lenin opposed the use of the term "minister" in the new Soviet Government, calling it "Such a vile, hackneyed word." [11] Although the appellation of "commissariat" was adopted in 1917 and used until 1946, the designations of "minister" and "ministry" were adopted in that year and are now used exclusively for these offices in the Soviet Union.

This list of similarities between the new and old regime, although far from complete, is nevertheless impressive. However, one must avoid the inference that current practices are simply duplicates of the past, or that the borrowings have been more important than the creations. As one of the greatest American anthropologists has pointed out, "every culture, every era, exploits some few out of a great number of possibilities. . . . These interpenetrations of traits occur and disappear, and the history of culture is in considerable degree a history of their nature and fates and associations." [12] There are significant departures from pedagogical tradition visible in the Soviet Union, and these disparities must be considered along with the adaptations. For example, the Soviet regime, quite unlike its predecessor, has encouraged the growth of several types of teachers' organizations–social, economic and professional. It is reported that all teachers are members of one or another of the four trade unions of educational workers, and a large number participate in various other pedagogical societies.[13]

More interesting than either the outright Soviet imitations or renunciations of the past are the instances where certain phases of a custom are almost completely assimilated at the same time that other aspects are vociferously denied. An outstanding example of this complex procedure is offered by the Soviet attitude toward the famous Tsarist slogan: Orthodoxy, Autocracy, and Nationalism. As has already been pointed out in this chapter and also in Chapter

One, the Soviet leaders are not at all reticent concerning the degree of political subservience demanded of the citizenry. Hardly a day passes without some expression in the Soviet press regarding the necessity of complete unanimity in political thought. No one even bothers to deny that ideological deviations are a cardinal sin in the U.S.S.R., and the long list of victims of many Soviet political purges in all walks of life bear eloquent testimony to the practical punishments meted out to offenders. Such has been the case since the very advent of the Soviet regime.[14]

"Nationalism," however, has undergone varying interpretations since 1917. Beginning with the most violent denunciation of all forms of this Tsarist concept, the Soviet Government and the Communist Party have year by year softened their attitude, until today "Soviet nationalism" has become a major aspect of patriotism. Love of the fatherland, willingness to fight and die for one's country, praise of the Soviet Union as the greatest of all nations, and even the admission of the superiority of the Great Russian people to all other Slavic folk—all these ideas are now preached openly in Soviet newspapers, theatres, and schools.[15]

But "Autocracy" has had a still different history, and one which is much more difficult to understand. Despite the fact that the word "dictatorship" has been used in every Soviet constitution to define the form of government, the leaders and often even the people strongly resent any implication that their ruling organs are in the least degree autocratic. That the chosen term "Soviet democracy" deludes not even the most friendly Western statesmen is indicated by the speech of President Franklin Roosevelt in 1940 when he declared that "The Soviet Union, as everybody who has the courage to face the facts knows, is run by a dictatorship as absolute as any other dictatorship in the world."[16]

Taken together, then, the trinity of concepts expressed

in the old slogan of Orthodoxy, Autocracy, and Nationalism have their somewhat different counterparts in the Soviet Union today. One American educator defined these elements several years ago as follows: "For religious orthodoxy there has been substituted economic orthodoxy, in place of the autonomy [*sic*] of the Tsar there has been established the autocracy of a Party, and the political and militaristic nationalism has been replaced by a class consciousness which for the present binds the Russian nation together as strongly as the old form."[17] One must remember that these words were written at a period in Soviet history when economic survival was the pre-eminent problem, and when Soviet nationalism possessed many aspects of a militant internationalism. Now, however, the international aspects of this nationalism, while undoubtedly still present, are commingled with so many purely nationalistic elements that the result is much closer to the Uvarov interpretation than it was in the 1930's. Moreover, with the passing of the economic crisis in the Soviet Union, orthodoxy has now become chiefly political, and appears to become more and more imbued with the fanaticism of earlier centuries.

There is some evidence that, of the three elements of the trinity, it is Orthodoxy which is the supreme law, the guiding principle, the *sine qua non* of Russian life in all ages and under all forms of government. As stated by an outstanding historian, "no story of Russia can be complete without taking account of [Church history]. Indeed it is at times difficult to distinguish the religious from the national; and though the Church never did its duty in education or in provision for public welfare, . . . Orthodoxy was itself the major part of Russian civilization, and has perhaps done more than anything else to shape the distinctive Russian consciousness."[18] The Soviet leaders have denied the existence of an autocracy and have frequently shifted their point of view on nationalism; but orthodoxy, whether political, economic, historical, or even aesthetic, appears as the lodestar of Russia today as well as the Russia of the years covered by this volume.

It is now time to summarize briefly some of the major conclusions which are indicated or implied in the materials presented in the preceding pages. No attempt will be made here to revaluate the outcomes of the various efforts made by the Tsarist regime to develop a more adequate system of education, nor to recapitulate the many contributions of that regime to its successor. Three hundred years of history constitute far too wide a web to be unraveled and rewoven in a few turns of the loom, and the designs intertwined therein are nearly always indistinct and frequently imperceptible. In any case, each reader must apply his own standards of the good, the bad, and the indifferent. Nevertheless, perhaps in this tapestry certain large configurations can be discerned with sufficient clarity to justify an attempt at interpretation.

There is much evidence that despite the most cataclysmic social upheaval that the world has ever known, the enduring character of Russian society has compelled a return to many pre-Revolution practices, not only in education but in other fields as well. It appears that many of the radical ideas imported from abroad, and blatantly espoused during the early years of the Soviet regime, have proven unassimilable in Russian culture and have been superseded by indigenous concepts which two decades ago were outlawed and despised.

It also appears that Tsarist Russia had developed many of the social organizations, administrative channels, and patterns of procedure which the new regime was able to turn to its own use almost immediately upon its seizure of power. Revolutionary talk about "smashing the old order of things" may have been good internal propaganda for a nation in flux, but behind the scenes the structure of the new state was rapidly being built upon the remnants of the old.

There is also offered, perhaps, at least a partial explanation of the abysmal failure of the Imperial regime to unify the Russian people, despite repeated efforts toward that end. As the gulf between Government and the people widened, mutual understanding became more and more difficult, and finally impossible. Although officials and laymen continued to use common terms of speech, there was an increasing tendency toward confusion in the respective interpretation of these terms. When the crisis came, the government found itself unable to convince the people of the need for concerted action. The people had long since lost faith in the sincerity of official proclamations, and the bureaucracy had long since lost all sensitivity to the real needs of its citizens.

Thus once more was illustrated Lord Acton's maxim regarding absolute power, for Russian autocracy invariably became less secure as it became more despotic. Perhaps in this pattern lies the greatest portent of all.

Table 1

Number of Schools, Teachers and Pupils in Russia (1782–1800)

YEAR	NUMBER OF SCHOOLS	NUMBER OF TEACHERS	NUMBER OF PUPILS		
			BOYS	GIRLS	TOTAL
1782	8	26	474	44	518
1783	9	28	654	77	731
1784	11	33	1,082	152	1,234
1785	12	38	1,282	209	1,491
1786	165	394	10,230	858	11,088
1787	218	525	11,968	1,571	13,539
1788	227	520	13,635	924	14,559
1789	225	516	13,187	1,202	14,389
1790	269	629	15,604	921	16,525
1791	288	700	16,723	1,064	17,787
1792	302	718	16,322	1,178	17,500
1793	311	738	16,165	1,132	17,297
1794	302	767	15,540	1,080	16,620
1795	307	716	16,035	1,062	17,097
1796	316	744	16,220	1,121	17,341
1797	285	644	14,457	1,171	15,628
1798	284	752	15,396	1,405	16,801
1799	277	705	15,754	1,561	17,315
1800	315	790	18,128	1,787	19,915

Table 2

Salaries of Administrative Officials in the Ministry of Public Education (1802–03)

(in rubles per year)

ITEM	SALARY	HOUSING ALLOWANCE	TOTAL
Minister of Public Education	12,000	5,000	17,000
Assistant Minister	4,000	2,000	6,000
Director of Department of Public Instruction	3,000	500	3,500
Budget for Entire Department of Public Instruction (12 persons)	21,225		
Curator of each Circuit	2,000		
Travel Allowance for all Six Curators	10,000		

Table 3

Model Budget of the Universities at St. Petersburg, Moscow, Kazan, and Kharkov (1803–04)

(in rubles per year)

ITEM	PER PERSON	TOTAL
Professors (28)	2,000	56,000
Adjuncts (12)	800	9,600
Language Teachers (3)	600	1,800
Masters in Ped. Inst. (12)	400	4,800
Student-Candidates (12)	300	3,600
State-supported Students (40)	200	8,000
Supplementary Wages to Professors Assigned to Special Duties:		
Rector	600	600
Deans (5)	300	1,500
Academic Secretary	300	300
Director of Ped. Inst.	500	500
Director of Clinical Inst. and Univ. Physician	500	500
Press Censor	450	450
Inspector of State Students	400	400
Librarian	400	400
Student Library Assistants		500
Student Secretarial Assistants	200	200
Library		1,000
Anatomical Exhibits and Caretaker		800
Botanical Garden and Caretaker		1,000
Chemistry Lab. and Laborant		1,000
Observatory		500
Physics Office		500
Natural History Office		600
Clinical Institute		5,000
Bursar	500	500
Secretarial & Clerical Aid for Bursar		900
Superintendent	450	450
Sending Personnel on Surveys of other Schools		5,000
Clerical Supplies		600
Journals & Newspapers		500
Foreign Censuses		200
Foreign Travel by Adjuncts to Improve Abilities		2,000
Establishing a Press		2,000
Priests & Church Support		1,000
Wages & Gratuities for Watchman		1,000
Teachers of Art, Dance, & Music		1,500
Pensions of Academic Officials & Widows		6,000
Maintenance of Edifice, Heating & Lighting, Cleaning, etc.		8,800
Total for one Univ.		130,000
For all four Universities: St. Petersburg, Moscow, Kazan, and Kharkov		520,000

(Universities of Dorpat & Vilna not included—see Table 4 for budget of University of Vilna)

Table 4
Actual Salary Budget of the University of Vilna (1803–04)

(in rubles per year)

POSITION	SALARY PER PERSON	TOTAL	
Rector of the University	1,200	1,200	
Deans of the Four Divisions (supplement to salary of Professor)	300	1,200	
Secretary of the University	450	450	
Secretary of the Board of Directors of the University	450	450	
Professors of Main Courses (32)	1,000	32,000	
Teachers of Auxiliary Courses (32)	500	16,000	
Adjuncts (12)	500	6,000	
Press Censors (4)	600	2,400	
Language Teachers (4)	?	1,500	
Art and Gymnastics Teachers (4)	?	1,800	
Total Salary Budget for Faculty		63,000	
Total University Budget			105,000

Table 5

Model Budget of Most Gymnasiums[1] *(1803–04)*

(in rubles per year)

ITEM	Class I Gymnasium[2]		Class II Gymnasium[3]		Class III Gymnasium[4]	
	PER PERSON	TOTAL	PER PERSON	TOTAL	PER PERSON	TOTAL
Directors (1)	1,000	1,000	900	900	800	800
Teachers (4)	750	3,000	650	2,600	550	2,200
Language Teachers (2)	400	800	400	800	400	800
Drawing Teacher (1)	300	300	300	300	300	300
For Library	—	250	—	250	—	250
For Operation and Maintenance	—	900	—	900	—	900
Total for each Gymnasium[5]		6,250		5,750		5,250

[1] Gymnasiums in the following *guberniyas* are *not* included in the list: Finland, Esthonia, Lithuania, Kurland, Vilna, Grodno, Minsk, Volinsk, Podolsk, and Kiev (except the one gymnasium at Kiev operated by State funds).

[2] Class I Gymnasiums at Arkhangel, Vologda, Vyatka, Irkutsk, Olonetz, Perm, St. Petersburg, and Tobolsk. Total budget for these eight, 50,000 rubles.

[3] Class II Gymnasiums at Vitebsk, Vladimir, Kaluga, Kursk, Kostroma, Moscow, Mogilev, Novgorod, Orlov, Orenburg, Pskov, Smolensk, Tver, Tula, and Yaroslavl. Total budget for these fifteen, 86,250 rubles.

[4] Class III Gymnasiums (19) at Astrakhan, Voronezh, Kiev (only one operated by State funds), Kazan, Kavkaz, Nizhegorod, Nikolaevsk, Ekaterinoslav, Poltava, Penza, Ryazan, Saratov, Simbirsk, Slobodsk-Ukraine, Tavrichesk, Tambov, Chernigov, Don Cossack area, Black-Sea Cossack area. Total for these nineteen, 99,750 rubles.

[5] Total amount budgeted for the 42 gymnasiums in these three classes, 236,000 rubles.

Table 6

Actual Budget of Seven Gymnasiums With HIGH Teacher Salaries[1] *(1804–05)*

(in rubles per year)

ITEM	PER PERSON	TOTAL
Director's salary and travel allowance	1,500	1,500
Teachers (6)	800	4,800
Drawing Teacher, who may also supervise the pupils	600	600
For upkeep of Library	—	200
For upkeep of Physics Laboratory	—	100
For prizes for pupils	—	150
For servants and other needs of students	—	400
Total budget for each of the seven gymnasiums		7,750

[1] Includes four gymnasiums at Dorpat, and others at Riga, Revel, and Vyborg.

Table 7

Actual Budget of Four Gymnasiums With LOW Teacher Salaries[1] *(1804–05)*

(in rubles per year)

ITEM	PER PERSON	TOTAL
Director of Gymnasium	800	800
Assistant Director (Supplement to salary of Senior Teacher chosen)	120	120
Senior teachers of Physics, Mathematics, Moralization and Law, Literature, Geography and History (5)	400	2,000
Senior teachers of Polish and Latin Grammar for 1st class (1) and for 2nd Class (1)	300	600
Confessor and Preacher	300	300
Junior teachers of languages (Russian, French, German) (3)	240	720
Junior Teacher of Drawing (1)	240	240
Library upkeep and study aids	—	240
Heating, lighting and maintenance of building	—	680
Pensions of Employees	—	3,000
Emergency Expenses	—	1,000
Total budget for each of four gymnasiums		9,700

[1] Includes gymnasiums at Vilna, Minsk, Grodno, and Krementz.

Table 8

Model Budget of 405 District Schools[1] (1803–04)

(in rubles per year)

ITEM	CLASS I SCHOOLS[2] PER PERSON	TOTAL	CLASS II SCHOOLS[3] PER PERSON	TOTAL	CLASS III SCHOOLS[4] PER PERSON	TOTAL
Principal (1)	400	400	350	350	300	300
Teachers (2)	300	600	275	550	250	500
Instruction in Divine Law	100	100	80	80	75	75
Instruction in Drawing	100	100	80	80	75	75
Operation and Maintenance	—	400	—	350	—	300
Total for each school[5]		1,600		1,410		1,250

[1] District Schools in the following *guberniyas* are *not* included in the list: Finland, Esthonia, Lithuania, Kurland, Vilna, Grodno, Minsk, Volinsk, Podolsk, and Kiev (except the one such school at Kiev operated by State funds).

[2] Class I Schools in these *guberniyas:* Arkhangel 7, Vologda 10, Vyatka 10, Irkutsk 15, Olonetz 7, Perm 12, St. Petersburg 11, Tobolsk 16. Total amount budgeted for 88 schools in this class, 140,800 rubles.

[3] Class II Schools in these *guberniyas:* Vitebsk 8, Vladimir 10, Kaluga 11, Kostroma 12, Kursk 14, Mogilev 12, Novgorod 10, Orenburg 12, Orlov 12, Pskov 8, Smolensk 12, Moscow 13, Tula 12, Tver 9, Yaroslavl 10. Total amount budgeted for 165 schools in this class, 232,650 rubles.

[4] Class III Schools in these *guberniyas:* Astrakhan and Kavkaz 9, Voronezh 13, Kazan 10, Kiev (state) 1, Nizhegorod 10, Ekaterinoslav 6, Nikolaevsk 5, Penza 13, Poltava 12, Ryazan 12, Saratov 8, Simbirsk 10, Slobodsk-Ukraine 10, Tavrichesk 7, Tambov 12, Chernigov 12, Don Cossack Area 1, Black-Sea Cossack Area 1. Total amount budgeted for 152 schools in this class, 190,000 rubles.

[5] Total amount budgeted for 405 District Schools, 563,450 rubles.

Table 9

Actual Budget of Thirty District Schools With HIGH Teacher Salaries[1] *(1804–05)*

(in rubles per year)

ITEM	PER PERSON	TOTAL
Teachers (3)	500	1,500
Drawing Teacher, who may also supervise the pupils	400	400
Books and technical models	—	200
Prizes for pupils	—	100
Servants and other expenses	—	200
Total budget for each of these schools		2,400

[1] Includes thirty district schools in the Educational Circuits of Dorpat, Kurland, Lithuania, Esthonia, and Vyborg.

Table 10

Actual Budget of Many District Schools With LOW Teacher Salaries[1] *(1804–05)*

(in rubles per year)

ITEM	PER PERSON	TOTAL
Principal of school	320	320
Senior teachers (4)—one for each class	300	1,200
Confessor and Preacher	300	300
Junior teachers (3) (Russian, Drawing, French *or* German)	200	600
Maintenance of school (books, heating, etc.)	—	400
Total budget for each of the schools		2,820

[1] Large number of district schools in Vilna Circuit and others.

Table 11

State Appropriation for Public Education (1803–04)

(in rubles)

Appropriation for District Schools (405)	563,450
Appropriation for Gymnasiums (42)	236,000
Appropriation for Universities (4)	520,000
Total appropriation for all Public Education	1,319,450

Table 12

Number of Students in Gymnasiums and Higher Educational Establishments (1830–1858)

YEAR	NO. STUDENTS IN UNIVERSITIES	NO. STUDENTS IN OTHER HIGHER EDUC. ESTAB.	NO. STUDENTS IN GYMNASIUMS	NO. OF GYMNASIUMS	TOTAL NO. OF STUDENTS
1830	3317	?	?	62	?
1831	2201	?	?	61	?
1837	2307	593	16,506	69	19,406
1838	2446	397	17,403	70	20,246
1839	2465	299	16,753	72	19,517
1840	2740	1,069	16,854	73	19,663
1841	2858	706	16,896	74	20,460
1842	2884	604	17,006	74	20,494
1843	2966	513	17,890	74	21,369
1844	3274	480	19,453	74	23,207
1845	3516	473	20,436	75	24,425
1846	3826	513	20,820	75	25,159
1847	4004	508	21,082	75	25,602
1848	4006	461	19,496	75	23,963
1849	3956	498	19,428	74	23,882
1850	3018	503	18,764	74	22,285
1851	3116	494	18,192	74	21,802
1852	3112	489	18,327	76	21,928
1853	3443	524	17,868	76	21,835
1854	3551	446	17,827	76	21,824
1855	3659	366	17,817	76	21,842
1856	4168	314	19,098	77	23,580
1857	4714	285	20,274	77	25,273
1858	4884	317	22,270	78	27,471

Table 13
Number of Pupils in District and Parish Schools (1830–1858)

YEAR	NO. OF DISTRICT SCHOOLS	NO. OF PUPILS	NO. OF PARISH SCHOOLS	NO. OF PUPILS	NO. OF PRIVATE SCHOOLS	NO. OF PUPILS	TOTAL NO. OF PUPILS
1830	416		718		402		79,420 [1]
1831	392		469		345		68,367 [1]
1837	427		840		436		73,260
1838	430		873		485		74,823
1839	435		911		475		75,602
1840	439		983		486		77,898
1841	442		1,021		481		77,030
1842	445		1,067		521		79,261
1843	445		1,059		562		83,999
1844	447		1,070		607		85,447
1845	447		1,047		585		83,966
1846	449		1,011		594		85,774
1847	451		1,010		597		88,931
1848	450		1,050		601		87,012
1849	431	27,198	1,065	43,203	599	15,244	85,645
1850	433	26,262	1,062	44,397	567	20,472	91,131
1851	434	25,834	1,068	44,723	592	23,358	93,915
1852	440	27,937	1,077	47,441	602	20,518	95,896
1853	440	27,725	1,125	48,832	633	20,946	97,503
1854	439	27,992	1,140	49,937	640	19,592	97,521
1855	439	27,309	1,106	49,101	614	17,888	94,298
1856	438	27,600	1,085	49,934	615	17,781	95,315
1857	437	28,266	1,095	52,815	637	14,608	95,689
1858	431	28,358	1,129	53,659	668	15,297	97,314

[1] Includes enrollment in gymnasiums and universities.

Table 14

Faculty Salaries in the Teachers Gymnasium at St. Petersburg[1] *(1804)*

(in rubles per year)

POSITION	SALARY	HOUSING ALLOWANCE	TOTAL
Director of Teachers Gymnasium	2,500		2,500
Professor of Physics	2,000	500	2,500
Professor of Philosophy	2,000	500	2,500
Lecturer on Aesthetics	1,500		1,500
Acting Professor of General History[2]	1,200	300	1,500
Acting Professor of Natural History[2]	700		700
Acting Professor of Geography[2]	700		700
Acting Professor of Mathematics[2]	700		700
Teacher of German Language	1,000		1,000
Teacher of French Language	1,000		1,000
Teacher of Drawing and Design	700		700
Total Faculty Salaries and Allowances for 11 Persons			15,300

[1] Later renamed the Main Pedagogical Institute.
[2] These posts appear to be held by temporary incumbents while better-qualified persons are being sought.

Table 15

Model Budget of Pedagogical Institutes Attached to Universities (1804–05)

(in rubles per year)

POSITION	PER PERSON	HOUSING ALLOWANCE	TOTAL
Director of Pedagogical Institute	2,500		2,500
Professors (3)	2,000	500	7,500
Lecturer on Aesthetics	1,500		1,500
Acting Professor of General History	1,200	300	1,500
Acting Professor of Natural History	700	(residence provided)	700

(Continued on page 273)

Table 15 (Continued)

POSITION	PER PERSON	HOUSING ALLOWANCE	TOTAL
Acting Professor of Mathematics	700	(residence provided)	
Acting Professor of Geography	700	300	1,000
Supplementary salary for one of the above three assigned as Inspector of Students	300		300
Teacher of German Language	1,000		1,000
Teacher of French Language	1,000		1,000
Teacher of Drawing and Design	700		700
Librarian (Supplement)	300		300
Total Salaries and Allowances for these 13 members of faculty			18,700

ITEM	TOTAL
Food for 100 students	8,400
Clothing for 100 students	7,680
Emergency needs of 100 students	1,800
Student supplies	1,000
Housekeeper	450
Doctor's visits to sick	200
Medication and treatment of students in city hospital	200
Senior Watchman	180
His uniform	25
Guard Watchmen (3)	100 each
Their uniforms	20 each

ITEM	TOTAL
Cooks (2), Baker (1), Laborers (7)	120 for all
(Food is supplied the cooks and the baker in addition to salaries)	
Firewood	1,548
Lighting	350
Miscellaneous: food, linen, laundry, baths	2,835
Total Expenses Other Than Faculty	26,228

TOTAL BUDGET 44,928

Table 16

Budget of the Main Pedagogical Institute at St. Petersburg (1816–17)

(in rubles per year)

ITEM	SALARY OR COST	HOUSING ALLOWANCE
Director, if not among Professors	3,000	1,200
if from among Professors	500 [1]	
Ordinary Professor	2,000	500
Extraordinary Professor	1,600	500

(Continued on page 274)

Table 16 (Continued)

ITEM	SALARY OR COST	HOUSING ALLOWANCE
Adjunct substituting for Professor	1,000	200
Masters and Lecturers (6)	700	150
Senior Professors (one for each Section)	200 [1]	
Additional Adjuncts (6)	800	
Teachers of Fine Arts and Gymnastics (all)	3,000	
Assistant in Physics	400	
Laborant in Chemistry	500	
Librarian, when member of faculty	500 [1]	
Conference Secretary	1,500	500
Administrative Counselor	1,500	
Administrative Secretary	1,200	
Cashier or Bursar	1,000	
Chief Steward	1,200	
Clerk of Director's office	1,000	
Adminstrative expenses (translations, correspondence, etc.)	3,500	
Inspector, if from staff	400 [1]	
if not from staff	1,500	
Assistant Director	800	
Doctor or Physician	800	200
Pensions for staff	6,000	
Maintenance of library and laboratories	5,000	
Inspections of schools in circuit	4,000	
Maintenance of chemistry laboratory	1,000	
Maintenance of infirmary	2,000	
Subscriptions to Russian and foreign newspapers and journals	500	
Maintenance of 100 pupils	30,000	
Maintenance and travel of outstanding students visiting abroad for study and experience	8,000	
Heating, lighting, cleaning of building, and fire-fighting equipment	12,000	
Salaries and gratuities to menials such as cook, porter, etc.	4,000	
Travel expenses of pupils from distant towns	6,000	
Unforeseen expenses	3,000	
TOTAL BUDGET	165,200	

Of this total: for instructional salaries	43,000
for faculty housing	12,000
Total for 33 faculty salaries and allowances	55,000

[1] Supplement to regular salary in another capacity.

Table 17

Budget of the Second Division of the Main Pedagogical Institute (1817–18)

(in rubles per year)

POSITION	AMOUNT	ITEM	AMOUNT
Inspector	2,000	For study aids, books, etc.	2,000
Assistant Inspector	1,200	Maintenance of 30 pupils	9,000
Teacher of Divine Law	600	Heating and Lighting of Building	8,000 [1]
Teacher of Calligraphy	600	Housekeeper	600
Teacher of Russian Language	800	Bookkeeper	600
Teacher of Mathematics	800	Office expenses	700
Teacher of History and Geography	800	For maintenance of servants and emergency expenses	2,300

Total faculty salaries: 6,800 rubles Other expenses: 23,200 rubles

Total budget for Second Division: 30,000 rubles

[1] "The greater part of this sum may be utilized for augmenting the number of pupils whenever the Main Pedagogical Institute obtains a proper building."

Table 18

Budget of the Main Pedagogical Institute (1828–29)

(in rubles per year)

ITEM	SALARY OR COST	ALLOWANCES	TOTAL
Director of the Institute	4,000	2,000	6,000
Inspector	4,000	residence	4,000
Ordinary Professors (17)	3,500	1,000	4,500
Teacher of Divine Law	1,500		1,500
Adjuncts (6)	1,500	500	2,000
Teacher of Art	2,000		2,000
Deans (3) supplement to salary of Ordinary Professor	500		5,000
Academic Secretary	400 [1]		
Librarian	400 [1]		
Senior Supervisor	2,000		2,000
Room Supervisors (5)	1,200		1,200
Administrative Counselor	3,000		3,000
Administrative Secretary	1,800		1,800
Bookkeeper	1,500		1,500
Executor-Steward	1,200	600	1,800
Office expenses of Conference	2,000		
Office expenses of Administration	3,000		
Secretary to Director	1,000		1,000
Office expenses of Director	200		
Doctor or Physician	1,000		1,000
Maintenance of 100 student scholarships	500 each		50,000
Infirmary and medicines	3,000		
Maintenance of Library and laboratories	10,000		
Subscriptions to Russian and foreign publications	800		
Travel expenses of scholarship students from distant towns	4,000		
Travel abroad for outstanding students	8,000		
Salaries and tips for menials	4,000		
TOTAL BUDGET			207,400

[1] Supplement to regular salary in another capacity.

Table 19
Social Origins of Students in the St. Petersburg Educational Circuit (1853)

TYPE OF INSTITUTION	TOTAL NUMBER OF STUDENTS	NUMBER FROM NOBILITY	NUMBER FROM OTHER CLASSES	PER CENT NOBILITY
University	424	299	125	73%
Gymnasiums	2831	2265	566	80
District Schools	4686	1814	2872	38
Urban Parish Schools	7613	883	6730	12
Private and Boarding Schools	6153	2960	3192	48

Table 20
Course of Study in Gymnasiums (1864)

SUBJECT	GYMNASIUMS WITH 2 ANCIENT LANGUAGES	GYMNASIUMS WITH 1 ANCIENT LANGUAGE	REAL-GYMNASIUMS
	(Number of hours per week in each subject)		
Divine Law	14	14	14
Russian Language & Literature	24	24	25
Latin Language	34	39	—
Greek Language	24	—	—
French or German Language	19	German 19 French 19	German 24 French 22
Mathematics	22	22	25
History	14	14	14
Geography	8	8	8
Natural History	6	6	23
Physics and Cosmography	6	6	9
Penmanship, Drawing, Designing	13	13	20
All Subjects	184	184	184

Table 21

Representative Ranks, Salaries and Classes of Duty in All Russian Universities Except Dorpat (1863)

	Number of Such Posts in Each University					Allowances for Each Post (In Silver Rubles)				
TITLE OR RANK	ST. P.	MOSCOW	KHARKOV	KAZAN	ST. VLAD. (KIEV)	SALARY	FOOD	ROOM	TOTAL	CLASS OF DUTY[1]
Rector	1	1	1	1	1	1500	—	given	1500	IV
Prorector (or Inspector)	1	1	1	1	1	1000	—	given	1000	V
Dean	4	4	4	4	4	600	—	—	600	V
Professor of Divine Law	1	1	1	1	1	2400	300	300	3000	–
Ordinary Professor	34	39	39	39	39	2400	300	300	3000	V
Extraordinary Professor	16	18	18	18	18	1600	200	200	2000	VI
Docent	24	31	31	31	31	900	150	150	1200	VII
Lecturer of For. Lang.	4	4	4	4	4	800	100	100	1000	VIII
Ordinary Faculty Clinician	–	6	6	6	6	480	120	—	600	–
Ordinary Hospital Clinician	–	2	2	2	2	480	120	—	600	–
Laboratory Technician	4	6	6	6	6	650	150	—	800	VIII
Librarian	1	1	1	1	1	1200	300	given	1500	VI
Library Assistant	3	3	3	3	3	480	120	—	600	VIII
Mechanic	1	1	1	1	1	450	—	—	450	XIV
Asst. Prorector	3	3	3	3	3	600	200	—	800	VIII
Feldschers in Clinic	–	6	6	6	6	200	40	given	240	–

[1] "Class of Duty" established the order of precedence for several types of privileges such as housing, source of funds for pension and allowances, etc. Although the classes of teaching posts sometimes varied from decade to decade, they remained fairly stable. Note, however, that at this period (1863) Inspectors are Class V, whereas they were Class VII in the decree on precedence issued by Tsar Alexander I in 1818.

Table 22

Increase in Salaries of Gymnasium and District School Officials and Teachers (1828–1859)

POSITION	SALARY IN RUBLES 1828[1]	1859	AMOUNT OF INCREASE[1]	PERCENT OF INCREASE
Directors of Gymnasiums				
in St. Petersburg	858	1000	142	16.5%
in Moscow	772	1000	228	29.5
in Class I gyms. in provinces	715	900	185	25.8
in Class II gyms. in provinces	643	850	207	32.1
in Class III gyms. in provinces	572	800	228	39.8
Inspectors of Gymnasiums				
in St. Petersburg	715	850	135	18.8
in Moscow	643	850	207	32.1
in Class I gyms. in provinces	572	800	228	39.8
in Class II gyms. in provinces	515	750	235	45.6
in Class III gyms. in provinces	458	700	242	52.8
Senior Teachers in Gymnasiums				
in St. Petersburg	643	750	107	16.6
in Moscow	558	750	192	34.4
in Class I gyms. in provinces	536	700	164	30.5
in Class II gyms. in provinces	465	650	185	39.7
in Class III gyms. in provinces	393	600	207	52.6
Principals (Smotriteli) of District Schools				
in St. Petersburg	343	500	157	45.7
in Moscow	300	500	200	66.6
in Class I schools in provinces	286	450	164	57.3
in Class II schools in provinces	250	400	150	60.0
in Class III schools in provinces	214	350	136	63.5
Teachers of District Schools				
in St. Petersburg	257	400	143	55.6
in Moscow	236	400	164	69.4
in Class I schools in provinces	214	350	136	63.5
in Class II schools in provinces	200	330	130	65.0
in Class III schools in provinces	179	300	121	67.5

[1] Figures in these columns are in terms of nearest whole ruble.

Table 23

Curriculum of the Molodechno Teachers Seminary (1864–65)

SUBJECT	NUMBER OF HOURS PER WEEK — IN THE SEMINARY: junior class (first year)	senior class (second year)	IN THE LOCAL PUBLIC SCHOOL
Divine Law	4	3	4
Methods		2	
Russian Language	5	4	4
Slavonic Language	2	1	2
Geography	2	2	
History	2	2	
Natural History	3	3	
Arithmetic	4	3	4
Geometry, geodesy and linear drawing	2	2	
Singing	2	2	2
Penmanship	2	2	4
All subjects	28	26	20

Table 24
Budget of the Molodechno Teachers Seminary (1864-65)

POST OR ITEM	NUMBER OF POSTS	ALLOWANCES IN RUBLES SALARY	FOOD	TOTAL	CLASS OF DUTY [2]
Director	1	1,000	500	1,500[1]	VI
Teacher of Divine Law	1	600	300	900[1]	
Preceptor (Nastavnik)	2	600	300	1,800[1]	IX
Teacher of Public School	1	450	—	450[1]	
Teaching of Singing	1	100	—	100	
Feldscher	1	100	—	100	
Watchman	1	60	—	60	
Office employees	2	60	—	120	
Student stipends	60	80	—	4,800	
Study aids for stipend holders	60	5		300	
Rewards to graduates				100	
Basic Library				100	
Office expenses				50	
Medical supplies				100	
Maintenance, etc.				600	
Unforeseen expenses				200	
TOTAL BUDGET				11,280	

[1] Living quarters, supplied by the State, supplement these salaries.
[2] Class of Duty determined priority in housing, source of pension funds, etc. This became increasingly important later in the century, when the Tsarist government decided against the setting aside of "poor lands" or "school lands," as was done in Germany and Switzerland, for the benefit of the schoolmaster, who in those nations cultivated them with the aid of his pupils and extracted thereby a meager supplement to his wages. [Cf. M. M. Kovalevsky, *Modern Customs and Ancient Laws of Russia* (London: David Nutt, 1891), p. 112.]

Table 25

Number of Church-Parish Schools and Pupils (1831-1894)

YEAR	NUMBER OF SCHOOLS[1]	NUMBER OF PUPILS	YEAR	NUMBER OF SCHOOLS	NUMBER OF PUPILS
1831	100	1,860	1880	4,348	108,990
1840	2,500	19,000	1884	4,540	112,114
1845	3,764	?	1885	8,351	202,350
1850	4,610	88,512	1886	11,693	318,652
1853	4,820	98,260	1887	14,471	408,721
1860	7,907	133,666	1888	17,025	478,300
1865	No reliable reports		1890	21,840	626,100
1870	No reliable reports		1894	31,835	981,076
1875	7,402	205,559			

[1] This column includes both church-parish and literacy schools; it was only in 1880 that the two types were separated for statistical purposes. Therefore, the apparent decline between 1875 and 1880 did not actually occur.

Table 26

Literacy Status of Young People (7–14 years old) in the Russian Empire in 1897

AGE IN YEARS	MALES ALL	MALES LITERATE	MALES ILLITERATE	FEMALES ALL	FEMALES LITERATE	FEMALES ILLITERATE
7	1,529,948	99,883	1,430,065	1,561,743	65,590	1,492,153
8	1,586,402	241,009	1,345,393	1,587,753	143,430	1,444,323
9	1,372,774	391,426	981,348	1,362,844	204,536	1,158,308
10	1,582,027	569,081	1,012,946	1,549,621	278,751	1,270,870
11	1,205,566	553,418	652,148	1,180,777	262,342	918,435
12	1,637,597	746,155	891,442	1,598,221	338,819	1,259,402
13	1,318,828	643,025	675,803	1,312,476	295,459	1,017,017
14	1,285,721	630,902	654,819	1,297,667	299,533	998,134
TOTAL	11,518,863	3,874,899	7,643,964	11,451,102	1,892,460	9,558,642
%	100%	31%	69%	100%	16.5%	83.5%

RECAPITULATION

YOUTHS OF BOTH SEXES, 7-14 YEARS

All	22,969,965	100%
Literate	5,767,359	25%
Illiterate	17,202,606	75%

Table 27

Literacy in Russia, by Areas and Sex, in 1897

	% Literate in Entire Population			% Literate in the Cities		
AREA	MALES	FEMALES	BOTH SEXES	MALES	FEMALES	BOTH SEXES
European Russia	32.6	13.7	22.9	58.5	38.3	48.9
Tsarist Poland	34.2	26.8	30.5	50.5	38.6	44.7
Caucasus	18.2	6.0	12.4	42.4	22.3	33.7
Siberia	19.2	5.1	12.3	48.0	28.3	39.4
Central Asia	7.9	2.2	5.3	24.9	10.3	18.5
The Empire	29.3	13.1	21.1	54.0	35.6	45.3

Table 28

Rate of Growth in Literacy in Russia, by Areas and Sex (1800–1897)

	% NOT Literate in 1897		Average Decennial Growth in Literacy for 19th Century		Average Decennial Growth in Literacy 1867-1897	
AREA	MALE	FEMALE	MALE	FEMALE	MALE	FEMALE
Eur. Russia	67.4	86.3	5.5	1.8	5.2	3.2
Tsarist Poland	65.8	73.2	3.8	3.1	1.8	1.0
Caucasus	81.8	94.0	1.9	1.0	0.3	1.9
Siberia	80.8	94.9	1.9	0.8	0.6	2.0
Cent. Asia	92.1	97.8	0.2	0.3	0.1	0.7

Table 29

Level of Education in Russia, by Class and Sex, in 1897

EXTENT OF EDUCATION	NOBLE AND OFFICIAL	CHRISTIAN CLERGY	URBAN	RURAL	FOREIGN SUBJECTS	OTHERS
MALES	%	%	%	%	%	%
Literate	73.2	77.8	50.1	27.4	38.8	6.8
General higher	7.8	1.9	0.3	0.0	0.5	0.02
Special higher	2.2	0.1	0.1	0.0	0.3	0.01
Special secondary	2.6	0.9	0.5	0.1	0.4	0.1
General secondary	19.7	51.9	2.6	0.1	3.9	0.2
Military higher	0.5	0.01	0.0	0.0	0.02	0.0
Military secondary	7.4	0.2	0.1	0.0	0.1	0.01
FEMALES						
Literate	69.2	66.6	31.1	9.7	39.0	2.2
General higher	0.5	0.1	0.02	0.0	0.1	0.01
Special higher	0.04	0.01	0.0	0.0	0.0	0.0
Special secondary	0.5	0.3	0.1	0.0	0.1	0.02
General secondary	23.4	11.7	2.5	0.1	5.1	0.2

Table 30

Number of Persons in Russia with Secondary or Higher Education, by Level and Sex, in 1897

TYPE OF INSTITUTION ATTENDED	NUMBER OF PERSONS HAVING ATTENDED	% FROM EACH TYPE OF INST.	% OF POPULATION OF THAT SEX	% LIVING IN RURAL AREAS
MALES				
University and other higher	97,961	11.5	0.16	16.7
Special and technical higher	29,656	3.5	0.05	21.3
Military higher	4,181	0.5	0.01	11.8
Special secondary	86,655	10.2	0.14	38.8
General secondary	558,038	65.7	0.89	33.5
Military secondary	72,441	8.6	0.12	17.3
Total Males from all	848,932	—	1.4	?
FEMALES				
University and other higher	6,360	1.2	0.01	12.7
Special and technical higher	619	0.1	0.01	19.7
Special secondary	13,293	2.5	0.02	23.0
General secondary	514,939	97.5	0.82	20.4
Total Females from all	535,211	—	0.8	?
Total Persons from all	1,384,143	—	1.1	?

Table 31

Per Cent of Total Population of Russia with General Secondary or Higher Education in 1897

	ALL CLASSES (%)		URBAN (%)		RURAL (%)	
AGE GROUP	UNIVERSITY	GEN. SEC.	UNIVERSITY	GEN. SEC.	UNIVERSITY	GEN. SEC.
MALES						
Under 10	—	0.04	—	0.1	—	0.005
10 - 19	0.02	1.3	0.04	4.1	0.001	0.2
20 - 29	0.3	1.2	0.8	4.1	0.01	0.2
30 - 39	0.4	1.2	0.5	3.7	0.005	0.1
40 - 49	0.3	1.2	0.3	3.3	0.004	0.1
50 - 59	0.3	1.1	0.2	1.9	0.002	0.5
60 & over	0.2	1.0	0.1	1.3	0.002	0.004
FEMALES						
Under 10	—	0.1	—	0.3	—	0.01
10 - 19	0.003	1.3	0.06	4.7	0.0002	0.1
20 - 29	0.02	1.6	0.05	4.9	0.0007	0.1
30 - 39	0.03	1.3	0.05	3.2	0.0006	0.07
40 - 49	0.02	0.7	0.02	1.5	0.0004	0.02
50 - 59	0.005	0.4	0.007	0.7	—	0.01
60 & over	0.003	0.3	0.004	0.5	—	0.006

Table 32

Enrollments in All Russian Universities (excluding Poland and Finland) (1808–1912)

YEAR	ST. PETERSBURG (1819)	MOSCOW (1755)	VILNA (1802-31) KIEV (1835)	KAZAN (1804)	KHARKOV (1804)	DORPAT (1632) (1802)	ODESSA (1865)	TOMSK (1888)	SARATOV (1909)	TOTAL
1808	—	135	525	40	82	193	—	—	—	975
1824	51	820	927	118	337	365	—	—	—	2,618
1835	285	419	120	252	342	567	—	—	—	1,985
1855	399	1,203	616	340	483	618	—	—	—	3,659
1865	785	1,741	555	413	588	560	—	—	—	4,641
1875	1,223	1,201	772	512	430	735	281	—	—	5,151
1881	2,155	2,504	1,337	825	937	1,164	422	—	—	9,344
1885	2,340	3,179	1,589	969	1,372	1,485	610	—	—	11,544
1894	2,675	3,761	2,453	816	1,090	1,496	506	377	—	13,169
1900	3,613	4,562	2,602	906	1,506	1,647	954	557	—	16,357
1904	4,652	5,810	3,099	1,308	1,792	1,872	2,162	811	—	21,506
1906	7,442	8,419	4,179	2,821	3,216	1,902	2,456	998	—	29,443
1909	8;663	10,086	4,857	3,049	4,936	2,415	3,232	1,110	92	38,440
1911	8,227	9,242	4,098	3,487	5,274	2,749	3,193	1,347	289	37,901
1912	7,282	9,390	4,857	2,955	3,315	2,251	2,756	892	412	34,538

(In 1916, these same nine universities had a total enrollment of 35,695)

NOTE: Figures directly beneath names of the universities indicate dates of founding; in the case of Dorpat, the first figure is date of founding and second is date the institution was brought under Russian control.

Table 33

Enrollment in all Russian Institutions of Higher Learning for Men, except Universities (1913)

(excluding Poland and Finland)

NAME AND LOCATION OF INSTITUTION	YEAR FOUNDED	NUMBER OF STUDENTS			
		1899	1902	1907	1912-13
Institute of Mining (SP)	1773	480	550	664	640
Military-Medical Academy (SP)	1799	768	750	750	900
Forestry Institute (SP)	1803	501	516	565	560
Bezborodko Lyceum (Nezhin)	1805	87	81	98	131
Institute of Ways of Communications (SP)	1810	886	894	900	1,384
Commercial Academy (M)	1810	403	?	?	4,261
Alexander's Lyceum (SP)	1811	106	?	?	290
Lazerev Institute (M)	1815	36	59	130	141
Technological Institute (SP)	1828	1,016	1,109	1,610	2,525
Higher Technical School (M)	1830	865	1,989	2,000	3,000
School of Law (SP)	1835	112	330	330	350
Institute of Civil Engineers (SP)	1842	353	530	510	810
Riga Polytechnic Institute	1862	1,446	1,701	1,750	2,088
Petrovskii Agricultural Academy (M)	1865	198	225	500	1,000
Historico-Philological Institute (SP)	1867	94	88	107	134
Demidov Lyceum (Yaroslavl)	1868	281	456	665	669
Nicholas' Lyceum (M)	1869	24	?	201	277
Archeological Institute (SP)	1879	195	?	?	542
Kharkov Technological Institute	1885	812	1,000	1,200	1,400
Electrotechnical Institute (SP)	1886	143	300	362	750

School of Engineering (M)	1896	236	380	567	580
Kiev Polytechnic Institute	1898	598	846	1,370	2,500
Ekaterinoslav Mining Institute	1899	—	128	250	480
Vladivostok Oriental Lang. Inst.	1899	—	76	125	127
Tomsk Technological Institute	1900	—	100	812	1,171
Polytechnic Institute Sosnovka (SP)	1902	—	—	700	5,215
Psycho-Neurological Institute (SP) [1]	1907	—	—	—	2,590
Novocherkassk Polytechnic Institute	1907	—	—	—	704
Shaniavskii University (M) [2]	1908	—	—	—	3,669
Oriental Academy (SP)	1909	—	—	—	102

Recapitulation: of the 30 institutions listed, 14 were located in St. Petersburg and 7 in Moscow.

(SP) located in St. Petersburg
(M) located in Moscow

[1] Private institution
[2] Municipal institution

NOTE: In addition to the 30 listed institutions, there were also 4 theological academies, 3 military academies, 1 academy of art, and 2 musical academies. See Table 32 for list of universities.

Table 34

Social Origins of Students in Russian Institutions of Higher Learning (1880–1914)

SOCIAL ORIGIN	7 UNIVERSITIES IN 1880 %	9 UNIVERSITIES IN 1914 %	5 HIGHER TECHNICAL STATE INSTITUTES IN 1914 %
Gentry and officials	46.6	36.1	24.5
Clergy	23.4	10.3	2.4
Merchants and Citizens	14.3	14.8	19.1
Workers and Craftsmen	12.4	24.3	31.6
Peasants	3.3	14.5	22.4

Table 35

Number of Students in All Schools of the Russian Empire (excluding Finland) in Relation to Total Population (1801–1914)

YEAR	POPULATION (in THOUSANDS)	APPROXIMATE NO. OF STUDENTS (IN THOUSANDS)	NO. OF STUDENTS PER 10,000 INHABITANTS: IN ALL SCHOOLS	IN SECONDARY SCHOOLS	IN HIGHER SCHOOLS
1801	37,540	45	12	1.0	0.1
1825	52,285	200	38	3.8	0.7
1835	60,185	240	40	3.8	0.5
1845	65,237	300	46	4.0	0.5
1855	71,108	400	56	3.7	0.8
1865	75,125	800	105	6.0	0.9
1875	90,218	1,200	132	11.1	1.1
1880	97,705	1,600	162	16.3	1.5
1885	108,787	1,900	174	14.7	1.5
1890	117,787	2,500	212	13.5	1.3
1895	123,920	2,800	226	13.3	1.3
1900	132,960	4,500	346	19.7	2.0
1905	143,980	5,600	388	24.1	3.5
1910	160,748	7,200	498	31.0	5.0
1914	175,140	9,500	545	36.0	7.5

Table 36

Zemstvo Educational Expenditures in Relation to Total Zemstvo Budgets (1868–1914)

YEAR	TOTAL EXP.	EDUC. EXP.	% OF EDUC. EXP. TO TOTAL EXP.
	(in thousands of rubles)		
1868	15,028	738	5.0
1871	21,509	1,600	7.4
1875	28,820	3,550	12.3
1880	36,317	5,200	14.3
1885	43,248	6,832	16.0
1890	48,347	7,226	14.9
1895	63,667	9,129	14.4
1900	89,142	15,971	17.9
1905	124,185	25,314	20.4
1910	171,687	42,882	24.9
1911	191,707	52,278	27.3
1912	252,615	74,418	29.5
1913	290,560	90,129	31.0
1914	336,373	104,597	31.1

NOTE: Figures for 1868-1911, incl., are for 34 *zemstvo* provinces; figures for 1912-1914, incl., are for 40 *zemstvo* provinces.

Table 37

Ministry of Public Education Expenditures in Relation to Total Expenditures of Tsarist Government (1795–1917)

YEAR	TOTAL GOVT. EXP.	MPE EXP.	% MPE EXP. OF TOTAL
	(in thousands of rubles)		
1795	56,860	782	1.4 (before estab. of MPE)
1805	125,449	2,601	2.1
1815	271,246 (war)	2,352	0.9
1825	413,460	8,601	2.1
1835	167,741 (silver)	6,831 (paper)	
		2,060 (silver)	1.2
1845	224,083	2,755 (hereafter in silver)	1.2
1855	525,970 (war)	2,910	0.6
1866	438,493	6,769	1.5
1870	563,897	10,131	1.8

(Continued on page 292)

Table 37 (Continued)

YEAR	TOTAL GOVT. EXP.		MPE EXP.	% MPE EXP. OF TOTAL
	(in thousands of rubles)			
1875	604,857		14,630	2.4
1880	793,384		16,786	2.1
1882	788,371		18,935	2.4
1885	913,138		20,446	2.2
1890	1,056,512		22,938	2.2
1895	1,520,819		23,600	1.6
1897	1,494,598		26,476	1.8
1900	1,873,772		33,181	1.8
1902	2,135,668		36,624	1.7
1904	2,737,697	(war)	42,433	1.6
1906	3,212,697		44,122	1.4
1907	2,564,608		45,907	1.8
1908	2,660,854	(First Duma)	53,149	2.0
1909	2,607,537		63,937	2.5
1910	2,596,660		76,011	3.0
1911	2,845,691		97,575	3.5
1912	3,171,061		117,337	3.7
1913	3,382,913		142,739	4.2
1914	3,558,000	(war)	155,292	4.4
1915	3,234,000		158,915	4.9
1916	3,646,000		165,160	4.5
1917	?		214,000[1]	?

NOTE: Above table focuses *only* upon Government expenditures for education through the Ministry of Public Education, which was the chief but not the sole agency for such expenditures. That other ministries devoted portions of their budgets to educational matters has been shown heretofore in this volume and is clearly indicated by the following supplementary table:

EDUCATIONAL EXPENDITURES OF ALL GOVERNMENT MINISTRIES (in rubles)			
1912	170,205,966	or	6.37 % of total govt. Exp.
1913	202,772,083	or	6.73 % of total govt. Exp.
1914	238,605,156	or	7.21 % of total govt. Exp.
1915	225,117,345	or	7.34 % of total govt. Exp.
1916	270,774,622	or	8.24 % of total govt. Exp.

[1] This figure from separate source as indicated in Reference Note to this table.

Table 38

Educational Expenditures of All Government Ministries (1916)

(in rubles)

Ministry of Public Education		165,159,780
Scientific Societies	2,868,760	
Universities	10,687,760	
Secondary & Special	38,477,337	
Primary	72,336,609	
Teaching Staff	3,686,158	
Buildings and Repairs	11,697,223	
Ministry of Interior		446,435
Holy Synod Church Schools		22,152,766
Ministry of Finance (Art and Educ.)		132,328
Ministry of Justice		967,977
Ways of Communication		1,056,856
Commerce and Industry (Science and Educ.)		4,586,724
Ministry of Agriculture		9,380,975
Ministry of War		20,864,803
Ministry of Marine		2,331,803
GRAND TOTAL		246,580,415

NOTE: Figures in above table are given chiefly for comparison with those in Table 37 on preceding page of this volume. It will be noted that the expenditures by the Ministry of Public Education are in agreement in both tables, but that the Grand Total above is more than 24 million rubles less than the 1916 figure shown in the supplementary section of Table 37. Moreover, the above figures do not add to the totals given and therefore cannot be considered reliable; but they can serve as an indication of the important role in education played by other ministries.

Table 39

Secondary School Curriculum under the Plan of the Ministry of Public Education (Ignatiev Plan) (1915)

SUBJECT	STUDY HOURS PER WEEK ACCORDING TO TYPE OF SCHOOL AND GRADE														
	NEW HUMANITARIAN					CLASSICAL HUMANITARIAN					REAL-SCHOOL				
A. Educational Group	IV	V	VI	VII	all	IV	V	VI	VII	all	IV	V	VI	VII	all
1. Divine Law	2	2	2	2	8	2	2	2	2	8	2	2	2	2	8
2. Russian language	5	5	4	5	19	5	3	4	4	16	5	4	3	4	16
3. History	3	3	4	4	14	3	3	3	3	12	2	3	3	3	11
4. Mathematics;	4	4	4	3	14	4	3	3	2	12	4	4	4	5	17
for math majors											4	6	6	6	22
5. Physics (cosmography)	2	3	2	2/2	11	2	2	2	2/1	9	2	2	4	3/2	15
6. Chemistry												2			2
7. Logic				2	2				2	2			2		2
8. Modern language	5	5	4	4	18	2	4	5	4	15	4	3	3	3	13
9. Geography	2	2	2		6	2	2			4	2	2	2		6
10. Natural Science;			2		2						2	2	2	3	9
for math majors														2	2
11. Ancient language						5	6	6	6	23					
Total for Group	23	24	24	24	94	25	25	25	26	101	23	24	25	25	99
											for math majors				97

B. Nurtural Group															
1. Practical work in Physics and Chemistry	1	1			2	1				1					
2. Physical exercise	3	3	3	3	12	3	3	3	3	12	3	3	3	3	12
3. Drawing;	1				1						2				2
for math majors											3				3
4. Familiarity with Artistic Works			1	1	2			1	1	2					
5. Designing													2		2
6. Practical Works in Physics											1			1	2
7. Practical Work in Chemistry												2			2
8. Practical Work in Natural Science;											1	1	1		3
for math majors														1	1
Total for Group	5	4	4	4	17	4	3	4	4	15	7	6	6	5	24
											for math majors				22
GRAND TOTAL	28	28	28	28		29	28	29	30		30	30	31	30	

Table 40

List of All Ministers of Public Education in Russia (1802–1917)

Years	Minister	Years	Minister
[1782–1799]	Count P. V Zavadovskii	1866–1880	Count D. A. Tolstoi
1802–1810	Count P. V. Zavadovskii	1880–1881	A. A. Saburov
1810–1816	Count A. K. Razumovskii	1881–1882	Baron A. P. Nikolai
1816–1824	Prince A. N. Golitsyn	1882–1897	Count T. D. Delianov
1824–1828	Admiral A. S. Shishkov	1898–1901	N. P. Bogolepov
1828–1833	Prince K. A. Liven	1901–1902	General P. S. Vannovskii
1833–1849	Count S. S. Uvarov	1902–1904	G. E. Sänger
1850–1853	Prince P. A. Shirinskii-Shikhmatov	1904–1905	General V. G. Glazov
1854–1858	A. S. Norov	1905–1906	Count I. I. Tolstoi
1858–1861	E. P. Kovalevskii	1906–1908	P. M. Kaufmann
1861	Count E. V. Putiatin	1908–1910	A. N. Schwarz
1862–1866	A. V. Golovnin	1910–1914	L. A. Kasso
		1915–1916	Count P. N. Ignatiev
		1916–1917	N. K. Kulchitskii

Notes on Above Table

a) From the creation of the Ministry of Public Education in 1802 until the overthrow of the regime in 1917, five Tsars headed the Government. In the same period, there were 25 Ministers of Public Education. Average number of Ministers of Public Education per Tsar is five.

b) Longest term of service (29 years) held by original incumbent, Count Zavadovskii, if his pre-Ministerial tenure of 20 years is included; next longest terms were held by Count Uvarov (17 years) and Count Delianov (16 years); no other Minister served even a full decade.

c) Average term of service for Ministers is about 4½ years. Average term of service after 1880 is just over 2 years: in 27 years under the last two Tsars there were thirteen Ministers of Public Education.

Table 41

List of Sovereigns of the Russian Empire (1500–1917)

1462–1505	Ivan III	1725–1727	Catherine I
1505–1533	Vasili III	1727–1730	Peter II
1533–1584	Ivan IV	1730–1740	Anne
1584–1598	Fedor I	1740–1741	Ivan VI
1598–1605	Boris Godunov	1741–1762	Elizabeth
1605–1606	Dmitri I	1762	Peter III
1606–1610	Vasili IV (Shuiski)	1762–1796	Catherine II
1610–1612	Wladislaw (VII) of Poland	1796–1801	Paul I
1613–1645	Mikhail Romanov	1801–1825	Alexander I
1645–1676	Alexis	1825–1855	Nicholas I
1676–1682	Fedor II	1855–1881	Alexander II
1682–1689	Ivan V and Peter I	1881–1894	Alexander III
1689–1725	Peter I	1894–1917	Nicholas II

Table 42

Statistics on Elementary and Secondary Schools in the Russian Empire in 1911

	Under the Jurisdiction of			
ITEM	MIN. PUB. EDUC.	HOLY SYNOD	OTHER	TOTAL
No. of schools	59,682	37,922	2,691	100,295
No. of ordained teacher-priests	27,621	20,374	1,101	49,096
No. of teachers (male)	45,143	23,291	2,432	70,866
No. of teachers (female)	57,255	22,860	3,196	83,311
No. of teachers (total)	102,398	46,151	5,628	154,177
No. pupils attending school on Jan. 18, 1911				
Male	2,871,299	1,199,694	128,571	4,199,564
Female	1,314,779	593,735	72,432	1,980,946
Total	4,186,078	1,793,429	201,003	6,180,510
No. of schools owning property	35,427	26,425	1,890	63,742
Value of this property in rubles	150,597,598	43,604,493	10,768,993	204,971,084
No. of schools on rented property	19,118	6,281	498	25,897
Yearly rental costs in rubles	5,266,768	298,499	170,044	5,735,311
Expenditures for schools in 1911, in rubles	70,583,094	15,841,324	4,373,781	90,798,199

SOURCES OF DATA IN APPENDIX

Table No.

1. S. A. Kniazkov and N. I. Serbov. *Ocherk istorii narodnogo obrazovaniia v Rossii do epokhi reform Aleksandra II* [Historical Sketch of Public Education in Russia to the Epoch of the Reforms of Alexander II], (Moscow 1910), p. 148.

2. Addendum to decree #1 (20,406) of September 8, 1802; addendum to decree #5 (20,582) of January 7, 1803; addendum to decree #7 (20,598) of January 24, 1803. *Sbornik postanovlenii po ministerstvu narodnogo prosveshcheniia* [Collection of Decrees of the Ministry of Public Education]. (St. Petersburg: Imperial Academy of Sciences, 1864-1865), Vol. I, appendix B, pp. 1-2.

3. Decree #11 (20,666) of March 17, 1803. *Sborn. post. MNP*, I, pp. 31-32.

4. Addendum to decree #15 (20,765) of May 18, 1803. *Sborn. post. MNP*, I, appendix B, p. 2.

5. Decree #11 (20,666) of March 17, 1803. *Sborn. post. MNP*, I, pp. 33-34.

6. Addendum to decree #32 (21,220) of March 21, 1804. *Sborn. post. MNP*, I, appendix B, pp. 4-5.

7. Addendum to decree #15 (20,765) of May 18, 1803; addendum to decree #41 (21,428) of August 20, 1804. *Sborn. post. MNP*, I, appendix B, pp. 3-7.

8. Decree #11 (20,666) of March 17, 1803. *Sborn. post. MNP*, I, pp. 34-36.

9. Addendum to decree #32 (21,220) of March 21, 1804. *Sborn. post. MNP*, I, appendix B, pp. 4-5.

10. Addendum to decree #41 (21,428) of August 20, 1804. *Sborn. post. MNP*, I, appendix B, p. 7.

11. Decree #11 (20,666) of March 17, 1803. *Sborn. post. MNP*, I, pp. 34-36.

12. Kniazkov, *op. cit.*, p. 210.

13. *Ibid.*, pp. 221-222.

14. Addendum to decree #29 (21,135) of January 23, 1804. *Sborn. post. MNP*, I, appendix B, p. 94.

15. Addendum to decree #34 (21,265) of April 16, 1804. *Sborn. post. MNP*, I, appendix B, pp. 5-6. Note that total of second part is 80 rubles greater than actual sum of figures.

16. Addendum to decree #264 (26,573) of December 23, 1816. *Sborn. post. MNP*, I, appendix B, pp. 27-28.

17. Addendum to decree #302 (27,108) of October 25, 1817. *Sborn. post. MNP*, I, appendix B, p. 32.

18. Addendum to decree #62 (2315) of September 30, 1828. *Sborn. post. MNP*, II(1), appendix A, p. 1.

Table No.

19. Adapted from Kniazkov, *loc. cit.*, pp. 210, 221-222.

20. "Rules of Gymnasiums and Progymnasiums of the Ministry of Public Education" (1864). *Sborn. post. MNP*, III, p. 1301.

21. Addenda to decree #472 of June 18, 1863 ("General Regulations of Imperial Russian Universities"). *Sborn. post. MNP*, III, appendix, pp. 66-67.

22. Adapted from "Projected Budget for Gymnasiums and District Schools" which was approved by Tsar Alexander II on April 17, 1859. *Sborn. post. MNP*, III, appendix, pp. 89-130. This entry bears no number but is evidently addenda to decree #183 (34,386) of same date.

23. Addenda to decree #554 of June 25, 1864 ("On the Establishment of the Molodechno Teachers Seminary"). *Sborn. post. MNP*, III, appendix, p. 76.

24. *Ibid.*, p. 76.

25. Data from official sources as presented in N. Hans, *History of Russian Educational Policy (1701-1917)* (London: P. S. King & Son, Ltd., 1931), pp. 157-158.

26. V. Ivanovich (Charnolusskii). "Iz itogov pervoi russkoi vceobshchei perepisi" [From the Summaries of the First Russian General Census] in *Vestnik Vospitaniia* [Educational Herald] XVII, No. 1, January 1906, p. 48.

27. *Ibid.*, p. 42.

28. *Ibid.*, p. 45.

29. *Ibid.*, pp. 52-53.

30. *Ibid.*, p. 50.

31. *Ibid.*, p. 54.

32. Hans, *op. cit.*, p. 238.

33. Adapted from *ibid.*, pp. 239-240.

34. *Ibid.*, pp. 239-240.

35. *Ibid.*, p. 242.

36. *Ibid.*, p. 232.

37. *Ibid.*, pp. 229-230; figure for 1916 is from G. Vernadsky, *A History of Russia* (New Haven: Yale University Press, 1929), p. 195.

38. Leary, D. B. *Education and Autocracy in Russia.* (Buffalo, N.Y.: University of Buffalo, 1919), p. 121. Figures drawn from Russian Year Book of 1916.

39. *Zhurnal Ministerstva Narodnogo Prosveshcheniia* [Journal of the Ministry of Public Education, St. Petersburg], 1915, No. 11.

40. *Sborn. post. MNP*, preface. A similar table, with slightly different dates and spelling of names, appears in Hans, *loc. cit.*, p. 243.

41. Information drawn from several sources.

42. N. A. Zhelvakov, *Khrestomatiia po istorii pedagogiki* (Sourcebook in the History of Pedagogy). State Pedagogical Textbook Publishers, Moscow, 1936, IV (2), p. 334, from N. Chekhov, *Narodnoe obrazovanie v Rossii* [Public Education in Russia], p. 222.

Chapter 1
Introduction: The Enduring Past

[1] R. Beazley, N. Forbes, and G. A. Birkett, *Russia from the Varangians to the Bolsheviks* (Oxford, England: The Clarendon Press, 1918), pp. 556-557. This volume quotes the text of the Tsar's abdication manifesto and also the manifesto of the Grand Duke Mikhail asking public support for the Provisional Government.

[2] J. Kucharzewski, *The Origins of Modern Russia* (New York: The Polish Institute of Arts and Sciences in America, 1948), Preface, p. xi. This work is a condensation of the same author's seven-volume classic entitled *Od bialego carato do czarwonego* [From White Tsardom to Red] which was published in Warsaw 1923-1935. The Preface quoted was written especially for the 1948 abridged edition in English. (The Chaadaev quotation at the beginning of this volume is also from this edition.)

[3] *Ibid.*, pp. xi, xix.

[4] *Ibid.*, pp. xiii-xiv.

[5] *Ibid.*, p. vii: Introductory Note by S. Harrison Thomson of the University of Colorado.

[6] V. I. Lenin, "Where to Begin" and "What Is To Be Done" in *Selected Works* (12 volumes) (Moscow: Cooperative Publishing Society of Foreign Workers in the U.S.S.R., 1934-38), Vol. II (1900-1904), pp. 15-23 and especially pp. 148-154.

[7] M. M. Kovalevsky, *Modern Customs and Ancient Laws of Russia* (London: David Nutt, 1891), pp. 121-123. Alexander Kornilov, in his *Modern Russian History* (2 volumes) (New York: Alfred A. Knopf, 1924), Vol. II, p. 103 fn., calls Kovalevsky "the greatest authority on Russian institutions." For comments on similar practices in Novgorod in the twelfth and thirteenth centuries, see D. B. Leary, *Education and Autocracy in Russia* (Buffalo, N. Y.: University of Buffalo, 1919), p. 18; and Beazley, *op. cit.*, p. 46.

[8] Lenin, *op. cit.*, Vol. IX, pp. 467-483: "The Tasks of the Youth Leagues."

[9] *Ibid.* It is clear that Lenin was referring to *all past* knowledge, and not just that contributed by recent writers, Russian scholars, or revolutionary movements.

[10] W. S. Churchill, *Blood, Sweat, and Tears* (New York: G. P. Putnam's Sons, 1941), p. 173.

[11] W. Lippmann, *U. S. Foreign Policy* (Boston: Little, Brown & Co., 1943), pp. 100-101.

Chapter 2

The First Steps Toward Enlightenment

[1] "Rules of the School of the Lutsk Brotherhood," article 1, in M. I. Demkov, *Istoriia russkoi pedagogii* [History of the Russian Pedagogue] (2 volumes) (Revel, 1895), Chap. XV, pp. 149-155. A fuller account of them is found in the same author's *Russkaia pedagogika v glavneishikh ee predstaviteliakh* [Russian Pedagogy as Reflected in Its Most Important Representatives] (St. Petersburg, 1898).

[2] *Polnoe sobranie russkikh letopisei* [Complete Collection of Russian Chronicles] (St. Petersburg: Russian Archeographical Commission, 1841-1921), Vol. I (1846), p. 51.

[3] *Ibid.*, Vol. V, (1851), p. 136; Vol. I, p. 65.

[4] *Ibid.*, Vol. I, pp. 100-105.

[5] Letter to Metropolitan Simon: *Akty Istoricheskie* [Historical Acts] (St. Petersburg: Russian Archeographical Commission, 1841), Vol. I (1334-1598), No. 104, pp. 146-148.

[6] Vladimir G. Simkhovitch, "History of the School in Russia" in *The Educational Review* (May 1907), p. 489; see also Evgen N. Medynskii, *Istoriia russkoi pedagogiki* [History of Russian Pedagogy] (Moscow: State Pedagogical Textbook Publishers, 1936), p. 13: "Archbishop Gennadius could not find in all the Novgorod district enough literate people to take priestly orders."

[7] *Stoglav* (London: Trübner and Company, 1860), Chap. 26, pp. 68-69. "Stoglav" is the name given to an assembly which met in Moscow in 1551, during the reign of Ivan IV, and set up a number of regulations for the guidance of the Church. These rules were then organized into 100 divisions, or chapters (*stoglavy*); hence the title. See B. D. Grekov, *The Culture of Kiev Rus* (Moscow: Foreign Language Publishers, 1947), p. 146.

[8] Simkhovitch, *loc. cit.*, pp. 489-490.

[9] M. Kovalevsky, *Modern Customs and Ancient Laws of Russia* (London: David Nutt, 1891), pp. 204-205.

[10] "Domostroi," (in) Moskovskii Universitet [Moscow University] *Imperatorskoe obshchestvo istorii i drevnostei rossiiskikh* [Imperial Society of History and Ancient Russia] (Moscow: 1881), Vol. II (April-June 1821), pp. 1-202. See articles 1, 14, 15, 17, and especially 22 on pages 11-12, 40-49, 52-54, 63-64.

[11] As paraphrased in Simkhovitch, *loc. cit.*, p. 493.

[12] S. A. Kniazkov, and N. I. Serbov, *Ocherk istorii narodnogo obrazovaniia v Rossii do epokhi reform Aleksandra II* [Historical Sketch of Public Education in Russia to the Epoch of the Reforms of Alexander II] (Moscow: 1910), pp. 9, 13.

[13] N. V. Chekhov, *Tipy russkoi shkoly* [Types of Russian Schools] (Moscow: "MIR" Publishers, 1923), p. 12; see also A. P. Pinkevich, *Kratkii ocherk istorii pedagogiki* [Brief Sketches on the History of Pedagogy] (Kharkov: "Proletarii" Publishers, 1930), p. 266: "It is very likely that instruction was carried on during this early period in churches and monasteries, and also by certain individuals, . . . but of specially organized schools there were none"; and R. Beazley et al., *Russia From the Varangians to the Bolsheviks* (Oxford, England: The Clarendon Press, 1918), p. 192: "Schools did not exist; what schooling was given was entirely private, haphazard, and piecemeal."

[14] Chekhov, *loc. cit.*, p. 13 (italics in original).

[15] Beazley, *op. cit.*, pp. 31-32; for the analysis of early Kievian culture in greater detail, see M. Hrushevsky, *A History of Ukraine* (New Haven: Yale University Press, 1941), pp. 68-71, 79, 117-122.

[16] "Godunov, Boris Fedorovich," in *Encyclopaedia Britannica*, 14th edit., Vol. X, pp. 463-464.

[17] Beazley, *loc. cit.*, passim; Medynskii, *loc. cit.*, p. 17; Hrushevsky, *op. cit.*, pp. 197-205.

[18] Chekhov, *loc. cit.*, p. 13: "The nobility continued to give their children home instruction and only occasionally sent them to the university."

[19] *Ibid.*, p. 13; Medynskii, *loc. cit.*, p. 19, mentions only the first three types but agrees that they "differed only slightly."

[20] Chekhov, *loc. cit.*, p. 13.

[21] *Ibid.*, p. 14.

[22] *Ibid.*, p. 14.

[23] Medynskii, *loc. cit.*, pp. 27-28.

[24] See p. 11.

[25] "Rules of the School of the Lutsk Brotherhood," articles 5, 12: Demkov, *loc. cit.*, pp. 151-153.

[26] It should be borne in mind that all of the students lived outside the school premises.

[27] "Rules of the School of the Lutsk Brotherhood," p. 151, article 7.

[28] Evidently, in view of the sentence following, a euphemism indicating the advisability of corporal punishment.

[29] "Rules of the School of the Lutsk Brotherhood," p. 153, article 14.

[30] *Ibid.*, p. 153, article 15.

[31] *Ibid.*, pp. 149-150, article 1.

[32] *Ibid.*, pp. 150-151, article 2.

[33] *Ibid.*, p. 154, article 18.

[34] See first page of this chapter.

[35] "Rules of the School of the Lutsk Brotherhood," p. 155, article 20.

[36] *Ibid.*, p. 152, article 9.

[37] *Ibid.*, conclusion to "Rules."

[38] *Ibid.*, introduction to "Rules."

[39] K. Kharlampovich, *Zapadnorusskie pravoslavniia shkole XVI i nachala XVII vv* [Church Schools of Western Russia in the XVI and the early XVII Centuries] (Kazan: Imperial University Press, 1898), pp. 348-349.

[40] D. B. Leary, *Education and Autocracy in Russia* (Buffalo, N.Y.: University of Buffalo, 1919), p. 28.

[41] Kharlampovich, *loc. cit.*, pp. 356-363.

[42] "Privileges of the Moscow Academy," article 5, in N. I. Novikov, *Drevniaia rossiiskaia vivliofika* [Ancient Russian Library] (2nd ed.; Moscow, 1788), Vol. VI, p. 408. See also Simkhovitch, *loc. cit.*, p. 194.

[43] "Privileges of the Moscow Academy," article 3; note that the Lutsk Rules stipulated nothing regarding the forebears of the teacher.

[44] *Ibid.*, pp. 408, 411-412, articles 5, 10.

[45] *Ibid.*, p. 409, article 6.

[46] *Ibid.*, pp. 413-415, article 12.

[47] *Ibid.*, p. 415, article 13; death by burning was also the punishment for deserting the Orthodox faith and joining another.

[48] *Ibid.*, pp. 415-417, article 14.

[49] *Ibid.*, p. 417, article 15.

[50] *Ibid.*, pp. 418-420, articles 17, 18.

[51] *Ibid.*, pp. 402-405, article 1.

[52] N. A. Zhelvakov, *Khrestomatiia po istorii pedagogiki* [Sourcebook in the History of Pedagogy] (Moscow: State Pedagogical Textbook Publishers, 1936), Vol. IV, Part I, p. 84, notes on Section 1 of the text.

[53] Chekhov, *loc. cit.*, pp. 17-18.

[54] Pinkevich, *loc. cit.*, p. 268.

[55] Medynskii, *loc. cit.*, p. 31.

[56] Chekhov, *loc. cit.*, pp. 18-19.

[57] *Ibid.*, p. 19.

[58] *Ibid.*, p. 20.

[59] Simkhovitch, *loc. cit.*, p. 494.

Chapter 3

The Rise of the State Universities

[1] F. F. Veselago, *Ocherk istorii morskogo kadetskogo korpusa* [Historical Sketches on the Naval Cadet Corps] (St. Petersburg: 1852). Cited in Zhelvakov, *op. cit.*, p. 90.

[2] E. V. Medynskii, "Development of Educational Ideas in Russia," *Soviet War News* (London), No. 802 (March 3, 1944). This author states that even the Moscow title was borrowed.

[3] *Ibid.;* Leary, *op. cit.*, p. 32.

[4] Medynskii, "Development of Educational Ideas in Russia," *loc. cit.*

[5] Leary, *loc. cit.*, p. 32.

[6] *Ibid.*, p. 32; G. Vernadsky, *A History of Russia* (New York: New Home Library, 1944), p. 126.

[7] "Instructions to the Naval Academy at St. Petersburg," article 4, in *Polnoe sobranie zakonov rossiiskoi Imperii c 1649 g* [Complete Collection of Laws of the Russian Empire from the year 1649] (48 volumes) (St. Petersburg: 1830-1843), Vol. V (1713-1719), No. 2937, p. 174.

[8] Thomas G. Masaryk, *The Spirit of Russia* (2 volumes) (New York: The Macmillan Company, 1919), Vol. I, p. 65.

[9] "Instructions to the Naval Academy at St. Petersburg," article 5, in *Polnoe sobranie zakonov*, *loc. cit.*, p. 174.

[10] *Ibid.*, pp. 175-176, article 27.

[11] *Ibid.*, p. 174, article 6.

[12] See Chapter 2 of this volume.

[13] Chekhov, *loc. cit.*, pp. 20-21.

[14] B. Pares, *History of Russia* (New York: A. A. Knopf, 1944), p. 215; Beazley, *op. cit.*, p. 240.

[15] Chekhov, *loc. cit.*, p. 22.

[16] *Ibid.*, p. 23; Leary, *loc. cit.*, p. 33; see also Chapter 2 of this volume.

[17] Masaryk, *op. cit.*, Vol. I, p. 73.

[18] Pares, *loc. cit.*, pp. 207-208; the office remained vacant until Premier Joseph Stalin elevated the Metropolitan Sergius to the post in 1943. A Church Sobor had elected a Patriarch shortly after the 1917 November Revolution but he was not recognized by the Government.

[19] "Dukhovnyi Reglament" [Ecclesiastical Statutes] (St. Petersburg: 1776). Cited in Zhelvakov, *loc. cit.*, pp. 101-109.

[20] Pares, *loc. cit.*, p. 207.

[21] Zhelvakov, *op. cit.*, pp. 190-191: notes on Section II of the text. See also Masaryk, *loc. cit.*, p. 61.

[22] Ecclesiastical Statutes, *loc. cit.*

[23] Not to be confused with the project for the Academy of Sciences, which will be described later.

[24] Ecclesiastical Statutes, *loc. cit.*

[25] *Ibid.*, articles 1-2.

[26] *Ibid.*, article 3.

[27] *Ibid.*, article 4.

[28] *Ibid.*, article 7.

[29] See Chapter 2 of this volume.

[30] Ecclesiastical Statutes, article 7.

[31] Chekhov, *loc. cit.*, pp. 20-21; Leary, *loc. cit.*, pp. 32-33.

[32] Masaryk, *loc. cit.*, pp. 60, 73; Vernadsky, *loc. cit.*, p. 126.

[33] Leary, *loc. cit.*, p. 33.

[34] Chekhov, *loc. cit.*, p. 22.

[35] Pares, *loc. cit.*, p. 215; Beazley, *loc. cit.*, p. 240.

[36] Leary, *loc. cit.*, p. 34. Peter met Leibnitz during his second trip to western Europe in 1716, and it was then that the idea for a Russian Academy of Sciences was born. Leary implies that Peter was far from literate himself, but it is well established that he could read and write and had a fair knowledge of arithmetic. According to Masaryk, *loc. cit.*, p. 55, Peter was awarded an honorary doctorate by Oxford University and was also nominated for membership in the Académie Française.

[37] *Polnoe sobranie zakonov*, No. 4443, Vol. VII (1723-1727), p. 220: decree of January 28, 1724, especially articles 1 and 2.

[38] Chekhov, *loc. cit.*, p. 22; Leary, *loc. cit.*, p. 36; Simkhovitch, *loc. cit.*, pp. 498-499.

[39] Simkhovitch, *loc. cit.*, p. 499; Leary, *loc. cit.*, p. 36; Vernadsky, *loc. cit.*, pp. 126-129.

[40] Zhelvakov, *loc. cit.*, p. 191: notes on Section II of the text. According to Grekov, *op. cit.*, p. 152, Tatishchev (1686-1750) was the first Russian historian to make use of the ancient Russian annals.

[41] V. N. Tatishchev, *Razgovor o pol'ze nauk i uchilishch* [Dialogue on the Benefits of Science and the School], edited by N. Popov (Moscow: 1877).

[42] *Ibid.*, question 116, p. 156.

[43] See also Chekhov, *loc. cit.*, p. 24.

[44] "Decree of the Empress Anne on the Registry of Nobles in the Cadet Corps," 1731: *Polnoe sobranie zakonov*, No. 8894, Vol. VIII (1728-1732), pp. 569-570.

[45] Chekhov, *loc. cit.*, pp. 25-26.

[46] Leary, *loc. cit.*, p. 36.

[47] Beazley, *op. cit.*, pp. 265-266.

[48] Leary, *loc. cit.*, p. 36.

[49] Vernadsky, *loc. cit.*, p. 127.

[50] Leary, *loc. cit.*, p. 37; Simkhovitch, *loc. cit.*, p. 500.

[51] Leary, *loc. cit.*, p. 37.

[52] Simkhovitch, *loc. cit.*, p. 500.

[53] Zhelvakov, *loc. cit.*, p. 192: notes on Section II of the text.

[54] See Chapter 2 of this volume.

[55] Simkhovitch, *loc. cit.*, p. 500.

[56] See Chapter 2 of this volume.

[57] "Approved Plan for the Establishment of Moscow University," article 28: *Polnoe sobranie zakonov*, Vol. XIV, p. 292, No. 10346; see also Simkhovitch, *loc. cit.*, p. 500, and Leary, *loc. cit.*, p. 37.

[58] Leary, *loc. cit.*, pp. 36-37.

[59] Simkhovitch, *loc. cit.*, p. 499; Leary, *loc. cit.*, p. 36; see also Chapter 2 of this volume.

[60] Leary, *loc. cit.*, p. 137.

Chapter 4
The Creation of State Schools

[1] Chekhov, *op. cit.*, p. 27.

[2] "Rules of the Educational Society for Noble Girls," articles 1-42: *Uchrezhdenniia i ustavy, kasaiushchiesia do vospitaniia i obucheniia v Rossii iunoshestva oboeva pola* [Organization and Rules Concerning the Nurture and Training of Youth of Both Sexes in Russia], Vols. I and II (St. Petersburg: 1774). Cited in Zhelvakov, *op. cit.*, pp. 134-141; see also Leary, *op. cit.*, p. 42.

[3] "Rules," article 4.

[4] *Ibid.*, article 15.

[5] *Ibid.*, article 27.

[6] *Ibid.*, article 23.

[7] "Rules of the Noble Terrestial Cadet Corps for the Instruction of Well-Born Russian Youth," 1766: *Uchrezhdenniia i ustavy*, etc., *op. cit.*

[8] *Ibid.*, Section V, articles 1-3.

[9] *Ibid.*, Section VIII.

[10] Leary, *loc. cit.*, p. 41.

[11] A. Veselovskii, "Diderot," in *Entsiklopedicheskii slovar'* [Encyclopedic Dictionary] (St. Petersburg: I. A. Efron, 1893), Vol. X, pp. 581-588. An interesting aspect of Diderot's visit has only recently come to light in D. H. Gordon and N. L. Torrey, *The Censoring of Diderot's Encyclopédie* (New York: The Columbia University Press, 1947). On the basis of a copy found in Russia, these authors show how the work was censored in France.

[12] These boards, under various names, were to be identified with local school administration during the following two centuries; see subsequent chapters of this volume.

[13] Leary, *loc. cit.*, pp. 41-42; see also Masaryk, *op. cit.*, Vol. I, p. 79, for itemized account of Catherine's gifts of money to her lovers, totaling nearly 30 million rubles during her reign.

[14] O. Kaidanova-Bervy, *An Historical Sketch of Russian Popular Education*, Vol. I, Chap. 1. [The English translation of *Ocherki po istorii narodnogo obrazovaniia v Rossii i SSSR na osnove lichnogo opyta i nabliudenii*] (Berlin: Petropolis Verlag, 1938), 2 volumes. The translation was made under the auspices of the Russian Translation Project of the American Council of Learned Societies, Washington, D.C., and has not yet been published. References to this work are therefore to chapters only, since the pagination of the MSS is subject to change.

[15] Zhelvakov, *op. cit.*, p. 194: notes to Section II of the text.

[16] Kaidanova-Bervy, *loc. cit.*

[17] *Ibid.*; Hans Von Eckardt, *Russia* (New York: A. A. Knopf, 1932), p. 89.

[18] Leary, *loc. cit.*, pp. 43-44.

[19] *Ibid.*, pp. 43-44; Vernadsky, *op. cit.*, p. 129: the latter author comments further that "the greatest Russian historians of the XVIII century were not professional men of learning. . . . One . . . was an administrative officer; another a politician; and a third, a military man."

[20] Kaidanova-Bervy, *loc. cit.*

[21] N. I. Novikov, ed., *Drevniaia rossiiskaia vivliofika* [Ancient Russian Library] (2nd ed.; Moscow: Press of the Typographic Company, 1788-1791), 20 volumes.

[22] Kaidanova-Bervy, *loc. cit.*

[23] *Ibid.;* for corroboratory estimates of Novikov, see Beazley, *op. cit.*, p. 298, and Pares, *op. cit.*, pp. 253-254, 273-274.

[24] Simkhovitch, *loc. cit.*, p. 502.

[25] Leary, *loc. cit.*, pp. 41-42.

[26] *Ibid.*, pp. 41-42.

[27] Simkhovitch, *loc. cit.*, p. 502.

[28] *Ibid.*, p. 502.

[29] *Polnoe sobranie zakonov,* No. 16421, of August 5, 1786, Vol. XXII (1784-1788), pp. 646-669.

[30] *Ibid.*, p. 646: Preamble.

[31] *Ibid.*, articles 1, 24; Leary, *loc. cit.*, pp. 41-42; Simkhovitch, *loc. cit.*, pp. 502-503; Chekhov, *op cit.*, pp. 27-28.

[32] Leary, *loc. cit.*, pp. 41-42; see also earlier pages of this chapter.

[33] *Polnoe sobranie zakonov,* No. 16421, chap. two, sect. II, article 26; Leary, *loc. cit.*, pp. 41-42.

[34] *Pol. sob. zak.*, chap. one, sect. IV, articles 18-23.

[35] *Ibid.*, chap. three, sect. II, art. 49.

[36] *Ibid.*, chap. three, sect. I, art. 27, 30.

[37] *Ibid.*, chap. three, sect. I, art. 38; sect. II, art. 48.

[38] *Ibid.*, chap. three, sect. I, art. 28.

[39] *Ibid.*, chap. three, sect. II, art. 41-42; sect. I, art. 31-33.

[40] *Ibid.*, chap. three, sect. I, art. 29, 35, 37.

[41] *Ibid.*, chap. three, sect. I, art. 38, 34.

[42] *Ibid.*, chap. three, sect. II, art. 47.

[43] *Ibid.*, chap. three, sect. II, art. 46.

[44] *Ibid.*, chap. three, sect. I, art. 36.

[45] See Table No. 1 in Appendix.

[46] Leary, *loc. cit.*, p. 42.

[47] *Ibid.*, p. 43; Simkhovitch, *loc. cit.*, pp. 502-503.

[48] Leary, *loc. cit.*, p. 43.

[49] *Ibid.*, p. 43.

[50] *Ibid.*, p. 37.

[51] *Ibid.*, p. 43.

[52] Simkhovitch, *loc. cit.*, p. 499.

[53] Leary, *loc. cit.*, p. 42.

[54] *Pol. sob. zak.*, Vol. XXII, pp. 648-649, articles 23, 18-26; see also earlier pages of this chapter.

[55] See Table No 1 in Appendix.

[56] Leary. *loc. cit.*, p. 42.

[57] A. S. Voronov, *Iankovitch de-Mirievo:* cited in Zhelvakov, *op. cit.*, pp. 177-178.

[58] Leary, *loc. cit.*, p. 44; V. I. Semevskii, *Krestiane v tsarstvovanie imperatrytsy Ekaterina II* [The Peasantry in the Reign of Empress Catherine II] (St. Petersburg: 1901-1903), Vol. I, pp. 281-287.

[59] A. Kornilov, *Modern Russian History* (2 volumes) (New York: A. A. Knopf, 1924), Vol. I, pp. 25-26; the author also gives an economic classification of this population, as follows: peasantry, 94 per cent; lower urban, 2.5 per cent; merchants, 1.0 per cent; parish clergy, 1.0 per cent; nobles and officials, 1.5 per cent.

[60] *Ibid.;* Vernadsky, *op. cit.;* Pares, *op. cit.*

[61] Chekhov, *op. cit.*

[62] *Ibid.*, p. 24.

[63] *Ibid.*, p. 25.

[64] *Ibid.*, p. 26.

[65] See earlier pages of this chapter for mention of persecution of Novikov.

[66] Leary, *loc. cit.*, p. 41.

[67] See Note 59, above.

[68] Chekhov, *loc. cit.*, p. 27.

Chapter 5

The Forging of a School System

[1] Beazley, *op. cit.*, p. 350; Leary, *op. cit.*, p. 45.

[2] Cited in Zhelvakov, *op. cit.*, p. 195: introduction to Section III of text.

[3] Beazley, *loc. cit.*, p. 351; Leary, *loc. cit.*, p. 45.

[4] "Manifesto on the Establishment of Ministries," decree #1 (20,406) of Sept. 8, 1802: *Sbornik postanovlenii po ministerstvu narodnogo prosveshcheniia* [Collection of Decrees of the Ministry of Public Education], 3 volumes (St. Petersburg: Press of the Imperial Academy of Sciences, 1864-65), Vol. I (1802-1825), pp. 1-4.

[5] Zhelvakov, *op. cit.*, p. 330: notes on Section III of the text.

[6] The Empress Maria Feodorovna, the German second wife of Tsar Paul, survived not only her husband, but also her eldest son, Tsar Alexander I. When she died in 1828, her younger son, Tsar Nicholas I,

created a special department in the Ministry of Public Education to continue the separate supervision of these schools. In 1859 another Empress Maria, also German and the wife of Alexander II, took these schools under her own protection. (See Beazley, *op. cit.*, pp. 347, 397, 437, 588.)

[7] Leary, *loc. cit.*, pp. 46-50.

[8] Simkhovitch, *op. cit.*, p. 505; see also Kornilov, *op. cit.*, Vol. I, p. 187.

[9] See Table No. 1 in Appendix.

[10] Chekhov, *op. cit.*, p. 28.

[11] Zhelvakov, *loc. cit.*, p. 330: notes on Section III of the text.

[12] Beazley, *op. cit.*, p. 382.

[13] *Ibid.*, p. 382; Zhelvakov, *loc. cit.*, p. 330; according to Kornilov, *loc. cit.*, p. 187, "the quality of the pedagogical personnel [in the universities] was then quite high, chiefly owing to the invitation of foreign professors (about sixty), although they had to lecture in Latin, French or German; only half of the professors lectured in Russian."

[14] Leary, *loc. cit.*, pp. 50-51.

[15] "Regulations of Moscow, Kharkov, Kazan Universities," decree #45 (21,497) of Nov. 5, 1804: *Sborn. post. MNP*, Vol. I, pp. 289-290.

[16] Articles 47 and 48 of the Regulations state that "the Ordinary and Honorary Professors comprise the University Council or General Assembly, the chairman of which is the Rector," and that this body "serves as the highest authority on academic and legal affairs" of the University. Thus "Council" and "General Assembly" appear to be synonymous terms.

[17] *Ibid.*, article 125.

[18] See Note 16, above.

[19] "Regulations," article 127.

[20] *Ibid.*, article 128.

[21] *Ibid.*, article 130.

[22] *Ibid.*, articles 131-133.

[23] *Ibid.*, article 129.

[24] Decree #47 (21,501) of Nov. 5, 1804: *Sborn. post. MNP*, Vol. I, pp. 302-339.

[25] Simkhovitch, *loc. cit.*, p. 506; Leary, *loc. cit.*, pp. 50-51; Beazley, *loc. cit.*, pp. 382-383.

[26] Simkhovitch, *loc. cit.*, p. 506; Leary, *loc. cit.*, pp. 50-51.

[27] Simkhovitch, *loc. cit.*, p. 506.

[28] *Ibid.;* Leary, *loc. cit.*, pp. 50-51.

[29] Beazley, *loc. cit.*, p. 382.

[30] Chekhov, *loc. cit.*, pp. 28-29.

[31] "Regulations for Educational Establishments Under the Jurisdiction of the Universities," decree #47 (21,501) of Nov. 5, 1804, Sect. IV, article 32: *Sborn. post, MNP*, Vol. I, pp. 302-339.

[32] *Ibid.*, article 40.

[33] *Ibid.*, article 41.
[34] *Ibid.*, articles 42-43.
[35] *Ibid.*, article 44.
[36] *Ibid.*, articles 49, 100, 135.
[37] *Ibid.*, article 46; see also Chapter 4 of this volume.
[38] *Ibid.*, articles 51-52.
[39] *Ibid.*, article 53; see also earlier documents as described in previous chapters of this volume.
[40] See Tables 2-11, 14-15 in Appendix.
[41] "Regulations for Educational Establishments," articles 136, 101.
[42] *Ibid.*, article 50.
[43] Leary, *loc. cit.*, p. 51.
[44] Beazley, *op. cit.*, p. 382.
[45] I. P. Pnin, *Opyt o prosveshchenii otnocitel'no k Rossii* [Experiences in Education in Russia] in *Ivan Pnin–Sochineniia* [Collected Works of Ivan Pnin] (Moscow: 1934), pp. 123-124. Pnin (1773-1805) was long a member of a liberal St. Petersburg circle which had some influence on the formation of the Ministry of Public Education.
[46] Beazley, *loc. cit.*, p. 382; Vernadsky, *op. cit.*, p. 127; Kornilov, *op. cit.*, Vol. I, p. 111.
[47] Leary, *loc. cit.*, p. 52.
[48] Beazley, *loc. cit.*, p. 382.
[49] Simkhovitch, *loc. cit.*, p. 513.
[50] Beazley, *loc. cit.*, pp. 382-383; all three of the lycées established during this period ultimately became institutions of higher learning. The one at Tsarskoe Selo was renamed Alexander's Lycée in honor of its founder; the Richelieu Lycée was transformed into the University of Odessa in 1865; and the Bezborodko Lycée at Niezhin had achieved its higher status by 1913: see Table No. 33 in Appendix.
[51] Leary, *loc. cit.*, p. 52.
[52] *Ibid.*, p. 52; Simkhovitch, *loc. cit.*, p. 506; Chekhov, *loc. cit.*, pp. 28-29.
[53] Chekhov, *loc. cit.*, p. 29.
[54] S. V. Rozhdestvenskii, *Istoricheskii obzor deiatel'nosti ministerstva narodnogo prosveshcheniia (1802-1902)* [Historical Review of the Activities of the Ministry of Public Education, 1802-1902] St. Petersburg: 1902). Table is titled "Educational Establishments in Russia at the Beginning of the XIX Century" but comparisons with other sources indicate that the definite year is 1806: see Chekhov, *loc. cit.*, pp. 28-29, and T. Darlington, *Education in Russia,* Board of Education, Special Reports on Educational Subjects, Vol. 23 (London: Wyman & Sons, Ltd., 1909), p. 52.
[55] Leary, *loc. cit.*, p. 52.
[56] Chekhov, *loc. cit.*, p. 29.
[57] Leary, *loc. cit.*, p. 53.

[58] *Ibid.*, p. 53: Leary points out that Uvarov's ideas were incorporated almost intact into the educational reorganization of 1819.

[59] *Ibid.*, p. 54; Kornilov, *op. cit.*, Vol. I, pp. 188-189; Zhelvakov, *op. cit.*, pp. 330-331.

[60] Pares, *op. cit.*, pp. 308-309.

[61] Zhelvakov, *loc. cit.*, p. 330: notes on Section III of the text.

[62] Decree #301 (27,106) of Oct. 24, 1817: *Sborn. post. MNP*, Vol. I, pp. 971-972.

[63] "Circulated Proposals Regarding Subjects Taught in Gymnasiums, District and Parish Schools," decree #174 of June 5, 1819: *Sbornik rasporiazhenii po ministerstvu narodnogo prosveshcheniia* [Collection of Edicts of the Ministry of Public Education] (St. Petersburg: 1866-67), Vol. I, (1802-1834), pp. 385-389.

[64] Cited in Darlington, *loc. cit.*, p. 55; see also Leary, *loc. cit.*, p. 54.

[65] Leary, *loc. cit.*, p. 55.

[66] B. Pares, *Russia and Reform* (New York: Dutton & Co., 1907), pp. 191-192.

[67] Leary, *loc. cit.*, p. 55; Beazley, *loc. cit.*, p. 383.

[68] Decree #374 of January 17, 1820: *Sborn. post. MNP*, Vol. I, pp. 1199-1209.

[69] Pares, *Russia and Reform*, p. 192.

[70] Leary, *loc. cit.*, p. 55.

[71] Pares, *Russia and Reform*, p. 192.

[72] Beazley, *loc. cit.*, p. 382; Darlington, *loc. cit.*, pp. 55-57.

[73] Leary, *loc. cit.*, p. 55.

[74] Darlington, *loc. cit.*, pp. 59-60.

[75] Simkhovitch, *loc. cit.*, p. 513.

[76] *Ibid.*, p. 506; Vernadsky, *loc. cit.*, p. 127.

[77] Simkhovitch, *loc. cit.*, p. 506; Vernadsky, *loc. cit.*, p. 127.

[78] Simkhovitch, *loc. cit.*, p. 506.

[79] Decree #340 (27,646) of Jan. 20, 1819: *Sborn. post. MNP*, Vol. I, pp. 1134-1145.

[80] *Ibid.*, article 1.

[81] *Ibid.*, articles 2-7.

[82] *Ibid.*, articles 9-14.

[83] *Ibid.*, article 18.

[84] *Ibid.*, article 43.

[85] Decree #302 (27,108) of Oct. 25, 1817: *Sborn. post. MNP*, Vol. I, pp. 1011-1019.

[86] *Ibid.*; see also Table No. 17 in Appendix.

Chapter 6

The Long Period of Reaction

[1] B. Pares, *History of Russia*, pp. 308-309.

[2] Pares, *Russia and Reform*, pp. 272-274.

[3] *Sborn. raspor. MNP*, Vol. I (1802-1834), pp. 527-530, article 251, September 11, 1824.

[4] *Ibid.*, Vol. I, pp. 531-538, article 254, December 11, 1824.

[5] *Ibid.*, Vol. I, pp. 531-538; note similarity even of phraseology between this document and the "Instructions" of Magnitskii, described in Chapter 5 of this volume.

[6] Pares, *Russia and Reform*, pp. 272-274.

[7] Leary, *loc. cit.*, p. 62; Simkhovitch, *loc. cit.*, p. 507; Beazley, *op. cit.*, p. 405.

[8] "Rescript of Nicholas I Regarding the Fundaments of the New Structure of Educational Establishments," dated August 19, 1827: *Sborn. raspor. MNP*, Vol. I, *loc. cit.;* see also Leary, *loc. cit.*, p. 62, Simkhovitch, *loc. cit.*, p. 507 and *Sborn. post. MNP*, Vol. II (1) 1825-39, p. 35.

[9] Decree #66 (2502) of Dec. 8, 1828: *Sborn. post. MNP*, Vol. II (1), 1825-39, pp. 150-209.

[10] Simkhovitch, *loc. cit.*, p. 507.

[11] *Ibid.*, pp. 507-508.

[12] Pares, *Russia and Reform*, p. 194.

[13] "Rules of Gymnasiums and Schools Under the Jurisdiction of the Universities," decree #66 (2502) of Dec. 8, 1828: *Sborn. post. MNP*, Vol. II (1), pp. 150-209, articles 11, 35, 50; Peter I had awarded tenth rank to teachers, and Catherine II frequently bestowed even higher rank upon them.

[14] *Ibid.*, article 36.

[15] *Ibid.*, article 31.

[16] *Ibid.*, articles 30, 32, 161, 314.

[17] *Ibid.*, article 272.

[18] Article 137 states that "the nobility of the province in which the gymnasium is located elects from its own midst an Honorary Trustee." Although this official's authority varied in the several provinces, he was always privileged to carry his opinions to the Minister of Public Education himself.

[19] "Rules of Gymnasiums and Schools Under the Jurisdiction of the Universities" (1928), article 11.

[20] *Ibid.*, article 36.

[21] *Ibid.*, article 200.

[22] *Ibid.*, article 141.

[23] *Ibid.*, articles 95-96.

[24] *Ibid.*, article 99.

[25] *Ibid.*, article 100.

[26] *Ibid.*, article 106.

[27] *Ibid.*, article 37.

[28] *Ibid.*, article 298.

[29] Simkhovitch, *loc. cit.*, p. 507. That their suppression was seriously considered is revealed in Darlington, *op. cit.*, pp. 71-72.

[30] "Rules of Gymnasiums and Schools Under the Jurisdiction of the Universities" (1828), *op. cit.*, chapter 8, articles 307-325.

[31] *Ibid.*, article 311. That all private boarding schools of this era did not deserve these encomiums is indicated by a description of some of these institutions in the memoirs of V. N. Karpov: "In these years [1830-40], to maintain a private boarding school was an extremely profitable profession, because it was necessary to pay 700-1000 rubles a year in order to place a son or daughter in the school for full maintenance. In addition to this demand, each male or female boarder brought a dowry to the boarding school, consisting of a silver spoon, knife and fork, six napkins, and two table cloths. If we bear in mind that in a boarding school having a good reputation there were not less than 200 pupils, we see that it received at one time 200 silver knives, 200 silver spoons, 100 dozen napkins, and more than 33 dozen tablecloths. But don't forget that in boarding schools silver spoons become German silver, knives often lose their silver handles, forks are without prongs, the napkins mended, and the tablecloths have great patches. It would be interesting to know where this mass of new spoons, knives, napkins and other items, brought as dowry to the boarding school, are hidden." from *Khar'kovskaia starina iz vospominanii starozhilia* [Old Times in Kharkov from the Memoirs of A Long-Time Resident] (Kharkov: Iuzhnii Krai, 1900), p. 227.

[32] "Rules," articles 314, 318, 315, 322, 317.

[33] *Ibid.*, article 311.

[34] *Ibid.*, articles 308, 316, 317.

[35] *Ibid.*, articles 320-321.

[36] *Ibid.*, articles 324-325.

[37] Simkhovitch, *loc. cit.*, p. 506.

[38] See first pages of this chapter.

[39] Darlington, *op. cit.*, p. 59; see also Chapter 4 of this volume.

[40] Cited in Beazley, *loc. cit.*, p. 405: "This formula—Altar, Throne, and People—remained the watchword of reaction throughout the remainder of the century."

[41] *Ibid.*, p. 405.

[42] *Ibid.*

[43] *Ibid.*, p. 406; Leary, *loc. cit.*, p. 64.

[44] Decree #363 (8337) of July 26, 1835: *Sborn. post. MNP*, Vol. II (1), pp. 767-768.

[45] *Ibid.*, article 150.

[46] *Ibid.*, article 151.

[47] *Ibid.*, article 152.
[48] *Ibid.*, articles 155-158.
[49] *Ibid.*, article 154.
[50] *Ibid.*, article 159.
[51] Decree #383 (8664) of Dec. 9, 1835: *Sborn. post. MNP*, Vol. II (1), pp. 793-804.
[52] *Ibid.*, introduction to the decree. The restrictions outlined here are but one example of the prejudices of the educational hierarchy in St. Petersburg, composed largely of men whose entire orientation was toward metropolitan standards of social position and culture. An exception to this rule was Count Uvarov, the new Minister of Public Education, who had traveled a great deal in Siberia in connection with his archeological explorations. Undoubtedly, his personal influence had much to do with the expansion of educational facilities in this region during his tenure of office in the Ministry (1833-49), the longest in Russian history.
[53] Decree #383, introduction to the decree.
[54] Beazley, *loc. cit.*, p. 407.
[55] Beazley, *loc. cit.*, p. 407.
[56] Simkhovitch, *loc. cit.*, p. 507: Leary, *loc. cit.*, p. 64.
[57] Simkhovitch, *loc. cit.*, p. 507.
[58] *Ibid.*, p. 507; Leary, *loc. cit.*, p. 64; Pares, *Russia and Reform*, p. 194.
[59] Simkhovitch, *loc. cit.*, p. 507, states that one acknowledged reason for the increased tuition rates was to keep out poor people "whom education may make dissatisfied with their lot, or with that of their friends."
[60] *Ibid.*, p. 507; Leary, *loc. cit.*, p. 64.
[61] Leary, *loc. cit.*, p. 64.
[62] *Ibid.*, p. 65.
[63] *Ibid.*; Beazley, *loc. cit.*, p. 408.
[64] Simkhovitch, *loc. cit.*, p. 508.
[65] Leary, *loc. cit.*, p. 65.
[66] Chekhov, *op. cit.*, pp. 31-32.
[67] *Ibid.*, pp. 31-35; Leary, *loc. cit.*, p. 65.
[68] G. T. Robinson, *Rural Russia Under the Old Regime* (New York: Longmans, Green, 1932), pp. 44-45.
[69] Vernadsky, *op. cit.*, p. 127.
[70] See Tables Nos. 12 and 13 in Appendix.
[71] Vernadsky, *loc. cit.*, pp. 127-128; Darlington, *op. cit.*, p. 38; Pares, *Russia and Reform*, p. 190.
[72] "Conditions for Examinations for Academic Degrees," decree #484 (10,188) of April 28, 1837: *Sborn. post. MNP*, Vol. II (1), pp. 984-988 and appendix A, pp. 46-47.
[73] *Ibid.*, articles 1-3.
[74] *Ibid.*, articles 5, 11.
[75] *Ibid.*, articles 6, 12.

[76] *Ibid.*, articles 7-8.
[77] *Ibid.*, articles 9-10.
[78] *Ibid.*, articles 13-17 and addendum to decree, item A.
[79] *Ibid.*, article 18.
[80] *Ibid.*, article 22.
[81] *Ibid.*, article 23.
[82] Decree #211 (6366) of Aug. 1, 1833: *Sborn. post. MNP*, Vol. II (1), pp. 458-460.
[83] "Regulations for the Imperial University of St. Vladimir," decree #798 (15,730) of June 9, 1842: *Sborn. post. MNP*, Vol. II (2), (1840-55), p. 234, articles 34-36.
[84] Decree #850 (16,984) of June 28, 1843: *Sborn. post. MNP*, Vol. II (2), pp. 289-293.
[85] Decree #665 (13,137) of Jan. 28, 1840: *Sborn. post. MNP*, Vol. II (2), p. 5. Many important incidents in the history of the Main Pedagogical Institute at St. Petersburg have been omitted from this and preceding sections of the volume because this institution receives special consideration in Chapter 7.
[86] Decree #1175 (24,597) of Nov. 5, 1850: *Sborn. post. MNP*, Vol. II (2), pp. 1026-1027.
[87] The 1840 decree (see reference note 85 above) listed this salary at 1000 silver rubles a year, which was about half that of Ordinary Professors in other subjects.
[88] *Ibid.*
[89] Decree #1186 (24,867) of Jan. 23, 1851: *Sborn. post. MNP*, Vol. II (2), pp. 1047-1051.
[90] *Ibid.*, articles 3-7.
[91] *Ibid.*, article 8.
[92] *Ibid.*, articles 9-12.
[93] *Ibid.*, articles 13-18.
[94] Leary, *loc. cit.*, p. 63.
[95] *Ibid.*, p. 66.
[96] Cited in Pares, *Russia and Reform*, p. 188.
[97] Beazley, *loc. cit.*, p. 406.

Chapter 7

Brief History of the Main Pedagogical Institute at St. Petersburg

[1] Notes to decree #158 of Nov. 15, 1858: *Sborn. post. MNP*, Vol. III (1855-64), pp. 294-299.
[2] *Ibid.;* also see Preface to decree #302 (27,108) of Oct. 25, 1817: *Sborn. post. MNP*, Vol. I, pp. 1011-1019.

[3] Decree #25 (20,769a) of May 20, 1803: *Sborn. post. MNP*, Vol. I, pp. 186-187.

[4] *Ibid.*

[5] See partial budget for Teachers Gymnasium in Table No. 14 in Appendix; for budgetary data on state universities and the Ministry of Public Education, see Tables Nos. 2, 3 and 4.

[6] Decree #34 (21,265) of April 16, 1804: *Sborn. post. MNP*, Vol. I, pp. 205-228.

[7] *Ibid.*, articles 1-2.

[8] *Ibid.*, articles 3-4.

[9] *Ibid.*, articles 5-9.

[10] *Ibid.*, articles 35, 15, 51, 120-123.

[11] *Ibid.*, articles 16-20.

[12] *Ibid.*, article 57.

[13] See Table No. 15 in Appendix.

[14] Decree #98 (23,035) of May, 23, 1808: *Sborn. post. MNP*, Vol. I, pp. 458-474.

[15] Decree #20 (20,863) of July 25, 1803, articles 100-101: *Sborn. post. MNP*, Vol. I, p. 94.

[16] Decree #163 (24,662) of June 2, 1811: *Sborn. post. MNP*, Vol. I, pp. 636-637.

[17] For example, the Imperial Lycée at Tsarskoe Selo; see decree #265 (26,584) of Dec. 30, 1816: *Sborn. post. MNP*, Vol. I, pp. 875-876.

[18] "Formation of the Main Pedagogical Institute," decree # 264 (26,573) of Dec. 23, 1816: *Sborn. post. MNP*, Vol. I, pp. 829-874.

[19] *Ibid.*, article 2.

[20] *Ibid.*, article 3.

[21] *Ibid.*, article 6.

[22] *Ibid.*, article 32.

[23] *Ibid.*, article 53.

[24] *Ibid.*, articles 44, 32.

[25] *Ibid.*, articles 35-36.

[26] *Ibid.*, article 49.

[27] *Ibid.*, articles 38-41.

[28] *Ibid.*, article 42.

[29] *Ibid.*, articles 53-55; see also Table No. 16 in Appendix.

[30] *Ibid.*, article 56.

[31] See Chapter 5 of this volume for the general implications of these changes.

[32] "On the Establishment of a Second Division in the Main Pedagogical Institute for the Training of Teachers for the Parish and District Schools," decree #302 (27,108) of Oct. 25, 1817: *Sborn. post. MNP*, Vol. I, pp. 1020-1022, article 1.

[33] *Ibid.*, article 2; it should be noted, however, that the budget implies that more pupils may be accommodated later. (See note to Table No. 17 in Appendix.)

[34] *Ibid.*, articles 4, 3.

[35] *Ibid.*, article 5.

[36] *Ibid.*, articles 19-20.

[37] *Ibid.*, articles 8-11; it is interesting to note that this first decree of the new amalgamated ministry persists in referring to the office merely as the Ministry of Public Education.

[38] *Ibid.*, articles 12-13.

[39] *Ibid.*, article 18.

[40] *Ibid.*, articles 17, 21.

[41] *Ibid.*, article 6.

[42] See Table No 17 in Appendix, as well as Tables Nos. 14, 15, 16.

[43] "On the Establishment of a Second Division," (1817), articles 5-6.

[44] *Ibid.*, article 7.

[45] For background of this and subsequent statements, see Chapter 5 of this volume.

[46] Darlington, *op. cit.*, p. 49.

[47] *Ibid.*, pp. 56-59.

[48] "On the Establishment of a University in St. Petersburg," decree #344 (27,675) of Feb. 8, 1819: *Sborn. post. MNP*, Vol. I, pp. 1152-1160.

[49] *Ibid.*, articles 1-3.

[50] *Ibid.*, articles 4, 11, 13.

[51] *Ibid.*, article 34.

[52] Notes to Decree #158 of Nov. 15, 1858: *Sborn. post. MNP*, Vol. III, pp. 296-297.

[53] Darlington, *loc. cit.*, p. 66.

[54] Decree #61 (2314) of Sept. 30, 1828: *Sborn. post. MNP*, Vol. II (1), pp. 112-113.

[55] Decree # 62 (2315) of Sept. 30, 1828: *Sborn. post. MNP* Vol. II (1), pp. 113-146.

[56] *Ibid.*, articles 1, 3.

[57] *Ibid.*, articles 9, 13, 17.

[58] *Ibid.*, articles 16, 20, 24, 33.

[59] *Ibid.*, article 25.

[60] *Ibid.*, article 36.

[61] *Ibid.*, articles 153-159, 37-38.

[62] See Table No. 18 in Appendix.

[63] See the duties of Monitors in gymnasiums, as described in Chapter 6 of this volume.

[64] See Table No. 18 in Appendix.

[65] Decree #157 (5296) of April 16, 1832: *Sborn. post. MNP*, Vol. II (1), p. 382.

[66] Decree #525 (10,845) of Dec. 30, 1837: *Sborn. post. MNP*, Vol. II (1), pp. 1029-1030.

[67] See Table No. 18 in Appendix.

[68] Notes to decree # 158 of Nov. 15, 1858: *Sborn. post. MNP*, Vol. III, pp. 294-299.

[69] Decree #665 (13,137) of Jan. 28, 1840: *Sborn. post. MNP*, Vol. II (2), p. 5.

[70] Decree #1175 (24,597) of Nov. 5, 1850: *Sborn. post. MNP*, Vol. II (2), pp. 1026-1027; see also Chapter 5 of this volume.

[71] Notes to decree #158 of Nov. 15, 1858: *Sborn. post. MNP*, Vol. III, pp. 294-299.

[72] *Ibid.*

[73] *Ibid.*

[74] *Ibid.*

[75] *Ibid.*; the Main Pedagogical Institute enjoyed the use of the entire sum for four years, but at the end of that time one-fourth of the appropriation was returned to the Pedagogical Institute of the University and assigned to the Faculty of Eastern Languages.

[76] "Instructions to the Director and the Inspector of the Main Pedagogical Institute," decree #1186 of Jan. 23, 1851: *Sborn. post. MNP*, Vol. II (2), pp. 1047-1051; see also Chapter 6 of this volume.

[77] Notes to decree #158 of Nov. 15, 1858: *Sborn. post. MNP*, Vol. III, pp. 294-299.

[78] Decree #35 (30,124) of Feb. 3, 1856: *Sborn. post. MNP*, Vol. III, p. 47.

[79] Decree #158 of Nov. 15, 1858: *Sborn. post. MNP*, Vol. III, pp. 294-296.

Chapter 8

The Great Reforms

[1] Beazley, et al. *Russia from the Varangians to the Bolsheviks* (Oxford, England: The Clarendon Press, 1918), p. 426.

[2] E. N. Medynskii, *Istoriia russkoi pedagogiki* [History of Russian Pedagogy] (Moscow: State Pedagogical Textbook Publishers, 1936), p. 235.

[3] N. V. Chekhov, *Tipy russkoi shkoly* [Types of Russian Schools] (Moscow: "MIR" Publishers, 1923), p. 33.

[4] See Chapter 6 of this volume.

[5] Chekhov, *loc. cit.*, pp. 34-35.

[6] See Chapter 6 of this volume.

[7] M. Kovalevsky, *Modern Customs and Ancient Laws of Russia* (London: David Nutt, 1891), p. 227. It will be recalled that several of the large landholders of France took much the same attitude in the decade 1780-1789.

[8] See especially G. T. Robinson, *Rural Russia Under the Old Regime* (New York: Longmans, Green and Co., 1932), passim. According to

one Soviet authority, since 1826 there had been peasant revolts in 45 out of the 47 guberniyas in European Russia, involving 2,000 villages: E. A. Morokhovets, *Krest'ianskaia reforma* 1861g (The Peasant Reform of 1861), (Moscow: State Socio-Economic Publishers, 1937), p. 126.

9 B. Pares, *Russia and Reform* (New York: E. P. Dutton and Co., 1907), p. 52.

10 E. Noble, *Russia and the Russians* (New York: Houghton, Mifflin and Co., 1901), pp. 136-137.

11 Pares, *loc. cit.*, p. 52.

12 *Ibid.*

13 T. Woody, *New Minds, New Men* (New York: The Macmillan Co., 1932), p. 30.

14 N. Hans, *History of Russian Educational Policy, 1701-1917* (London: P. S. King and Son, Ltd., 1931), p. 232: figures given are compiled from tables therein.

15 Pares, *loc. cit.*, pp. 51-52; Noble, *loc. cit.*, p. 136; Woody, *loc. cit.*, pp. 30-31.

16 Hans, *loc. cit.*, pp. 238-242.

17 *Ibid.*, p. 293.

18 See Table No. 19 in Appendix.

19 D. B. Leary, *Education and Autocracy in Russia* (Buffalo, N.Y.: University of Buffalo, 1919), p. 75.

20 Beazley, *loc. cit.*, pp. 435-436; the ideas from which these students took their inspiration will be analyzed in Chapter 9 of this volume.

21 A. Kornilov, *Modern Russian History* (New York: Alfred A. Knopf, 1924), Vol. II, p. 91.

22 Beazley, *loc. cit.*, p. 436; Kornilov, *loc. cit.*, pp. 91-92.

23 Beazley, *loc. cit.*, p. 436.

24 *Sbornik postanovlenii po ministerstvu narodnogo proveshcheniia*, Vol. 1, Preface. According to Zhelvakov, *op. cit.*, Vol. IV., Part II, pp. 551-552 (notes to section IV of text), Golovnin was regarded in most Russian circles as a liberal thinker.

25 V. G. Simkhovitch, "The History of the School in Russia," p. 510; also Beazley, *loc. cit.*, p. 436; Kornilov, *loc. cit.*, pp. 92-93; Leary, *loc. cit.*, p. 75.

26 For description of 1804 Statutes, see Chapter 5 of this volume; for 1835 Statutes, see Chapter 6.

27 Leary, *loc. cit.*, pp. 75-76; Beazley, *loc. cit.*, p. 436; Simkhovitch, *loc. cit.*, pp. 510-511. See also Table No. 21 in Appendix for data on chairs and salaries.

28 Kornilov, *loc. cit.*, p. 93; Leary, *loc. cit.*, pp. 75-76; Simkhovitch, *loc. cit.*, p. 511; Beazley, *loc. cit.*, p. 436.

29 Decree # 487 of July 13, 1863: *Sborn. post. MNP*, Vol. III, p. 1048.

30 Decree #557 of July 11, 1864: *Sborn. post. MNP*, Vol. III, pp. 1199-1201. See Chapter 6 for description of the regulations cited, which were confirmed on June 9, 1842, although the University of St. Vladimir

was legally established on December 25, 1833; see also Table No. 21 in Appendix for additional data on pensions.

[31] Decree #470 of June 18, 1863: *Sborn. post. MNP*, Vol. III.

[32] Beazley, *loc. cit.*, p. 437. In 1867, the entire financial responsibility was to be thrown on the *zemstvos:* see O. Kaidanova-Bervy, *An Historical Sketch of Russian Popular Education*, Vol. One, Part II, Chapter 1.

[33] "Conditions in Elementary Public Schools," article 1: *Sborn. post. MNP*, Vol. III, p. 1226.

[34] *Ibid.*, article 2.

[35] Kaidanova-Bervy, *loc. cit.*

[36] Hans, *loc. cit.*, p. 232.

[37] "Rules of Gymnasiums and Progymnasiums under the Ministry of Public Education," article 1: *Sborn. post. MNP*, Vol. III, p. 1301.

[38] Beazley, *loc. cit.*, p. 437; Noble, *loc. cit.*, p. 137.

[39] See Table No. 20 in Appendix.

[40] See tables in Hans, *loc. cit.*, p. 242; see also A. Rambaud, *History of Russia* (3 volumes) (Boston: Estes and Lauriat, 1872-1882), Vol. II, pp. 697-699.

[41] Pares, *op. cit.*, pp. 198-199.

[42] See tables in Hans, *loc. cit.*, pp. 238-240.

[43] Simkhovitch, *loc. cit.*, p. 511.

[44] Beazley, *loc. cit.*, p. 437; Leary, *loc. cit.*, p. 78.

[45] Pares, *loc. cit.*, p. 198, citing Rambaud, *loc. cit.*, pp. 697-698.

[46] Pares, *loc. cit.*, p. 198.

[47] Leary, *loc. cit.*, p. 78; Beazley, *op. cit.*, p. 446.

[48] See also Hans, *loc. cit.*, p. 293.

[49] Kaidanova-Bervy, *loc. cit.*, Vol. One, Part II, Chapter 1; also comparison of tables in Beazley, *op. cit.*, p. 488 and Hans, *loc. cit.*, pp. 198-199.

[50] Pares, *loc. cit.*, pp. 198-199.

[51] Kaidanova-Bervy, *loc. cit.*

[52] Beazley, *op. cit.*, p. 444.

[53] The first was Prince Golitsyn (1816-24), whose theories and practices are described at length in Chapter 5.

[54] T. A. Kuzminskaya, *Tolstoy As I Knew Him* (New York: The Macmillan Co., 1947), pp. 144-146. The author of this work was the favorite sister-in-law of Leo Tolstoi and is the prototype of 'Natasha' in *War and Peace*.

[55] Beazley, *op. cit.*, p. 445.

[56] "Rules," etc., Chapter I, article 1: *Sborn. post. MNP*, Vol. V, pp. 431-464. See also quotation of 1864 Rules earlier in this chapter.

[57] Beazley, *loc. cit.*, p. 446.

[58] *Ibid.*

[59] *Ibid.*

[60] Imperial Rescript of December 25, 1873: cited in Kaidanova-Bervy, *loc. cit.*

[61] "Conditions in Elementary Public Schools," (1874), article 1: *Sborn. post. MNP*, Vol. VI, pp. 223-234.

[62] *Ibid.*, article 2.

[63] Tolstoi was Procurator of the Holy Synod as well as Minister of Public Education.

[64] "Conditions in Elementary Public Schools," (1874), article 14.

[65] Beazley, *loc. cit.*, p. 447.

[66] *Ibid.*, p. 447.

[67] Decree of the Ministry of Public Education: cited in Kaidanova-Bervy, *loc. cit.*

[68] Kaidanova-Bervy, *loc. cit.*

[69] Kornilov, *op. cit.*, Vol. II, pp. 248-266; Beazley, *op. cit.*, pp. 470-472; G. Vernadsky, *A History of Russia*, p. 166; B. Pares, *A History of Russia*, pp. 391-393.

[70] Beazley, *loc. cit.*, pp. 471-473.

[71] Pares, *History of Russia*, pp. 394, 410-412; Kornilov, *loc. cit.*, Vol. II, pp. 260-266.

[72] Beazley, *loc. cit.*, p. 473; Kornilov, *loc. cit.*, p. 261.

[73] Simkhovitch, *loc. cit.*, p. 512.

[74] Kornilov, *loc. cit.*, p. 261.

[75] "On the Curtailment of Gymnasium Education," *Sborn. post. MNP*, Vol. X, pp. 880-883: cited in T. Darlington, *Education in Russia*, p. 147.

[76] Kornilov, *op. cit.*, pp. 249 *et seq.*

[77] *Ibid.*, p. 261; Beazley, *loc. cit.*, p. 473.

[78] Kaidanova-Bervy, *loc. cit.*

[79] Cited in Kaidanova-Bervy, *loc. cit.*; however, this author gives the incorrect date for publication of the Rules.

[80] "Rules of the Church-Parish Schools," (1884), article 1: *Pravila i programmy dlia tserkovno prikhodskikh shkol i Shkol gramoty* (2nd ed., St. Petersburg, 1894), p. 3.

[81] "Rules of the Church-Parish Schools," article 5.

[82] *Ibid.*, articles 5, 8.

[83] *Ibid.*, articles 12, 13.

[84] *Ibid.*, articles 15-18.

[85] Kaidanova-Bervy, *loc. cit.* For data showing great growth of such schools after the adoption of the Rules of 1884, see Table No. 25 in Appendix.

[86] "Rules of the Church-Parish Schools," article 6; see Chapter 6 of this volume for brief description of the literacy schools. It is also significant that, in 1891, the Holy Synod took over the administration of the Sunday Schools described early in this chapter: Darlington, *loc. cit.*, p. 146.

[87] "Regulations of Real-Schools," (1888); *Sborn. post. MNP*, Vol. XI, pp. 29-56.

[88] Noble, *op. cit.*, p. 173.
[89] Darlington, *loc. cit.*, pp. 146-147.
[90] Pares, *Russia and Reform,* p. 65.
[91] Noble, *loc. cit.*, p. 173.
[92] Pares, *loc. cit.*, p. 64.
[93] Noble, *loc. cit.*, pp. 173-174.
[94] Cited in Kornilov, *op. cit.*, Vol. II, p. 284.
[95] Darlington, *loc. cit.*, p. 147.
[96] Pares, *loc. cit.*, pp. 66-67.
[97] Decree #409 of July 4, 1862: *Sborn. post. MNP,* Vol. III, pp. 781-782.
[98] See Table No. 22 in Appendix.
[99] Decree #233 (35,578) of March 20, 1860: *Sborn. post. MNP,* Vol. III, pp. 460-472, article 1.
[100] *Ibid.*, article 2.
[101] *Ibid.*, article 3. This arrangement was modified when universities were established at Odessa (1864) and Tomsk (1888).
[102] *Ibid.*, articles 4, 5.
[103] Decree #279 (36,533) of January 11, 1861: *Sborn. post. MNP,* Vol. III, pp. 552-561, article 1.
[104] *Ibid.*, article 4.
[105] *Ibid.*, article 8.
[106] *Ibid.*, article 14.
[107] *Ibid.*, article 17.
[108] Decree #476 of June 25, 1863: *Sborn. post. MNP,* Vol. III, pp. 1029-1032.
[109] Decree #485 of July 2, 1863: *Sborn. post. MNP,* Vol. III, pp. 1042-1045.
[110] Decree #447 of January 3, 1863: *Sborn. post. MNP,* Vol. III, p. 846.
[111] Decrees #554-555 of June 25, 1864: *Sborn. post. MNP,* Vol. III, pp. 1174-1175, 1175-1199.
[112] See Table No. 23 in Appendix: comparisons can be made with descriptions of curricula in Chapter 7.
[113] See Table No. 24 in Appendix.
[114] "Conditions in City Schools," decree of May 31, 1872, article 20: *Sborn. post. MNP,* Vol. V, pp. 1178-1189.
[115] "Basic Code for Industrial Schools" (1888) article 23: *Sborn. post. MNP,* Vol. X, pp. 1088-1099.
[116] *Ibid.*, article 24.
[117] Hans, *op. cit.*, pp. 163-164.
[118] Darlington, *op. cit.*, p. 89.
[119] Hans, *op. cit.*, p. 137.
[120] *Ibid.*, p.137. The new "Statute for Ladies Seminaries" was published on May 24, 1871.
[121] Hans, *loc. cit.*, p. 137.
[122] Kaidanova-Bervy, *loc. cit.*

Chapter 9

The Beginning of the End

[1] Professor James Mavor in a letter to Alexander S. Kaun, cited in A. Kornilov, *Modern Russian History* (2 volumes) (New York: Alfred A. Knopf, 1924), Vol. II, p. 274.

[2] V. Ivanovich, (Charnolusskii). "Iz itogov pervoi russkoi vceobshchei perepisi" [From Summaries of the First Russian General Census] in *Vestnik Vospitaniia* [Educational Herald], Vol. XVII, no. 1 (January 1906), pp. 38-55.

[3] *Ibid.*, p. 40.

[4] See Table No. 26 in Appendix.

[5] See Table No. 27 in Appendix.

[6] See Table No. 27 in Appendix.

[7] See Table No. 29 in Appendix.

[8] See Table No. 28 in Appendix.

[9] V. I. Gurko, *Features and Figures of the Past: Government and Opinion in the Reign of Nicholas II.* (Hoover Library on War, Revolution and Peace. Publication No. 14) Palo Alto (Calif.): Stanford University Press, 1939, p. 20.

[10] Statement attributed to Professor George Vernadsky in A. Kornilov, *Modern Russian History* (New York: Alfred A. Knopf, 1924), Vol. II p. 331.

[11] A. J. Sack, *The Birth of the Russian Democracy* (New York: Russian Information Bureau, 1918), p. 85. Both author and publisher were supporters of the Provisional Government and strongly opposed the Bolshevik regime from its inception.

[12] Kornilov, *op. cit.*, pp. 290-291. The number of students arrested constituted about 10 per cent of the total enrollment: see Table No. 32 in Appendix.

[13] See Table No. 32. It is true that there were several hundred additional students at the University of Warsaw, but their ties with Russian students were not close enough to concern them. In like manner, the approximately 10,000 students in various Russian technical institutes and specialized academies (see Table No. 33) took little interest in political squabbles until later in the regime.

[14] Kornilov, *loc. cit.*, p. 291; Sack, *loc. cit.*, p. 85; D. B. Leary, *Education and Autocracy in Russia* (Buffalo, N. Y.: University of Buffalo, 1919), p. 106.

[15] Kornilov, *loc. cit.*, p. 292; Sack, *loc. cit.*, p. 85.

[16] Leary, *loc. cit.*, p. 106.

[17] Kornilov, *loc. cit.*, p. 292; Gurko, *op. cit.*, p. 589 (editor's notes).

[18] Gurko, *op. cit.*, p. 6.

[73] Quoted in Hans, *loc. cit.*, p. 220.

[74] Pares, *op. cit.*, p. 203.

[75] Hans, *loc. cit.*, p. 220; see also Table No. 40 in Appendix.

[76] Ignatiev, *op. cit.*, pp. 146-148, 151.

[77] Florinsky, *op. cit.*, p. 8; Vernadsky, *op. cit.*, pp. 184-186; Beazley, *op. cit.*, p. 570.

[78] Beazley, *op. cit.*, p. 547.

[79] G. T. Robinson, *Rural Russia Under the Old Regime* (New York: Longmans, Green and Co., 1932), p. 256.

[80] *Ibid.*, p. 256; Beazley, *loc. cit.*, p. 547 and 547 fn.

[81] Robinson, *loc. cit.*, pp. 256-257; see also Table No. 37 in Appendix.

[82] Vernadsky, *loc. cit.*, p. 195.

[83] See Table No. 37 in Appendix.

[84] Gurko, *op. cit.*, p. 599 (editor's notes).

[85] *Ibid.*, pp. 599-600.

[86] Woody, *loc. cit.*, p. 30.

[87] Gurko, *loc. cit.*, pp. 600-601 (editor's notes).

[88] *Ibid.*, pp. 600-601.

[89] Beazley, *op. cit.*, pp. 485-487; Woody, *loc. cit.*, p. 31.

[90] See Table No. 35 in Appendix; it is worthy of note that during approximately these same years, there was also a slight drop in relative *zemstvo* expenditures for education (see Table No. 36).

[91] Gurko, *op. cit.*, pp. 238-239.

[92] Vernadsky, *loc. cit.*, p. 204.

[93] *Ibid.*, p. 204; Woody, *loc. cit.*, p. 31; Gurko, *op. cit.*, p. 601 (editor's notes).

[94] See Table No. 36 in Appendix.

[95] Compare Tables Nos. 36 and 37 in Appendix.

[96] Florinsky, *loc. cit.*, pp. 11-12; Vernadsky, *loc. cit.*, p. 205.

[97] Beazley, *loc. cit.*, p. 490.

[98] Hans, *op. cit.*, p. 163.

[99] Gurko, *op. cit.*, p. 63.

[100] Vernadsky, *loc. cit.*, p. 204.

[101] Gurko, *loc. cit.*, p. 63.

[102] *Ibid.*, p. 238.

[103] Florinsky, *loc. cit.*, p. 12.

[104] P. Crowson, *History of the Russian People* (New York: Longmans, Green and Co., 1948), pp. 38-51, dates the beginning of the separation of Gentry and People with the early seventeenth century, and believes that the chasm became unbridgeable under Peter I and Catherine II.

Chapter 10

The Status of Teachers During the Last Two Decades of Tsardom

[1] M. T. Florinsky, *The End of the Russian Empire* (New Haven: Yale University Press, 1931), pp. 222-223.

[2] *Autobiography of Andrew Dickson White* (2 vols.) (New York: The Century Co., 1922), Vol. II, pp. 5-7. See also E. Noble, *Russia and the Russians* (Boston: Houghton, Mifflin and Co., 1901), pp. 173-174.

[3] D. B. Leary, *Education and Autocracy in Russia* (Buffalo, N. Y.: University of Buffalo, 1919), p. 102.

[4] Cited in V. G. Simkhovitch, "History of the School in Russia" in *The Educational Review* (May 1907), p. 521.

[5] *Ibid.*, p. 522; for data on cost of living during the period 1895-1900, see David Shub, *Lenin—A Biography* (New York: Doubleday and Co., Inc., 1948), p. 31.

[6] A. S. Rappoport, *Home Life in Russia* (New York: The Macmillan Co., 1913), pp. 140-141.

[7] B. Pares, *Russia and Reform* (New York: E. P. Dutton and Co., 1907), pp. 380-381.

[8] Rappoport, *loc. cit.*, p. 142.

[9] Leary, *loc. cit.*, p. 102.

[10] V. I. Gurko, *Features and Figures of the Past* (Palo Alto: Stanford University Press, 1939), p. 245.

[11] Leary, *loc. cit.*, p. 103.

[12] "Rechi, doklady, stat'i E. P. Kovalevskogo" [Speeches, Reports and Articles of E. P. Kovalevskii] in *Narodnoe obrazovanie i tserkovnoe dostoianie v III Gosudarstvenom Dume* [Public Education and Church Property in the Third State Duma], Parts II and III, pp. 180-185: cited in N. A. Zhelvakov, *Khrestomatiia po istorii pedagogiki* [Sourcebook in the History of Pedagogy] (Moscow: State Pedagogical Textbook Publishers, 1936), Vol. IV, Part II, p. 325.

[13] P. J. Novgorotsev, "Universities and Higher Technical Schools" in P. N. Ignatiev (ed.), *Russian Schools and Universities in the World War* (New Haven: Yale University Press, 1929), pp. 140-141.

[14] *Ibid.*, p. 141; see also Table No. 34 in Appendix for data on social composition of student bodies in 1914.

[15] Rappoport, *loc. cit.*, p. 141.

[16] A. J. Sack, *Birth of the Russian Democracy*, pp. 126-133: complete story of the case is found therein, with full account of Zinaida's defense at her own trial, from which account the quotations used have been taken.

[17] P. Romanov, "Mart-Mai 1917 Goda" [March-May 1917] in *Krasnyi*

Arkhiv [Red Archives] (Moscow: State Publishing House, Vol. XV, September 1926), pp. 53-56.

[18] *Ibid.*, pp. 53-56.

[19] N. N. Ilin, *Pedagogicheskoe obrazovanie za granitsei i u nas* [Pedagogical Training Abroad and in Russia] (Moscow: Educational Workers Press, 1927), p. 88 fn.

[20] E. N. Medynskii, *Istoriia russkoi pedagogiki* [History of Russian Pedagogy] (Moscow: State Pedagogical Textbook Publishers, 1936), p. 423.

[21] A. P. Pinkevich, *Science and Education in the U.S.S.R.* (London: Victor Gollancz, Ltd., 1934), p. 66.

[22] Pares, *op. cit.*, pp. 210-211, 412-414.

[23] For a complete and detailed account of training methods in both Ministry and *zemstvo* institutions up to 1917, see the excellent article by A. Arsen'ev entitled "Pedagogicheskaia praktika v dorevolutsionnykh uchitel'skikh seminariiakh Rossii" [Pedagogical Practice in Pre-Revolutionary Russian Teachers' Seminaries] in *Sovetskaia Pedagogika* [Soviet Pedagogy], September 1938, No. 9, pp. 91-109.

[24] Pares, *loc. cit.*, pp. 210-211. The only later revision of the procedure described came in 1911 when the Director and preceptors of the seminary began to take a more active part in the supervision of practice teaching: see Arsen'ev, *loc. cit.*, and also the ideas of K. D. Ushinskii as described in Chapter 11 of this volume.

[25] *Ibid.*, pp. 412-414.

[26] G. Vernadsky, *A History of Russia* (New Haven: Yale University Press, 1929), p. 205.

[27] Cited in T. Darlington, *Education in Russia* (London: Wyman and Sons, Ltd., 1909), p. 157; see also Leary, *loc. cit.*, pp. 103-104.

[28] Cited in T. Woody, *New Minds, New Men* (New York: The Macmillan Co., 1932), p. 32.

[29] Rappoport, *loc. cit.*, p. 140.

[30] Woody, *loc. cit.*, p. 32.

[31] Pares, *loc. cit.*, pp. 412-414.

[32] See Table No. 42 in Appendix.

[33] W. H. Bruford, *Chekhov and His Russia* (New York: Oxford University Press, 1947), p. 92.

[34] *Ibid.*, pp. 98-99.

[35] Simkhovitch, *loc. cit.*, p. 517: the statistics in this monograph are based on the Report of the St. Petersburg Committee on Literacy, issued in 1895.

[36] Woody, *loc. cit.*, p. 34.

[37] Cited in A. Kornilov, *Modern Russian History* (2 vols.) (New York: Alfred A. Knopf, 1924), Vol. II, pp. 330-331. (Total corrected.)

[38] *Ibid.*, p. 330.

[39] Cited in A. S. Rappoport, *Pioneers of the Russian Revolution* (New York: Brentano's, 1919), p. 135.

[40] *Ibid.*, especially Chapters VII-X, incl.; Sack, *op. cit.*, passim; Gurko, *op. cit.*, pp. 626-645 (editor's notes).

[41] Woody, *loc. cit.*, pp. 34-35.

[42] Rappoport, *Home Life in Russia*, pp. 138-139.

[43] See Table No. 42 in Appendix.

[44] "Conditions in Advanced Elementary Schools," decree of June 25, 1912, Chapter I, article 7, in *Zhurnal Ministerstva Narodnogo Prosveshcheniia* [Journal of the Ministry of Public Education], Part XLI, 1912, no. 9 (September), p. 23.

[45] Cited in G. T. Robinson, *Rural Russia Under the Old Regime* (New York: Longmans, Green and Co., 1932), p. 310 (notes to Chapter XII of the book).

[46] Kornilov, *loc. cit.*, p. 332: figures are based on an official report of the medical section of the Ministry of Public Education. A penetrating article on this question was written in 1911 by N. K. Krupskaia, the wife of V. I. Lenin, and appears in her *Voprosy narodnogo obrazovaniia* [Questions of Public Education] (Moscow: Communist Book Publishers, 1918), pp. 171-181.

[47] Cited in Kornilov, *loc. cit.*, p. 332 from *Modern Russia* by George Alexinsky.

[48] Pares, *loc. cit.*, pp. 215-216.

[49] Gurko, *op. cit.*, p. 183.

Chapter 11

Pioneers in Russian Educational Philosophy

[1] Lomonosov's prestige is even greater in Russia today than it was during his own time. In an interview regarding the celebration of the 220th anniversary of the founding of the Academy, Vladimir Komarov, President of the Academy of Sciences of the U.S.S.R., stated that "the first period of our Academy's existence was so closely connected with the beginning, content, and results of Lomonosov's activity, that it might rightly be called the Lomonosov period": *Information Bulletin* of the Embassy of the U.S.S.R., Washington, D. C., Vol. V. no. 16 (February 8, 1945), p. 7.

[2] See Chapter 4 of this volume; also E. N. Medynskii, *Istoriia russkoi pedagogiki* [History of Russian Pedagogy] (Moscow: State Pedagogical Textbook Publishers, 1936), pp. 94-97; also O. Kaidanova-Bervy, *An Historical Sketch of Russian Popular Education*, Vol. I, Part I, chapter 1.

[3] T. G. Masaryk, *The Spirit of Russia* (2 vols.) (New York: The Macmillan Company, 1919), Vol. I, pp. 76-77; J. Lavrin, *An Introduction to the Russian Novel* (New York: McGraw-Hill Co., 1947), p. 8. Radishchev's book was entitled *A Voyage from Petersburg to Moscow*

and was published in 1790. When Catherine II read it she was horrified at its "radical" implications, and declared that its author was "more dangerous even than Benjamin Franklin." See E. Tartak, "The Liberal Tradition in Russia: A. Herzen and V. Soloveff" in F. Gross (ed.), *European Ideologies* (New York: Philosophical Library, 1948), pp. 310-323.

[4] Lavrin, *op. cit.*, pp. 42-43; Masaryk, *op. cit.*, Vol. I, pp. 112, 121; A. S. Rappoport, *Pioneers of the Russian Revolution* (New York: Brentano's, 1919), pp. 135-151.

[5] Rappoport, *loc. cit.;* see also "P. Y. Chaadayev" by V. Virginski in *VOKS Bulletin* (Moscow, U.S.S.R.) No. 5, 1947, pp. 36-43; N. Berdyaev, *The Russian Idea* (New York: The Macmillan Company, 1948), pp. 34-38.

[6] *Ibid.*, p. 79; A. Kornilov, *Modern Russian History* (New York: Alfred A. Knopf, 1924), Vol. I, pp. 289-293, 301-305; Masaryk, *op. cit.*, Vol. I, pp. 350-378; Lavrin, *op. cit.*, passim.

[7] Quoted in E. N. Medynskii, "Development of Educational Ideas in Russia," in *Soviet War News* (Press Department of the Soviet Embassy in London), No. 802, March 3, 1944. Despite this emphasis upon individualism, Berdyaev, *op. cit.*, p. 103, concludes that Belinskii "arrived at a world outlook which may be regarded as the basis of Russian socialism. . . . [This] new device was social organization—'social organization or death.'"

[8] I. G. Avtukhov, "Pedagogicheskie vzgliady V. G. Belinskii" [Pedagogical Views of V. G. Belinskii] in *Sovetskaia Pedagogika* [Soviet Pedagogy] No. 6 (June 1938), pp. 100-107.

[9] Rappoport, *op. cit.*, pp. 145-148; Masaryk, *op. cit.*, Vol. I, chapter 12.

[10] Sh. I. Ganelin, "A. I. Gertsen kak pedagog-prosvetite'," [A. I. Hertzen as Educator] in *Sovetskaia Pedagogika,* No. 1, 1938, pp. 109-116.

[11] Medynskii, "Development of Educational Ideas in Russia," *loc. cit.*

[12] Medynskii, *Istorii russkoi pedagogiki, op. cit.*, pp. 212-220; Rappoport, *op. cit.*, p. 180. Chernyshevskii's writings on education have been published in one volume entitled *N. G. Chernyshevskii, Izbrannye pedagogicheskie vyskazyvaniia* [Collected Pedagogical Opinions of N. G. Chernyshevskii] (Moscow: State Pedagogical Textbook Publishers, 1936).

[13] Rappoport, *loc. cit.*, pp. 148-151; Masaryk, *op. cit.*, Vol. II, chapter 14.

[14] Medynskii, *Istorii*, etc., *loc. cit.*, pp. 215-220.

[15] *Ibid.*, pp. 220-225; Kornilov, *op. cit.*, Vol. II, pp. 207-217; Masaryk, *op. cit.*, Vol. II, chapter 14; Dobroliubov's writings on education have been published in one volume entitled *N. A. Dobroliubov, Izbrannye pedagogicheskie vyskazyvaniia* [Collected Pedagogical Opinions of N. A. Dobroliubov] (Moscow: State Pedagogical Textbook Publishers, 1936).

[16] N. A. Dobroliubov, "Bcerossiiskie illiuzii, razrushaemye rozgami" [Abolition of Corporal Punishment—An All-Russian Illusion] (1860) in *Izbrannye, op. cit.*, pp. 294-316.

[17] Kaidanova-Bervy, *op. cit.*, Vol. I, Part I, chapter 3; Medynskii, *Istorii,* etc., *op. cit.*, Chapter VII, takes a much less favorable view of Pirogov.

[18] Kaidanova-Bervy, *op. cit.*, Vol. I, Part I, chapter 5.

[19] Rappoport, *op. cit.*, p. 186; Berdyaev, *op. cit.*, p. 106; Beazley, et al., *Russia from the Varangians to the Bolsheviks* (Oxford, Eng.: The Clarendon Press, 1918), p. 442.

[20] Rappoport, *loc. cit.*, p. 179: based on data on L. Kulczycki, *Geschichte der russ. Revol.* (Gotha, 1910) Vol. I, p. 294; see also Masaryk, *op. cit.*, Vol. II, passim.

[21] P. J. Novgorotsev, "Universities and Higher Technical Schools" in P. N. Ignatiev (ed.), *Russian Schools and Universities in the World War* (New Haven: Yale University Press, 1929), p. 136.

[22] Rappoport, *loc. cit.*, p. 192.

[23] G. Vernadsky, *A History of Russia* (New Haven: Yale University Press, 1929), pp. 206-207; D. B. Leary, *Education and Autocracy in Russia* (Buffalo, N.Y.: University of Buffalo, 1919), pp. 73-74.

[24] Medynskii, "Development of Educational Ideas in Russia," *loc. cit.*

[25] Kaidanova-Bervy, *op. cit.*, Vol. I, Part I, chapter 3; Medynskii, *Istorii,* etc., *op. cit.*, Chapter VIII, pp. 180-211; for description of Moscow University at this period, see last page of Chapter 6 of this volume.

[26] See Chapter 6 of this volume.

[27] Kaidanova-Bervy, *loc. cit.;* Medynskii, *Istorii,* etc., *loc. cit.*

[28] *Ibid.*, pp. 181-182.

[29] Kaidanova-Bervy, *loc. cit.*

[30] *Ibid.*

[31] *Ibid.*

[32] *Ibid.;* see also N. A. Zhelvakov, *Khrestomatiia po istorii pedagogiki* [Sourcebook in the History of Pedagogy] (Moscow: State Pedagogical Textbook Publishers, 1936), Vol. IV, Part I, p. 253 (notes on Section IV of the text).

[33] Kaidanova-Bervy, *loc. cit.*

[34] Quoted in *ibid.*

[35] Quoted in *ibid.*

[36] Medynskii, *Istorii,* etc., *loc. cit.;* Pugachev's rebellion occurred in 1773 and was instrumental in swaying Catherine II from her earlier liberal ideas; see Chapter 4 of this volume.

[37] See Ushinskii's "Preface" to his greatest work: *Chelovek kak predmet vospitaniia–Opyt pedagogicheskoi antropologii* [Man as the Subject of Education–Experiences in Educational Anthropology] in K. D. Ushinskii, *Izbrannye pedagogicheskie sochineniia* [Selected Pedagogical Works] (Moscow: State Pedagogical Textbook Publishers, 1945), pp. 461-485.

[38] Quoted in Kaidanova-Bervy, *loc. cit.*

[39] See original article (1861) on this subject in Ushinskii, *Izb. ped. soch.*, *op. cit.*, pp. 204-217.

[40] Original article in *Ibid.*, pp. 87-105; this translation of the quotation is from Kaidanova-Bervy, *loc. cit.*

[41] Medynskii, *Istorii, loc. cit.*

[42] Ushinskii, (1857), "O pol'ze pedagogicheskoi literatury" [On the Use of Pedagogical Literature] in *Izb. ped. soch.*, pp. 35-52.

[43] *Ibid.*

[44] Medynskii, *Istorii*, etc., *loc. cit.*, p. 201; for a more recent but concurrent Soviet view of Ushinskii's psychological theories, see S. L. Rubinshtein, "Psychological Science and Education" in *Harvard Educational Review*, Vol. 18, no. 3. (Summer 1948), pp. 158-170.

[45] V. Ia. Struminskii, "K. D. Ushinskii i ego pedagogicheskoe nasledstvo" [K. D. Ushinskii and His Pedagogical Legacy] in Ushinskii, *Izb. ped. soch.*, pp. 546-547.

[46] Ushinskii, "*Proekt*," etc., *loc. cit.*

[47] *Ibid.*

[48] *Ibid.*

[49] *Ibid.*

[50] *Ibid.*

[51] *Ibid.*

[52] Medynskii, *Istorii*, etc., *loc. cit.*, p. 205.

[53] Kaidanova-Bervy, *loc. cit.*

[54] *Ibid.*

[55] Cited in Struminskii, *loc. cit.;* see also editorial in Pravda, Moscow, April 10, 1937, entitled "Velikii pedagog i ego tseniteli" [A Great Pedagogue and His Judges].

[56] Medynskii, *loc. cit.*, p. 190.

[57] Kaidanova-Bervy, *loc. cit.*

Chapter 12

The Educational Heritage of the U.S.S.R.

[1] E. N. Medynskii, "Development of Educational Ideas in Russia" in *Soviet War News* (Press Department of the Soviet Embassy in London), no. 802, March 3, 1944, p. 4.

[2] See A. M. Pankratova, *Istoriia S.S.S.R.* [History of the U.S.S.R.], 1948; A. B. Shestakov, *Kratkii Kurs Istorii SSSR* [Short Course in the History of the U.S.S.R.], 1937 and A. B. Shestakov, *Istoriia SSSR* [History of the U.S.S.R.], 1945. All of these volumes are textbooks for Soviet elementary and incomplete-secondary schools, and were published by the State Pedagogical Textbook Publishers in Moscow in the years indicated.

[3] Several Soviet articles on the Academy of Sciences are available in English. See "200th (220th) Anniversary of the Academy of Sciences To

Be Celebrated" in *Information Bulletin* of the Embassy of the U.S.S.R., Washington, D.C., Vol. V, no. 16 (February 8, 1945), p. 7; A. A. Baikov, *Twenty-five Years of the Academy of Sciences of the U.S.S.R.* (New York: American Russian Institute, 1944); V. P. Volgin, "Affiliates and Branches of the Academy of Sciences of the U.S.S.R." in *Pravda*, Moscow, June 25, 1947, and also appearing in English in *Soviet Press Translations* (Far Eastern and Russian Institute, University of Washington), Vol. II, no. 15 (September 15, 1947), pp. 116-117. A more objective but still favorable view is offered in G. Vernadsky, *Ancient Russia* (New Haven: Yale University Press, 1943), Chapter I.

[4] A. Chernov, "Lomonosov i Sovremennost'" [Lomonosov and Modern Times] in *Sovetskoe Studenchestvo* [Soviet Studentry], no. 9, November 1936, pp. 57-60. The first two articles in the previous reference (3) also contain descriptions of Lomonosov's scientific and educational activities.

[5] "Rules for School Children" in G. S. Counts and Nucia P. Lodge, "*I Want To Be Like Stalin*" (New York: John Day Co., 1947), appendix pp. 149-150. This volume consists of selections from a Soviet official textbook on Pedagogy, and abounds in instances revealing the current Soviet tendency to return to pre-Revolution concepts of education, methods of instruction, and interpretations of Russian nationalism.

[6] "V Sovete Ministrov SSSR" [In the Council of Ministers of the U.S.S.R.] in Izvestia, Moscow, no. 87 (9003), April 11, 1946, p. 2. This contains a list of 305 institutions of higher learning assigned to the jurisdiction of the newly created Ministry of Higher Education of the U.S.S.R. For data on earlier assignments, see A. P. Pinkevich, *Science and Education in the U.S.S.R.* (London: Victor Gollancz, Ltd., 1935), p. 79.

[7] G. Vernadsky, *A History of Russia* (New Haven: Yale University Press, 1929), p. 401.

[8] According to a pamphlet entitled *Higher Educational Establishments in the U.S.S.R.*, VOKS Information Bureau, Moscow, October 1939, nearly 90 per cent of all students in such institutions were then receiving stipends ranging from 120 to 200 rubles a month.

[9] William H. (E.) Johnson, "General Aims of Soviet Education" in *American Quarterly on the Soviet Union*, American Russian Institute, New York, Vol. I, no. 2 (July 1938), pp. 42-51.

[10] Pinkevich, *op. cit.*, pp. 84-85: "The lecture has been restored to its proper place as a means of furthering contact between the professor and the students." For later Soviet views on the same subject see Counts, *op. cit.*, passim.

[11] L. Trotsky, *My Life* (New York: Charles Scribner's Sons, 1930), pp. 337-338.

[12] R. Benedict, *Patterns of Culture* (New York: Penguin Books, Inc., 1946), pp. 33, 40.

[13] *The Trade Union of Soviet School Teachers* (Moscow: VOKS Information Bureau, no date).

[14] See T. Woody, *New Minds, New Men* (New York: The Macmillan Co., 1932), p. 454: "Since 1925, when a formal declaration was made by the Teachers Congress, expressing their loyalty to the ruling Party, there has been at least no open question of their acceptance of the principles and purposes of Communist education." See also a typical recent article by V. Svetlov, "The Ideological Training of Students Must be Improved" in *Izvestia*, Moscow, December 14, 1946, as translated in *Soviet Press Translations* (Far Eastern and Russian Institute, University of Washington), Vol. II, no. 5.

[15] See Counts, *op. cit.*, particularly the Introduction and Chapter III ("For Our Beloved Motherland").

[16] Address to the convention of the American Youth Congress held in Washington, D.C., in February 1940, as quoted in R. E. Sherwood, *Roosevelt and Hopkins* (New York: Harper and Brothers, 1948), p. 138.

[17] I. L. Kandel, *Comparative Education* (New York: Houghton Mifflin Co., 1933), p. 43.

[18] B. Pares, *A History of Russia* (4th ed. rev.; New York: Alfred A. Knopf, 1944) pp. vi-viii. It is also interesting to note certain organizational similarities between the Holy Synod of the later XIX century and the revived Patriarchate of today. The relationship of both these institutions to the Government, for example, is much the same. The Chief Procurator of the 1850's acted as liaison officer between the Church and the State, and was attached to the Council of Ministers, just as are the present chairmen of the two religious councils in the U.S.S.R. In each case, the main task of these officials is defined as the responsibility of seeing that church practices conform to civil law. And now the church in the U.S.S.R. is permitted to have its own schools, although these by no means compare in either number or authority with the schools of the Holy Synod. The fact that many major differences between the old Synod and the new Patriarchate exist should not be allowed to obscure the presence of important, and increasing, resemblances.

List of Reference Works Cited in Notes to this Volume

A. Primary Sources (in Russian)

Akty Istoricheskie (Historical Acts). Russian Archeographical Commission, St. Petersburg 1841. Vol. I (A.D. 1334-1598).

Chernyshevskii, N. G. *Izbrannye pedagogicheskie vyskazyvaniia.* (Collected Pedagogical Opinions). State Pedagogical Textbook Publishers, Moscow 1936. 208 p.

Dobroliubov, N. A. *Izbrannye pedagogicheskie vyskazyvaniia.* (Collected Pedagogical Opinions) State Pedagogical Textbook Publishers, Moscow 1936. 388 p.

"Domostroi" in *Imperatorskoe obshchestvo istorii i drevnostei rossiiskikh.* (Imperial Society of History and Ancient Russia). Chteniia Press, Moscow University, 1881. Vol. II, April-June 1821, pp. 1-202.

"Dukhovnyi Reglament" (Ecclesiastical Statutes) in Zhelvakov, N. A., *Khrestomatiia po istorii pedagogiki* (Sourcebook in the History of Pedagogy). State Pedagogical Textbook Publishers, Moscow 1936, Vol. IV (1), pp. 101-109.

Karpov, V. N. *Khar'kovskaia starina iz vospominanii starozhilia* (Old Times in Kharkov from the Memoirs of a Longtime Resident). Iuzhnii Krai Press, Kharkov 1900. 518 p.

Krupskaia, N. K. *Voprosy narodnogo obrazovaniia* (Questions of Public Education). Communist Book Publishers, Moscow 1918.

Novikov, N. I. (ed.) *Drevniaia rossiiskaia vivliofika* (Ancient Russian Library). Typographic Press, Moscow, 1788-1791. Second edition, 20 volumes.

Pankratova, A. M. *Istoriia SSSR* (History of the U.S.S.R.). Textbook for 8th grade of secondary schools. State Textbook Publishers for the Ministry of Public Education of the R.S.F.S.R., Moscow 1948. 3 volumes.

Pnin, Ivan. "Opyt o prosveshchenii otnocitel'no k Rossii" (Experiences in Education in Russia) in *Ivan Pnin—Sochineniia* (Collected Works of Ivan Pnin). State Publishing House, Moscow 1934, pp. 121-161.

Polnoe sobranie russkikh letopisei (Complete Collection of Russian Chronicles). Russian Archeographical Commission, St. Petersburg 1841-1921. 24 volumes. (vol. I, 1846; vol. V, 1851).

Polnoe sobranie zakonov rossiiskoi Imperii c 1649 g (Complete Collection of Laws of the Russian Empire from 1649). St. Petersburg 1830-1843. 48 volumes.

Pravila i programmy dlia tserkovno prikhodskikh shkol i shkol gramoty

(Rules and Programs for Church-Parish Schools and Literacy Schools). St. Petersburg 1894, second edition.

Romanov, P. "Mart-Mai 1917" (March to May 1917). *Krasnyi Arkhiv* (Red Archives)—Historical Journal of the Central Archives Office of the R.S.F.S.R.—vol. XV, September 1926.

Rozhdestvenskii, S. V. *Istoricheskii obzor deiatel'nosti ministerstva narodnogo prosveshcheniia, 1802-1902* (Historical Review of the Activities of the Ministry of Public Education, 1802-1902). Ministry of Public Education, St. Petersburg 1902. 785 p.

Sbornik postanovlenii po ministerstvu narodnogo prosveshcheniia (Collection of Decrees of the Ministry of Public Education). Imperial Academy of Sciences, St. Petersburg 1864-1865. 3 volumes.

Sbornik rasporiazhenii po ministerstvu narodnogo prosveshcheniia (Collection of Edicts of the Ministry of Public Education). St. Petersburg 1866-1867. 3 volumes.

Shestakov, A. B. *Kratkii kurs istorii SSSR* (Short Course in the History of the U.S.S.R.). Textbook for the 3rd and 4th grades of elementary schools. State Textbook Publishers for the Commissariat of Public Education of the R.S.F.S.R., Moscow 1937. 222 p.

———, *Istoriia SSSR* (History of the U.S.S.R.). Textbook for the 4th grade of elementary schools. State Textbook Publishers for the Commissariat of Public Education of the R.S.F.S.R., Moscow 1945. 280 p.

Stoglav (One Hundred Chapters of Laws). Trübner and Company, London 1860. 238 p.

Tatishchev, V. N. *Razgovor o pol'ze nauk i uchilishch* (Dialogue on the Benefits of Science and the School). University Press, Moscow 1877.

Uchrezhdenniia i ustavy, kasaiushchiesia do vospitaniia i obucheniia v Rossii iunoshestva oboeva pola (Organization and Rules Concerning the Nurture and Training of Youth of Both Sexes in Russia) in Zhelvakov, N. A. *Khrestomatiia po istorii pedagogiki* (Sourcebook in the History of Pedagogy). State Pedagogical Textbook Publishers, Moscow 1936, vol. IV (1), pp. 141-151.

Ushinskii, K. D. *Izbrannye pedagogicheskie sochineniia* (Collected Pedagogical Works). State Pedagogical Textbook Publishers, Moscow 1945.

Zhelvakov, N. A. *Khrestomatiia po istorii pedagogiki* (Sourcebook in the History of Pedagogy). State Pedagogical Textbook Publishers, Moscow 1936. (Note: The entire series under this title consists of four volumes; Zhelvakov is the editor of Volume IV, parts 1 and 2, which is devoted to the history of education in Russia from the beginnings to 1917).

B. Secondary Sources—Books and Pamphlets (in Russian)

Chekhov, N. V. *Tipy russkoi shkoly* (Types of Russian Schools). MIR Publishers, Moscow 1923. 148 p.

Demkov, M. I. *Istoria russkoi pedagogii* (History of the Russian Pedagogue). Revel 1895. 2 volumes.

Ilin, N. N. *Pedagogicheskoe obrazovanie za granitsei i u nas* (Pedagogical Training Abroad and in Russia). Educational Workers Press, Moscow 1927. 153 p.

Kaidanova-Bervy, Olga. *Ocherki po istorii narodnogo obrazovaniia v Rossii i SSSR na osnove lichnogo opyta i nabliudenii* (Sketches on the History of Public Education in Russia and the U.S.S.R. on the Basis of Personal Experiences and Observations). Petropolis Verlag, Berlin 1930. 2 volumes. (Note: Because the English translation of this work has not yet been published, it is listed here under sources in Russian).

Kharlampovich, K. *Zapadnorusskie pravoslavniia shkole XVI i nachala XVII vv.* (Church Schools of Western Russia in the XVI and early XVII Centuries). Imperial University Press, Kazan 1898.

Kniazkov, S. A. and N. I. Serbov. *Ocherk istorii narodnogo obrazovaniia v Rossii do epokhi reform Aleksandra II.* (Historical Sketch of Public Education in Russia to the Epoch of the Reforms of Alexander II). Moscow 1910.

Medynskii, E. N. *Istoriia russkoi pedagogiki* (History of Russian Pedagogy). State Pedagogical Textbook Publishers, Moscow 1936. 472 p.

Morokhovets, E. A. *Krestianskaia reforma 1861 g* (The Peasant Reform of 1861). State Socio-Economic Publishers, Moscow 1937. 163 p.

Pinkevich, A. P. *Kratkii ocherk istorii pedagogiki* (Brief Sketch of the History of Pedagogy). Proletarii Publishers, Kharkov 1930. 347 p.

Semevskii, V. I. *Krestiane v tsarstvovanie imperatrytsy Ekaterina II* (The Peasantry in the Reign of Empress Catherine II). St. Petersburg 1901-1903. 2 volumes.

Veselago, F. F. *Ocherk istorii morskogo kadetskogo korpusa* (Historical Sketch of the Naval Cadet Corps) in Zhelvakov, N. A. *Khrestomatiia po istorii pedagogiki* (Sourcebook in the History of Pedagogy). State Pedagogical Textbook Publishers, Moscow 1936, vol. IV (1), p. 90.

Voronov, A. S. *Iankovich de-Mirievo* in Zhelvakov, N. A. *Khrestomatiia po istorii pedagogiki* (Sourcebook in the History of Pedagogy). State Pedagogical Textbook Publishers, Moscow 1936, vol. IV (1), pp. 176-178.

C. Periodical Articles (in Russian)

Arsen'ev, A. "Pedagogicheskaia praktika v dorevoliutsionnykh uchitel'skikh seminariiakh Rossii" (Pedagogical Practice in Pre-Revolution Russian Teachers Seminaries). *Sovetskaia Pedagogika* (Soviet Pedagogy), September 1938, no. 9.

Avtukhov, I. G. "Pedagogicheskie vzgliady V. G. Belinskii" (Pedagogical Views of V. G. Belinskii). *Sovetskaia Pedagogika* (Soviet Pedagogy), June 1938, no. 6.

Chernov, A. "Lomonosov i sovremennost," (Lomonosov and Modern Times). *Sovetskoe Studenchestvo* (Soviet Studentry), November 1936, no. 9.

Ganelin, Sh. I. "A. I. Gertsen kak pedagog-prosvetiel'" (A. I. Hertzen as Educator). *Sovetskaia Pedagogika* (Soviet Pedagogy), 1938, no. 1.

Ivanovich, V. (Charnolusskii). "Iz itogov pervoi russkoi vceobshchei perepisi" (From the Summaries of the First Russian General Census). *Vestnik Vospitaniia* (Educational Herald), vol. XVII, no. 1, January 1906.

Veselovskii, A. "Diderot." *Entsiklopedicheskii Slovar'* (Encyclopedic Dictionary), vol. X, pp. 581-588. I. A. Efron, St. Petersburg 1893.

Izvestia (official organ of the Soviet Government), April 11, 1946, no. 87 (9003): "V Sovete Ministrov SSSR" (In the Council of Ministers of the U.S.S.R.).

Pravda (official organ of the Communist Party of the Soviet Union), April 10, 1937: "Velikii pedagog i ego tseniteli" (A Great Pedagogue and His Judges).

Zhurnal Ministerstva Narodnogo Prosveshcheniia (Journal of the Ministry of Public Education, St. Petersburg), part XLI, September 1912, no. 9.

D. Primary Sources (in English)

Bunyan, James and H. H. Fisher. *The Bolshevik Revolution*, 1917-1918. (Documents and Materials). Hoover War Library Publications, No. 3. Stanford University Press, Palo Alto (Calif.), 1934. 735 p.

Golder, Frank A. *Documents of Russian History, 1914-1917*. (Translated by Emanuel Aronsberg). The Century Historical Series. The Century Company, New York 1927. 663 p.

Lenin, V. I. *Selected Works*. Cooperative Publishing Society of Foreign Workers in the U.S.S.R., Moscow 1934-1938. 12 volumes.

Vernadsky, George (editor). *Medieval Russian Laws*. (Records of Civilization, Sources and Studies no. 41.) Columbia University Press, New York 1947.

E. Secondary Sources—Books and Pamphlets (in English)

Anonymous. *Higher Educational Establishments in the U.S.S.R.* VOKS Information Bureau, Moscow 1939 (October).

Anonymous. *The Trade Union of Soviet School Teachers*. VOKS Information Bureau, Moscow, no date.

Baikov, A. A. *Twenty-five Years of the Academy of Sciences of the U.S.S.R.* American Russian Institute, New York 1944. 40 p.

Beazley, Raymond, Nevill Forbes and G. A. Birkett. *Russia from the*

Varangians to the Bolsheviks. The Clarendon Press, Oxford (England) 1918. 601 p.

Benedict, Ruth. *Patterns of Culture.* Penguin Books, Inc., New York 1946. 272 p.

Berdyaev, Nicholas. *The Russian Idea.* The Macmillan Company, New York 1948. 255 p.

Bruford, W. H. *Chekhov and His Russia.* Oxford University Press, New York 1947.

Counts, George S. and Nucia P. Lodge "*I Want To Be Like Stalin.*" John Day and Company, New York 1947. 150 p.

Churchill, Winston S. *Blood, Sweat, and Tears.* G. P. Putnam's Sons, New York 1941. 462 p.

Crowson, Paul. *A History of the Russian People.* Longmans, Green and Company, New York 1948. 225 p.

Darlington, Thomas. *Education in Russia.* (Board of Education, Special Reports on Educational Subjects, vol. 23.) Printed for His Majesty's Stationery Office by Wyman and Sons, Ltd., London 1909. 569 p.

Florinsky, Michael T. *The End of the Russian Empire.* (Carnegie Endowment for International Peace, Division of Economics and History; Economic and Social History of the World War, Russian Series.) Yale University Press, New Haven 1931. 272 p.

Gordon, Douglas H. and Norman L. Torrey. *The Censoring of Diderot's Encyclopédie.* Columbia University Press, New York 1947.

Grekhov, B. D. *The Culture of Kiev Rus.* (Translated by Pauline Rose). Foreign Language Publishing House, Moscow 1947. 146 p.

Gurko, V. I. *Features and Figures of the Past.* Government and Opinion in the Reign of Nicholas II. (Hoover Library on War, Revolution, and Peace; publication no. 14.) Stanford University Press, Palo Alto (California) 1939. 760 p.

Hans, Nicholas. *History of Russian Educational Policy, 1701-1917.* P. S. King and Son, Ltd., London 1931. 255 p.

Hrushevsky, Michael. *A History of Ukraine.* (Edited by O. J. Frederiksen; preface by George Vernadsky). Published for the Ukrainian National Association by Yale University Press, New Haven 1941. 629 p.

Ignatiev, Paul N. *Russian Schools and Universities in the World War.* (Carnegie Endowment for International Peace, Division of Economics and History; Economic and Social History of the World War, Russian Series.) Yale University Press, New Haven 1929. 239 p. (Note: see also listings under Novgorotsev, P. J. and Odinetz, D. M.)

Kaidanova-Bervy, O. *An Historical Sketch of Russian Popular Education.* [The English translation of *Ocherki po istorii narodnogo obrazovaniia v Rossii i SSSR na osnove lichnogo opyta i nabliudenii*] Petropolis Verlag, Berlin, 1938. 2 volumes.

Kandel, Isaac L. *Comparative Education.* Houghton Mifflin Company, New York 1933. 922 p.

Kornilov, Alexander. *Modern Russian History.* From the Age of Catherine II to the Revolution of 1917. (Translated and extended by Alexander S. Kaun.) Alfred A. Knopf, New York 1924. 2 volumes.

Kovalevsky, Maxime M. *Modern Customs and Ancient Laws of Russia.* (The Ilchester Lectures for 1889-1890). David Nutt, London 1891. 250 p.

Kucharzewski, Jan. *The Origins of Modern Russia.* (Introductory Note by S. Harrison Thomson of the University of Colorado.) The Polish Institute of Arts and Sciences in America, New York 1948. 503 p.

Kuzminskaya, T. A. *Tolstoy As I Knew Him.* The Macmillan Company, New York 1947.

Lavrin, Janko. *An Introduction to the Russian Novel.* McGraw-Hill Company, New York 1947. 253 p.

Leary, Daniel B. *Education and Autocracy in Russia.* From the Origins to the Bolsheviki. College of Arts and Sciences, University of Buffalo (New York) 1919. 127 p.

Lippmann, Walter. *U. S. Foreign Policy—Shield of the Republic.* Little Brown & Company, Boston, 1943. 128 p.

Masaryk, Thomas G. *The Spirit of Russia* (Translated by Eden and Cedar Paul). The Macmillan Company, New York 1919. 2 volumes.

Noble, Edmund. *Russia and the Russians.* Houghton Mifflin and Company, New York, 1901.

Novgorotsev, Paul J. "Universities and Higher Technical Schools" in Ignatiev, Paul N. *Russian Schools and Universities in the World War.* (Carnegie Endowment for International Peace, Division of Economics and History; Economic and Social History of the World War, Russian Series). Yale University Press, New Haven 1929.

Odinetz, Dmitry M. "Primary and Secondary Schools" in Ignatiev, Paul N. *Russian Schools and Universities in the World War.* (See above item.)

Pares, Bernard. *History of Russia.* Alfred A. Knopf, New York 1944. 575 p.

———. *Russia and Reform.* E. P. Dutton and Company, New York 1907.

Pinkevich, A. P. *Science and Education in the U.S.S.R.* (New Soviet Library Series, no. 12.) Victor Gollancz, Ltd., London 1934. 176 p.

Rambaud, Alfred. *History of Russia.* From the Earliest Times to 1882. (Translated by L. B. Lang.) Estes and Lauriat, Boston 1879-1882. 3 volumes.

Rappoport, A. S. *Home Life in Russia.* The Macmillan Company, New York 1913. 284 p.

———. *Pioneers of the Russian Revolution,* Brentano's New York 1919. 281 p.

Robinson, Geroid T. *Rural Russia Under the Old Regime.* Longmans, Green and Company, New York 1932.

Sack, A. J. *The Birth of the Russian Democracy.* Russian Information Bureau, New York 1918.

Sherwood, Robert E. *Roosevelt and Hopkins—An Intimate History.* Harper and Brothers, New York 1948. 979 p.

Shub, David. *Lenin—A Biography.* Doubleday and Company, Inc., New York 1948. 438 p.

Tartak, Elias. "The Liberal Tradition in Russia: A. Herzen and V. Soloveff" in Gross, Felix (editor). *European Ideologies.* Philosophical Library, New York 1948.

Trotsky, Leon. *My Life.* Charles Scribner's Sons, New York 1930. 599 p.

Vernadsky, George. *A History of Russia.* Yale University Press, New Haven 1929 and 1944; New Home Library, New York 1944. 397 p.

———. *Ancient Russia.* (Volume I of a projected series of 10 volumes by Vernadsky and Michael Karpovich under the general title of *A History of Russia.*) Yale University Press, New Haven 1943. 370 p.

Von Eckardt, Hans. *Russia.* Alfred A. Knopf, New York 1932.

White, Andrew D. *Autobiography of Andrew Dickson White.* The Century Company, New York 1922. 2 volumes.

Woody, Thomas. *New Minds: New Men.* The Emergence of the Soviet Citizen. The Macmillan Company, New York 1932. 528 p.

F. Periodical Articles (in English)

Anonymous. "Godunov, Boris Fedorovich." *Encyclopaedia Britannica* (14th edition), vol. X, pp. 463-464.

Bernstein, Mikhail. "Higher Education in the U.S.S.R. During and After the War." *The Educational Forum,* vol. XII, no. 2, January 1948.

Johnson, William H. (E.) "General Aims of Soviet Education." *American Quarterly on the Soviet Union,* vol. I, no. 2, July 1938.

Komarov, Vladimir. "Two Hundredth (220th) Anniversary of the Academy of Sciences to be Celebrated." *Information Bulletin of the U.S.S.R.* (published by the Soviet Embassy in Washington, D.C.), vol. V, no. 16, February 8, 1945.

Medynskii, E. (N.) "Development of Educational Ideas in Russia." *Soviet War News* (published by the Press Department of the Soviet Embassy in London, England), no. 802, March 3, 1944.

Rubinshtein, S. L. "Psychological Science and Education." *Harvard Educational Review,* vol. 18, no. 3, Summer 1948 (translated by Ivan D. London from the original in *Sovetskaia Pedagogika,* vol. 9, no. 7, 1945).

Simkhovitch, Vladimir G. "The History of the School in Russia." *Educational Review,* vol. 33, May 1907, pp. 486-522.

Svetlov, V. "The Ideological Training of Students Must Be Improved." *Soviet Press Translations* (Far Eastern and Russian Institute, University of Washington), vol. II, no. 5 (translated from the original in *Izvestia,* December 14, 1946).

Virginskii, V. "P. Y. Chaadaev." *VOKS Bulletin* (published by the All-Union Society for Cultural Relations with Foreign Countries, Moscow), no. 5, 1947.

Index to Main Topics